RETHINKING CHONGQING

LONGINES

和安
满江
长江鱼庄
火锅鱼
满江红 游两江
长江鱼系列
一鱼多吃 各种特色炒菜
电话：15902327878

闲茶楼
茶
最低消费 8 元

CBEST重百电器

银行
通往北城天街

Published by:
Yale School of Architecture
180 York Street
New Haven, Connecticut 06520
www.architecture.yale.edu

Distributed by:
ActarD
151 Grand Street, 5th Floor
New York, New York 10013
www.actar-d.com

This book was made possible through the
Edward P. Bass Distinguished Visiting
Architecture Fellowship fund of the Yale School
of Architecture. It is the seventh in a series of
publications of the Bass fellowship published
through the Dean's office.

Editors:
Andrei Harwell, Critic in Architecture;
Nina Rappaport, Publications Director;
and Emmet Zeifman

Copy Editor: David Delp

Photography Credits:
William Gridley: Cover, 110, 112–117
Andrei Harwell: 57, 96, 112
Kohn Pedersen Fox Associates:
33, 34, 35, 36, 40, 41
Shui-On Land: 20, 21, 22, 24, 25, 26, 27, 29
Emmett Zeifman: 2, 4, 6, 12, 15, 17, 18, 30, 42, 45,
49, 50, 54, 61, 62, 64, 104, 105, 118, 170, 172

Chinese translation: Celeste Ma

Design: MGMT. design, Brooklyn, New York
Cover: Photograph by William Gridley

Library of Congress data: available upon request.
ISBN 978-0-9893317-4-6

RETHINKING CHONGQING: MIXED USE AND SUPER DENSE VINCENT LO/ KOHN PEDERSEN FOX ASSOCIATES

YALE SCHOOL OF ARCHITECTURE EDWARD P. BASS DISTINGUISHED VISITING ARCHITECTURE FELLOWSHIP

Edited by Andrei Harwell,
Nina Rappaport, and Emmett Zeifman

1.1.1.

Edward P. Bass Distinguished Visiting Architecture Fellowship

In 2003, Edward P. Bass, a 1967 graduate of Yale College who studied at the Yale School of Architecture as a member of the class of 1972, endowed this fellowship to bring property developers to the school to lead advanced studios in collaboration with design faculty. Mr. Bass is an environmentalist who sponsored the Biosphere 2 development in Oracle, Arizona, in 1991, and a developer responsible for the ongoing revitalization of the downtown portion of Fort Worth, Texas, where his Sundance Square, which combines restoration with new construction, has transformed a moribund urban core into a vibrant regional center. In all his work, Mr. Bass has been guided by the conviction that architecture is a socially engaged art operating at the intersection of grand visions and everyday realities.

The Bass fellowship ensures the school curriculum recognizes the role of the property developer as an integral part of the design process. The fellowship brings developers to Yale to work side by side with educators and architecture students in the studio, situating the discussion about architecture in the wider discourse of contemporary practice. The first Bass studio, led by Gerald Hines and Louis I. Kahn Visiting Professor Stefan Behnisch, in 2005, was documented in *Poetry, Property, and Place* (2006). The second Bass studio, in 2006, which teamed Stuart Lipton with Saarinen Visiting Professor Sir Richard Rogers ('62), engineer Chris Wise, and architect Malcolm Smith ('97), was documented in *Future-Proofing* (2007). *The Human City* (2008) records the Yale studio collaboration of Roger Madelin and Bishop Visiting Professor Demetri Porphyrios. *Urban Integration: Bishopsgate Goods Yard,* which documents the studio led by Nick Johnson and the FAT architecture partnership, was published in 2009, and, in 2010, Charles Atwood and architect David M. Schwarz's studio work was published in *Learning in Las Vegas. Urban Intersections: Sao Paulo* featured the work of a studio led by real estate developer Katherine Farley and adjunct professor Deborah Berke published in 2011. It is a pleasure to present the studio and investigations led by developer Vincent Lo of Hong Kong and partners Paul Katz, Jamie von Klemperer, and Forth Bagley in the firm of New York-based Kohn Pedersen Fox who were Saarinen Professors at Yale.

1.1.2.

Introduction

Rethinking Chongqing: Mixed Use and Super Dense—the seventh book to document the Edward P. Bass Distinguished Visiting Architecture Fellowship at the Yale School of Architecture—gathers the research and design proposals of the Yale studio taught by Vincent Lo, chairman of Shui On Land, and Paul Katz, James (Jamie) von Klemperer, and Forth Bagley (B.A. '02, M.Arch '05), principals and director, respectively, at Kohn Pedersen Fox, assisted by Andrei Harwell ('06) of the Yale faculty. Together the limits of high-density development and its intersection with urban infrastructure and design were tested on a key site in Chongqing.

Chongqing, one of China's four directly controlled municipalities, is experiencing dynamic growth. The city's dramatic topography, dense urban core, and complex transportation infrastructure presented the students with the opportunity to challenge conventional concepts of urban development by proposing one million square meters of new development, a daunting task.

The book begins with an interview with Edward P. Bass Distinguished Visiting Architecture Fellow Vincent Lo, followed by a separate interview with Eero Saarinen Visiting Professors Paul Katz, Jamie von Klemperer, and Forth Bagley. Following the studio brief and a summary of the architectural and urban problems put before the students, an essay by Wu Jiang, vice president of Tongi University, and an essay by Michel Hulshof and Daan Roggeveen, directors of the Go West Project, a multidisciplinary research studio, situate the urbanization of Chongqing in the context of contemporary China and provide a framework for understanding the project.

The diagrams and calculations of the "Precedents" section catalog the first three weeks of the term, when students were asked to develop detailed and comprehensive typological studies of mixed-use, high-density projects in Shanghai, Hong Kong, and Japan and prepare a detailed analysis of Shui On Land's pathbreaking redevelopment, Xintiandi, in Shanghai. In the fourth week of the term, students visited Shanghai and Chongqing and met and interviewed various

local officials. For example, Ling Yeuming, vice mayor, and Shirong Li, deputy director of the city's Foreign Trade and Economic Relations Commission, discussed with the studio the government's aspirations for the site and the future of Chongqing. Upon returning to New Haven, the students began their design work in earnest, each configuring their own program mix of residential, office, hospitality, and convention space—developed in consultation with a team from Shui On Land—around a new rail station and public space. The book organizes the student work by typological strategy: linked towers, megastructures, monumental spaces, and urban fabrics. Highlights of the final reviews provide insight from the studio leaders as well as architects and planners, including John Alschuler, Albert Chan, Marianne Kwok, Patricia Patkau ('78), Bill Pedersen, Alan Plattus, Demetri Porphyrios, and Alex Twining ('77).

The editors would like to acknowledge the students who participated in the studio whose cooperation was essential to this book: Yijie Dang, William Gridley, Keith Johns, Alfie Koetter, Kee Lew, Qiwei Liang, Katsunori Shigemi, Brian Spring, Danh Thai, and Emmett Zeifman. We would also like to extend thanks to our copy editor, David Delp; graphic designer, Sarah Gephart of MGMT. design; and translator Celeste Ma.

— Nina Rappaport, Andrei Harwell, and Emmett Zeifman

包装 画册
吊旗 杂志
宣传单 联单
手提袋 不干胶
名片 丝印
挂历 条幅
不锈钢字
镂空字
刻章
专业
刻章
刻章
电脑

2. STUDIO

2.1.1.

Interview with Vincent Lo

PP.2/3 Evening shoppers gather in the retail area in the center of Chonqging.

PP.4/5 Floating restaurants line the riverbanks of central Chongqing.

PP.4/5 The vast central plaza of a new commercial district in Chongqing.

P.12 A man eats a supper of noodles in a small restaurant in Chongqing.

P.15 Holiday decorations fill storefronts lining a small lane in central Chongqing.

P.17 A group of men warm themselves by an open fire in a commercial area of Chongqing.

P.18 A narrow residential lilong in central Shanghai.

Vincent Lo of Shu On Land discusses his role as a developer in China.

Nina Rappaport How and when did you first begin developing projects?

Vincent Lo My first development project was in 1976, working on a private-sector participation scheme for the Hong Kong government to provide affordable housing that qualified residents of the city could purchase. I learned most in the development of Xintiandi, as it was the first of its kind in Shanghai to combine preservation with a new food-and-entertainment hub in the city center. First, I had to understand what the market needed and could accept, because the concept was new to China. Since the successful launching of this project, my company has been invited by many other provinces to undertake similar projects in different municipalities.

NR What was it like to be a developer in Shanghai in 1985, at the initial growth period of Chinese cities? How were you different in your approach to development?

VL China was in the beginning stage of its reform and just starting to open up. The property market wasn't formed because the government allocated all housing, so there was little or no purchasing power.

Therefore, my first project was to invest, with the Communist Youth League, in the development of a small three-star hotel in the center of Shanghai. The market wasn't ready for developers from outside of China, and it was quite a few years before we ventured into property development projects there.

The Xintiandi portion of the Taipingqiao development in central Shanghai incorporates both renovated Shikumen-style buildings and new construction in brick and stone to create a contemporary interpretation of the traditional Shanghainese lilong neighborhood.

Projects were planned in cooperation with the government since the state had control of all land resources. With the reform policy taking root and the Chinese economy growing at a consistently rapid rate, a huge demand for quality office, commercial, and residential buildings developed. Since the completion of Shanghai's Xintiandi, Shui-On Land has worked closely with the government in identifying opportunities to cater to the needs of different cities. We undertook extensive research on the cities concerned, examining their economic infrastructures, histories, competitive strengths, resources, and opportunities and threats. Then, together with the government, we would propose the planning of a new landmark city-center redevelopment project.

NR How does one work with the government to coordinate projects? What is the process for acquiring development sites, and how do you organize contracts differently in China than for those in the United States? When you have partners, how do you coordinate the same process, especially in developing and expanding future markets?

The traditional low-rise urban fabric of of Shanghai's Xintiandi stands out against the high-rise development of central Shanghai. To the left of the image is the Taipingqiao Park that forms the hear of Shui-On's development.

PP.22/23 The first of three towers designed by KPF for the Chongqing International Trade and Commerce Center rises over the lake at the center of the Chongqing Tiandi development.

VL After identifying a site suitable for development, we work out a master plan and submit it to the government. After approval by the government departments concerned, the site is put up for tender or auction. Because we have already been working on the site for some time, we have a strong competitive edge over other developers in the acquisition of the site.

Land acquisition is very different than it is in the United States because there is no freehold land in China. Land can be leasehold only from the government. And when you go into a development cooperation with the government, typically the contract is like an agreement listing out only the basic terms. For example, our project in Shanghai, which would cost more than $4 billion, required only a six-page development agreement with the government thirteen years ago, and it has worked out wonderfully well. If we have development partners, we go through the same procedures, except the government expects my company to be the lead partner since they have worked with and have confidence in us.

A mix of high and midrise development provide a dense residential environment in Wuhan Tiandi.

The low-rise retail area of Wuhan Tiandi provides well-shaded pedestrian streets lined by restaurants and cafes.

NR Xintiandi is your most well-known project. What led you to the concept of preserving the central core, developing new buildings, and creating that unique environment? And how was the preservation of scale an important issue? How did you work with architects and the government to incorporate the preservation of historic sites into your plans?

VL Xintiandi was an innovative redevelopment concept for Shanghai and China. We undertook the project because of the existence in the neighborhood of the First Congress Hall of the Communist Party.

The government required us to preserve the streetscape and the ambience, and no tall buildings were to be allowed in the neighborhood. Therefore, we had to consider how to best make use of the historic shikumen, or stone gate housing that is unique to Shanghai, how to preserve and make use of these buildings in the modern age. Since shikumen architecture is not really suitable for today's residential or commercial use, we had to adapt it for food-and-entertainment purposes.

No one in China had experience in this type of work at the time, so we invited Benjamin Wood, an American architect, who was involved in the planning and design of Boston's Faneuil Hall, to work with Shui-On on the project. Wood spent a few months in Shanghai studying the stone-gate housing architecture and roaming the streets to get a feel for the local atmosphere so he could capture it in the design. We felt it was not advisable to just develop the project for tourists; our first target customers were the local people. So, we also engaged the services of a Tongji University professor, who is an expert on shikumen housing, to provide us with all the necessary details about the design and architecture. We also made use of old building materials that we had taken from the dilapi-

The Knowledge and Innovation Community (KIC) is a mixed-use devleopment that combines offices with residential buildings and recreational facilities in an attempt to foster a new technology hub in Shanghai.

dated buildings we had to demolish to construct the new ones. This gave Xintiandi an authentic look.

NR Why did you not hire a Chinese architect who is an expert on the historic buildings?

VL We did not hire a Chinese architect for the Xintiandi project because this kind of preservation and adaptation project was completely new to China, including in Hong Kong, so we invited Ben Wood, who has a very illustrious track record in the planning and design of these kinds of projects.

NR How do you combine the development side of your business with the construction side?

VL I started out as a building contractor and moved into the property development business later, but it is now the bulk of our business. We have separate management teams for the two businesses, and we make use of the expertise of our contracting arm in property development.

NR How have you influenced the government about its ideas for programs for development and economic growth?

VL In 2002, the Shanghai government wanted to enhance economic growth through technology and science, but it appeared to be a slogan without any substantive action plan. So, we took the initiative to put forward a proposal advocating the development of a community in Shanghai modeled after Silicon Valley, to promote innovation, high-tech, and academic research. We believed that, for innovation and high-tech to succeed, the support of the venture capital industry was required. The Shanghai government was excited by our proposal and invited us to identify a site and work out a detailed plan for its implementation.

I identified and chose the site for the development. The government formed a joint venture with Shui-On Land to undertake the project. In six years, the project is almost half finished and is known as the Knowledge and Innovation Community, in the Yangpu District in Shanghai.

NR What is your method for understanding and building flexibility into a project? Do you allow for future change in a development?

VL We don't build too much flexibility into our development projects because, before coming up with our master plans, we have undertaken

Modern residential towers overlook a central plaza in the KIC.

very extensive and elaborate studies to anticipate the needs and changes in the cities going forward. But should market conditions change dramatically, we don't expect to have much trouble convincing the government to amend the master plan.

Before we took on the Chongqing project, we had carried out a lot of research on Chongqing and had a very clear idea as to which way the city would develop and grow and what kind of facilities would be required in the future. We have built that all into our master plan, and we review the master plan on an annual basis. Thus far, after six years, there hasn't been any requirement to make an amendment to our original master plan. I started out as a building contactor and moved into the property development business later, but it is now the bulk of our business. We have separate management teams for the two businesses, and we make use of the expertise of our contracting arm in property development.

NR Had you ever taught architects before? And what were you most interested in sharing with them from your experience?

VL I had never taught architects before, but I have worked closely with them for over three decades. I hoped my teaching at Yale was informative in terms of understanding large-scale developments in Hong Kong and mainland China, how the market works, and how we work with government. I also hope that the students saw the projects from a property developer's viewpoint.

NR How do you think your approach can be applied, globally, to new development?

VL I don't believe the process of working in China is applicable to other parts of the world because it is in a unique position, with a huge market, a very high rate of economic growth, and an urgent need for a large volume of quality development.

NR As you are expanding into western China, what are the new challenges and opportunities there? What are the most difficult issues in China now in terms of the speed of change?

VL China began its reform policy in the eastern coastal region of the country, and after thirty years of substantial growth there is a huge disparity between the coastal region and the western part of the country. Therefore, the national government has made very strong and determined policies to speed up the growth and development of the west. We have been venturing into the central and western regions for almost ten years, and the cities have grown significantly during that time. The development is challenging in the sense that, as developers and investors, we have to judge the speed of change, and the Chinese government has often taken the world by surprise—including people, like me, who have experience in China—by making major decisions rapidly and then bringing them to fruition in a very short period of time. At this point, there are more opportunities in the western provinces because the growth rate is higher than in the coastal region. The most challenging issue is keeping up with the rapid changes and swift government policies.

Contemporary residential buildings surround preserved Lingnan-style architecture at the center of Foshan Tiandi.

PP.30/31 New high-rises line Century Avenue in the Pudong District of Shanghai.

2.1.2.

Interview with Kohn Pedersen Fox Associates

Jamie von Klemperer, Paul Katz, and Forth Bagley of Kohn Pedersen Fox Associates discuss their work in China.

Nina Rappaport Kohn Pedersen Fox has worked on numerous large-scale projects that are developer-driven. How would you say this work has informed your practice in terms of working with a client that is not the user of the building? What is your role in terms of guiding a building project's program and use?

Jamie von Klemperer Developers have a broader purview than simply attaching a single function to a building; the better ones have made a career of insinuating themselves into the functions. If the buildings contain retail, the developers get into the business of selling, merchandising, and branding. Or, if they are residential compounds, they become specialists in apartment and furniture layouts. As their architects, we have become experts in each of these programs. With the better developers it is like a tennis game, in which we might serve and initiate the idea, but they hit the ball back.

Paul Katz One of the nice things about working with developers is that almost all our clients are repeat clients. We don't spend a lot of time looking for new work, and, as a consequence of establishing these great relationships, we are able to start where we left off on their last project. It saves starting from scratch and, ultimately, leads to better, more sophisticated buildings.

NR The great client is often responsible for a daring design or new program type because they offer greater financial possibilities. When have you influenced a developer in changing the brief and helped them have a new vision that reorganizes programmatic uses in, for example, your projects in China? How did you start working there?

JvK A good example of how we have been able to influence the development paradigm is actually the story of how we started in China in the mid-1990s. At that time, Chinese local development expertise was fledgling. Our involvement was mostly through overseas developers in Hong Kong and Tokyo that had a strong footing in China and brought us into the new environment.

We first worked with a developer named Hang Lung to re-skin a building that was already under construction; it was a very modest project, but we added value through design. They then asked us to design Plaza 66, in Shanghai. The building defined the best level of office building for international business, and, at the time, it became a kind of Valhalla of luxury shopping in China.

The developer hadn't really anticipated the success, but soon mayors from other parts of China wanted the same building type. It quickly

Rising above the city, the distinctive tapering form of the Shanghai World Financial Center catches the light of the setting sun.

became a development brand. The expressions of form and the fluid circulation plan worked with the program, which the developer repeated in Tianjin, Shenyang, Wuhan, and ten other Chinese cities. If the developer were to do that before assigning the architect, the project would have lost all its dynamism.

Forth Bagley There are similar examples with other clients, too. People talk about China as if that country's rapid growth and urbanization were inevitable. There is nothing that said that China would grow the way it did. It is the result of architects like us and developers like Shui-On Land working with the government to solve problems and capitalize on the benefits of this unprecedented economic expansion.

NR With the second wave of development in China, at the time of the Beijing Olympics, did you feel a drastic change in the way your work was considered and the types of projects you were commissioned to undertake? How did you become more known?

JvK We had already been practicing in China, but, at that time, state-owned Chinese enterprises felt confident enough to hire us. Suddenly, Chinese companies commissioned us to do one-off headquarters projects. They looked at Plaza 66 and our Shanghai World Financial Center—which is now the tallest building in China and put us on the map in a way that no advertising ever could—and saw a proven track record. We never marketed in China. We did projects, talked to students, and gave lectures. Our books were bootlegged and translated into Chinese. We saw our work copied. At a certain point, we thought there must have been an edict that every major Chinese city should have a 400- meter-tall building because we were seeing requests to design them for places such as Shenzhen, Suzhou, Shenyang, Guangzhou, and Tianjin. At the end of the day, designing and delivering a collection of quality buildings was the best form of advertising.

NR How do you maintain your control—and not just deliver drawings—so that you see through the project to construction? How have you contributed to the change in building-construction culture?

PK Architects believe in making buildings that are physically solid, interesting, and durable, and that was a tough thing to achieve in China in 1994. If you built an average building, it stuck out. That is simply no longer true. When we started there we made a rule not to take projects with less than construction-document control for the exterior wall and public spaces. This approach was different from other firms, and it allowed us to maintain a level of control over detailing and execution that was unique.

The lapped panels of the facade of the International Commerce Center (ICC) in Kowloon, Hong Kong peel away from the building at the base to create a dramatic canopy at the entrance to the Ritz-Carlton Hotel.

The orientation of the curtainwall panels on the ICC tower in Hong Kong strikingly reflect the sunlight.

PP.36/37 A close-up photograph shows the detail of the lapped curtain wall panels at the base of the ICC tower.

Our New York City office, along with a certain group of engineers and contractors—an Italian exterior-wall company or a curtain-wall engineer from the Philippines—worked together to raise the level of construction.

There is a long chain of international export pioneers working in China.

JvK Absolutely, today, the tables are beginning to turn. The biggest curtain-wall company in the world is now in the northern Chinese city of Shenyang. KPF is adapting, too. While the design center of our firm is still very much in New York City, we've established offices in Hong Kong and Shanghai as well as elsewhere to help deliver these complicated projects.

NR Where have you been able to innovate in terms of new vertical urban-design developments?

JvK Innovation has happened, for us, in these tall-building projects because, when you have thirty thousand people flowing in and out of

a building each day, there are serious implications for connections to infrastructure and transit systems. Hong Kong and Japan, with their hyper density, provide the highest form of development of the idea. Our firm innovated in steps in these places.

PK Exactly. It has been incremental. What we've seen is that some of the gigantic departures from the design norm in China may not actually have the greatest influence. For example, one of the greatest buildings in China in the past decade is the CCTV. It is a masterpiece, but it has not led to a paradigm shift. Because it is such a giant step away from conventional development patterns rather than an incremental innovation, it has proved to be less influential in shaping the Chinese built environment.

NR How do you see solutions to increased density, especially in places like China, contributing to sustainability—something that has been talked about for years in terms of urban transit and preserving open space?

PK The subject of density is a deep focus for our firm because we really started as a tall-building firm. The tall building had been a white-bread, speculative, single-use tower; but, over time and particularly in the Asian context, the ability of the tower to become a mixed-use vertical city added a new dimension to the building type. The potency of plugging it into horizontal infrastructural networks made it a tree with roots that played a major role in the way city-center nodes were shaped. With the rising tide of sustainable investigation and the importance of density in favoring transit hubs and transportation centers as places to stack up program—not just twenty or forty stories but even higher—super-density has become the clearest and most potent solution for combating sprawl.

FB Examples of this phenomenon are three of our supertall towers now under construction in the Pearl River Delta: ICC in Hong Kong, Ping An IFC in Shenzhen, and the Chow Tai Fook Center in Guangzhou. Each of these towers is a 400-meter-plus, mixed-use supertall tower that announces a new central business district in its city and has connections to citywide subway networks. Once completed, they will all connect to a new high-speed-rail line, which allows the buildings to be connected in new ways. ICC's twenty thousand population in Hong Kong will be twenty minutes from Ping An IFC's twenty thousand population in Shenzhen—and the traveler never has to going outside.

PK When you have cities of eight million or ten million connected like that—with supertall towers placed strategically at the gateway to these connections—it changes what people expect from these buildings. They are no longer mere office buildings.

JvK At the other end of the spectrum, another example, is one of our projects in the middle of Shanghai. Jing An is built around a house that Mao Tse-tung lived in for six months in his youth, before the Communist Party took off. The project is on the scale of Rockefeller Center, with towers and base buildings, but it employs a freer form of building blocks, which are used to match a program that crescendos from the ground to a 300-meter-tall tower. The dream is for it to be a center for opera and culture as well as a base for corporations and a place to live.

NR How does such a major insertion into a historic area respond to context?

JvK That's an interesting question because Shanghai, as a former concession city, is a patchwork. It really wasn't a Chinese city; it was built by the French and the Russians, among others. The vernacular form of housing tracts built up in the early twentieth century developed an urban fabric of very large blocks. Zones were bounded by wide roads; inside the zones were organic occurrences of open spaces and alleyways, from public roads to semi-public streets and private gardens. We try to work on large projects in a way that recaptures, at a different scale, the DNA of that kind of public-private space. It's not for the sake of nostalgia; it is what really makes Shanghai a particularly alluring place in which to walk and live.

PK There's real value in not erasing that past. It's something Vincent Lo saw very early on. Visitors coming to Chinese cities generally encounter daunting seas of thirty-story buildings. It's part of our thinking in the United States that heritage is a positive; taking that and applying it in a fundamental way to the Chinese city has led to some of the most rewarding architectural results.

NR How did you come to work with Vincent Lo in the Yale studio?

PK Vincent Lo is one of the most active and dynamic developers practicing today. Vincent's Xintiandi development has done for Shanghai in the 2000s what Rockefeller Center did for New York City in the 1930s. It's impossible to overstate his impact on Shanghai and on the Chinese city, in general. We immediately thought of him when we decided to tackle the issue of high-density urbanism in western China for the Yale studio.

JvK Plus, he is genuinely interested in building on what he has achieved in Xintiandi—finding new models for development and positively contributing to the future growth of Chinese cities. He is open to the kinds of adventure that an architect should be interested in. Vincent is very well respected in the Chinese government.

FB You can't really talk about Chinese city planning without having these kinds of close relationships. He has opportunities to impart the change we hope the students will accomplish.

NR Do you think the studio could influence new typologies in China in terms of multi-functional train stations integrated into the city fabric?

JvK Yes. The site for the studio project is Chongqing's central train station. It is huge and very centrally located, but it is isolated. In China, transportation has tended to be kept separate from commercial development. We wanted to see what would happen if the students could build off the development model of Xintiandi—its blend of public and private spaces, program, and typologies—and increase its density to reflect the importance of the train station at the heart of the city center. How dense could we make it? How could this building respond to rapid urbanization and an increasingly globalized middle class? How could it advance the current development paradigm? In fact, this studio project could actually change architectural and urban history in China because we have a developer who thinks it is an intriguing idea.

PK What we're interested in studying with the students is the tip of this process of urbanization—in shaping and giving form to the moment this unprecedented growth meets globalization.

A rendering shows the new CTF Finance Center rising over the Zhujiang River in Guangzhou.

A mock-up of the curtain wall of the CTF Finance Center shows the terracotta fins that run up the facade of the tower.

A rendering shows the stepped crown of the CTF Financial Center tower in Guangzhou. The complex contains a hotel, luxury residences, and a series of outdoor terraces and gardens.

PP.42/43 A street cleaner pauses in a residential area of central Shanghai.

2.2.1.

Studio Brief

Summary of Studio Problem

Over the past fifteen years, the urban development model exemplified by Shanghai's Pudong Central Business District—large, mixed-use blocks set in isolation from one another—has become the dominant model for urban growth in China. It is now widely acknowledged among planners in China and the West that this model encourages urban sprawl and automobile use over consolidated, pedestrian-friendly, transit-oriented neighborhoods, while also privileging privatized open spaces over more accessible public parks and plazas. As urbanization and economic growth extends into China's western cities, local planners are looking for other models of urban development to create lasting, sustainable, and dynamic urban projects.

The success of development company Shui-On Land's innovative Xintiandi project as a mixed-use neighborhood in central Shanghai offers a richer, more sustainable model of development, with connections to public transit, pedestrian-friendly streets, and open public green spaces. The students studied Xintiandi and other mixed-use projects in the first half of the semester and then employed the lessons they learned in their proposals for a superdense, mixed-use development on the site of Chongqing's central rail station.

Guided by the combined expertise of developers and practicing architects, the Edward P. Bass Distinguished Visiting Architecture Fellowship seeks to ground innovative academic work in the realities of contemporary development. The intention of the Chongqing studio was to explore the limits of superdense, mixed-use development in a rapidly urbanizing city, serving as a test case, more broadly, for new development in western China. From the start, the Chongqing site, for which Shui-On Land and architect Kohn Pedersen Fox Associates are currently collaborating on a large-scale project, offered specific challenges related to its geography, infrastructure, and economy. The students were asked to pay careful attention to the mixed-use program and the site in order to produce new models of sustainable, livable urban space that could be both visionary and realistic. These projects surpass their precedents in density and mix of uses, suggesting new directions for development that address the radical pace and scale of urban growth in cities, such as Chongqing, in western China.

Context

Over the past twenty years, the Chinese economy has evolved, growing from one of the world's smallest to its second largest, behind only the United States. An unprecedented migration of millions of people from western and central China into burgeoning cities along the country's eastern seaboard has accompanied this rapid economic growth. This process—the largest mass migration in human history—has caused the country's cities to balloon in size, fundamentally reshaping their urban character.

In few cities has this transformation been as extreme as in Shanghai, a city which has undergone a process of urbanization unlike any in world history. In Pudong, where rice fields and small villages once stood across the Huangpu River from the historic city center, a new central business district (CBD) has a skyline that is as dramatic as any in the world's most established cities. This area, planned as a high-density city of the future, has influenced a generation of city master plans throughout China. Consequently, large, isolated blocks framed by overscaled boulevards—the basic urban form of Pudong—have become the norm for almost all new developments in major Chinese cities.

The megaproject—often derided as excessive, exuberant, and wasteful in the West—has emerged as China's dominant urban condition, providing an efficient legal, economic, and architectural solution to increasing the density of its cities. Though the legal rationale and perceived municipal economic benefits of these large parcel projects are clear, the architectural and urban implications have been less certain. While architects, through their work with developers, have designed buildings that have created fundamentally new paradigms for mixed-use superblocks, shattering assumptions about a single project's ability to produce a genuine internal urban realm, the wide boulevards, prescribed uses, and isolated nature of these blocks continually undermine the urban conditions established within individual sites.

As urban populations continue to grow and the limits of large, single-block development become apparent, China's city planners have begun to look for ways to enrich the existing development paradigm. No longer embracing the automobile-oriented American model of urban

The modern skyline of Pudong, Shanghai's Central Business District, as seen from the historic Bund, across the river.

growth, planners have increasingly turned to development models that are more complex and layered as a way to create sustainable, efficient, and vibrant cities.

Xintiandi

When it opened in 2001, Shui-On Land's Xintiandi project in Shanghai fundamentally reshaped expectations about the future of Chinese cities. The project combined new development and park space with the restoration and adaptation of a low-rise historic district, creating a remarkable hybrid of traditional, pedestrian-friendly urban fabric, modern high-density building stock, and a rich mix of programs that keep the neighborhood busy throughout the day and night. Never before had a developer in China attempted to preserve heritage architecture while integrating new development within an existing urban context, elevating the urban experience with a diverse mix of program types.

At Xintiandi, Shui-On Land merged one of modern China's most important historical sites—location of the first congress of the Communist Party—with hotel, retail, entertainment, residential, and office programs, a large public park, and internal city streets. The "Rockefeller Center of Shanghai" instantly became a destination for residents, tourists, and businesses and showed that developers could produce a sense of the 24-hour life of traditional city fabric within a single-owner, master-planned development.

With urbanization in China's eastern cities slowing, government officials have increasingly focused their attention on developing the economies and urban conditions of China's western cities. Places such as Chengdu, Wuhan, Nanning, and Chongqing are now playing host to the type of growth that occurred over the past two decades in their eastern counterparts.

With the successes and limits of the Pudong style of development now more fully understood, planners seeking alternate strategies to accommodate growth and produce urban density may look to Xintiandi as a model. How can this model be adapted to enliven high-density, urban blocks? What happens when other models and scales of mixed-use development and infrastructure planning are merged with this new model?

The Site

Hemmed in by mountains and isolated from the country's eastern seaboard, Chongqing's population of more than thirty million is spread across an area the size of South Carolina. Its historic downtown, perched on a hilly peninsula at the junction of the Yangtze and Jialing rivers, is home to roughly ten million inhabitants. Like Shanghai, Beijing, and Tianjin, Chongqing is one of China's four *zhíxiásh*, or "directly controlled municipalities" in official parlance. Often referred to simply as the "municipalities," these four cities enjoy a higher position than all other cities in the Chinese command economy and have wider powers of self-administration and planning control than sub-provincial cities, which are normally subject to provincial planning authority. Chongqing was made a municipality 1997, but has begun to thrive only recently, thanks to its growing manufacturing industries, primarily in the automotive and technology sectors, as well as investments in infrastructure and communication, which have propelled it to the top of the country's real estate development market. Much of the city's fabric is now being re-imagined and repositioned.

Chongqing Railway Station, the site of the studio project, is the city's principal rail terminal, which includes the areas above and below the adjacent rail lines as well as the nearby infrastructural assemblages and public open space. This site is a snarl of urban infrastructures that must be rationalized, reconfigured, and improved if it is to survive the city's growing pains. Tucked between the hills and the Jialing River and ringed by infrastructure, including towering elevated highways and rail lines, the site is a complex and important transportation node in the city, offering numerous connections to regional and local transit.

The municipal government invited Shui-On Land to tender for redeveloping Chongqing Railway Station. In turn, Shui-On Land asked the students, acting as its architects, to complete an analysis of the site and then design a series of schemes for development. The site was assigned a floor area ratio (FAR) of 20, but no restriction was given on program and height, which were determined by the individual students for each of their projects. The government noted that the tender would be evaluated on the design's ability to do the following:

- Provide a model of high-density development that can be successfully adapted to other cities in western China.
- Create a symbol of the city's continued growth, attractiveness, and prosperity.
- Promote public infrastructure and environmentally sound, sustainable lifestyles.
- Attract businesses, retail, and urban life to the downtown.

Method

Over the first half of the semester, the students studied Xintiandi and other mixed-use superblock developments, producing comprehensive analytic diagrams of their forms, programs, and relationships to the urban context. During this period, the students traveled to Shanghai and Chongqing to visit precedents and see the site. While in China, they also met with a senior team from Shui-On Land, the vice mayor of Chongqing, and other local officials to learn more about contemporary patterns of development, the history and economic conditions of Chongqing, and the project site itself. The students developed preliminary program distribution schemes for the Chongqing site and presented their initial briefs to the Shui-On Land senior team.

The precedent studies covered a comprehensive range of mixed-use and rail projects. Beginning in Shanghai, the students, in teams of two, compared Shui-On Land's approach in Xintiandi to previous mixed-use developments in Shanghai, focusing on the individual program types, adjacencies, and effects of Plaza 66, the Jing An Mixed-Use Development, People's Square, Shanghai IFC, and the Shanghai World Financial Center. Then, the student pairs undertook a comprehensive analysis of Xintiandi's multiple functions and typologies, including the residential towers, retail and entertainment areas, hotels, offices, and parks and cultural facilities.

After this in-depth look at Shanghai, the students expanded their knowledge of important and innovative mixed-use projects in Hong Kong and Japan, places that offered both complementary and contrasting contexts for understanding the potential of the site in Chongqing. Because of its density, emphasis on infrastructural connections, and integrated public and private sectors, Hong Kong provided a foil to the history of development in Shanghai. Further, Pacific Place, Hong Kong Station/IFC, Kowloon Station/ICC, The Landmark, and the Shun Tak Centre were analyzed for their program adjacencies, connections to transportation, and overall branding and design. Japanese mixed-use projects—Roppongi Hills, Tokyo Midtown, Nagoya Station, Tokyo Station, and Kyoto Station—also provided interesting lessons on the relationship between private and public development, particularly as integrated into the country's remarkable rail network.

Following their visit to Chongqing, the students began the design of their individual mixed-use projects. Working from a program brief and a set of urban aspirations developed in consultation with the studio critics, the students began by developing three design options for the project. By the mid-review, the students were expected to have developed one of these options into a scheme with a clear narrative relating their brief and program mix to the urban context. Following the mid-review, the students engaged in detailed design of their schemes—developing a diverse range of projects that included mixed-use supertall and superblock schemes informed by the typological studies of the Shanghai, Hong Kong, and international models researched in the first part of the semester. Taken together, the projects, many of which attempted to hybridize key precedents to maximize density and connectivity, pose an exciting set of questions about what might be possible for the future cities of western China.

The driver of a three-wheeled taxi in Chongqing.

The Shanghai World Financial Center towers over Shanghai at dusk.

PP.50/51 A new business center under construction in Chongqing.

2.3.1.

New Development in Chongqing: Challenges and Opportunities

—

Wu Jiang, Vice President, Tongji University

Over the past three decades, China has experienced a massive and rapid urbanization process that is unprecedented in human history. Increasing by a rate of 1 percent per year over this span, the urban population of China has grown to 50 percent from less than 20 percent of the total population. Today, this urban population is increasing by thirteen million people per year. If promising assumptions of Chinese economic growth over the next twenty to thirty years hold true, the scale and pace of Chinese urbanization will continue to grow steadily.

During these past thirty years of growth, Chinese urbanization was mainly concentrated in the eastern coastal zone. The Pearl River Delta (centered on Guangzhou and Shenzhen), the Yangtze River Delta (centered on Shanghai), and the Bohai Economic Rim (centered on Beijing and Tianjin) developed into megalopolitan areas that encompass numerous major and minor cities. Most significant architectural and urban projects were developed in these vast urban agglomerations. However, as rapid and sustained economic growth has spread urbanization processes to the midwestern region of China, the central government initiated its ambitious Western China Development policy to direct this trend.

The site for this graduate studio, jointly taught by Shui-On Land and Kohn Pedersen Fox Associates, is Chongqing, the largest city in western China. During the Second World War, Chongqing was made the provisional capital of the national government, which established Chongqing as a major Chinese city in politics, economics, and especially industry. Since then, the mountainous city has been an important urban and economic center in the upper reaches of the Yangtze River Economic Zone in western China. Recently, Chongqing has been designated as the fourth, directly governed municipality in China, following Beijing, Shanghai, and Tianjin. Today, this massive municipality—it is the largest of the four—of over 32 million people and 82,000 square kilometers, with the city of Chongqing at its heart, is entering into a new stage of development.

Like many western Chinese cities, Chongqing now faces the pressure of catching up with these three other, highly urbanized but more economically developed cities on China' east coast in order to compete with them economically on the national stage. There is a large development gap between the municipality of Chongqing, where nearly 50 percent of the population remains in the rural areas surrounding the city proper, and Beijing, Shanghai, and Tianjin. Among the municipalities, however, Chongqing enjoys its own development advantages: it has the highest population of the four and greater available land resources. Further, in the 1960s and 1970s, when major industrial facilities were relocated to western China, Chongqing was one of the cities to benefit, and it now has a solid industrial base that attracts China's top workers and talent. Today, the Western China Development policy of the Chinese central government offers Chongqing incredible opportunities to transform its economy and urban infrastructure.

Chongqing is situated in a mountainous region of western China and is known as "Mountain City." The historic and densely developed center of Chongqing is located on a peninsula of steep hills formed by the intersection of the Yangtze River and the Jialing River. Rapidly growing new urban centers now ring this geographically contained area. The geomorphology of Chongqing makes the spatial distribution of the city significantly different from the urban patterns found in Shanghai, Tianjin, and Beijing and poses a number of unique challenges for urban planning and design.

Modern development in Chongqing has largely consisted of point towers. Within the old city, the dramatic topography has created interesting spatial conditions for tower development as the steepness of the hills produces multiple ground planes from which a single building may be entered and linked to its urban context. In the rapidly growing perimeter areas, by contrast, these towers are more conventionally located in large, open lots that have been prepared for development. A complex network of expressways, as well as an emerging metro system, links these new areas to central Chongqing and one another, spanning the two rivers at multiple points.

As it develops Chongqing can refer to the successful economic lessons of urbanization on China's east coast. But will Chongqing achieve greater performance in terms of environmental protection, ecological maintenance, and cultural continuity? The congested, complex urban infrastructure must negotiate significant topographical challenges, such as crossing rivers and mountains; adequate rail and public transit systems are lacking, resulting in an overdependence on private cars; the topography and placement of infrastructure makes pedestrian activity difficult; the existing building stock in the city center is aging and insufficient to house the growing population and the emerging service economy. While the municipality is attempting to increase industrial production, transition to a more balanced mix of service and industrial economies, and accommodate the rapid urbanization of its still significant rural population, its planners want to preserve important concentrations of historic fabric and vernacular building typologies but also the incredibly beautiful—and architecturally challenging—terrain.

The Yale studio provided the students with an opportunity to confront the scale, constraints, and challenges of contemporary urban development. They were expected to engage not only the complex blend of topography and infrastructure existing on the project site of Chongqing's main rail station but also produce a brief for one million square meters of mixed-use development—that is, a superblock—that would guide their design work. The expertise of Shui-On Land, Kohn Pedersen Fox, and the faculty of Yale was crucial to developing ten well-rounded and thoughtful projects, each of which, in its own way, addresses the spatial and programmatic challenges presented by the ambitious scale of the studio.

Taken together, these design concepts break through the old, static image of Chongqing to create a lively urban character that respects the topography of the site. More important, the students successfully mixed comprehensive urban programs and vivid urban spaces into holistic architectural projects.

2.3.2.

The CBD Model: Canary Wharves in Central China

—

Michiel Hulshof and Daan Roggeveens

Journalist Michiel Hulshof is partner at Tertium, architect Daan Roggeveen is the founder of MORE Architecture, Shanghai and curator at University of Hong Kong/Shanghai Study Centre.

In 2009, they founded the Go West Project, a multidisciplinary research studio focusing on emerging megacities and published the book How the City Moved to Mr Sun: China's New Megacities, *in 2011.*

Chongqing and other cities in central and western China are competing vehemently with each other for foreign investment. China has transformed itself from a country of peasants to a nation of manufacturers; the time has now come to improve the high-end services industry. Just as the concept of the Special Economic Zone (SEZ) stimulated industrial development in the 1980s and 1990s, new Central Business Districts (CBDs) are being created to encourage the growth of the financial and service sectors. Administrators see a CBD as the crowning achievement in the transformation of their town to a modern metropolis.

Since Shanghai began the transformation of the district of Pudong into a center of international finance in the early 1990s, every ambitious Chinese city has wanted its own CBD: a district with an impressive skyline of high-rise office blocks containing the regional headquarters of

A "stick man" carries goods in central Chongqing.

multinationals, banks, legal firms, investors, insurers, and consultants. Beijing built the Chaoyang CBD, Guangzhou established the Tianhe CBD, and Tianjin developed the Binhai CBD. The concept is so popular that the abbreviation *CBD* has become a word in the Chinese language.

Like every self-respecting Chinese city, Chongqing has built its own urban-planning hall in the heart of the old city center, at the crossing of the Yangtze and Jialing rivers. It houses a massive model of the future city from which potential investors can pick from several CBDs that are to be constructed in the coming decades.

These new CBDs in central China should not be seen exclusively as a sign of China's rapid economic development. The numerous new business districts popping up all over the country could just as well be the result of the pitfalls of the Chinese model for urban development, as we saw in Wuhan, one of Chongqing's competitors in central China.

•••

We first met Professor Yu Yiding in the fall of 2009. The deputy director of the Wuhan planning authority smoked one local Red Golden Dragon cigarette after the other. Yu received us in an archetypical academic's office. Papers and reports covered his desk. The cabinet was crammed with books, a wooden globe, and cardboard boxes containing bottles of mineral water. In this remarkable atmosphere, he explained to us how the city of Wuhan embarked on a journey to become a financial center.

In the 1990s, when Yu worked as a professor at Wuhan University, discussions of moving the military Wangjiadun Airport began. Due to the rapid growth of the city, the runway and control tower had been swallowed up by the Wuhan urban area. Residential areas completely encircled the air force base. In 2002, Yu moved from Wuhan University to the Planning Authority. His timing was excellent. Less than a year later, Wuhan's People's Congress decided to raze Wangjiadun Airport. It was every city planner's dream: the sudden materialization of an empty zone seven square kilometers in size, twice as large as New York City's Central Park, in the center of Wuhan, a rapidly growing city of millions.

Yu had spent the preceding five years figuring out what to do with that enormous swath of vacant land. As he spoke to us, he took a map of Wuhan out of his desk and spread it out on a low wooden table. He pointed at the strategic position of the former airfield while he recounted the lively debates at the Planning Authority: "How could we use the area? We could turn it into a residential district, a park, or perhaps even a forest. But none of these ideas seemed quite right. The local authorities had spent a lot of money on shifting the air-base and wanted to recover the costs. It soon became clear we would have to do something else." Yu and his colleagues finally designated this new area in the heart of the city a Central Business District, every self-respecting Chinese city's dream.

•••

International consultancy firms are increasingly taking over the role of architects and planners in the first phase of the planning process in Chinese megacities. In Wuhan, McKinsey backed Yu and the local planners in building a Central Business District on the site of the air base. The consulting company studied thirty different business districts worldwide, from Tokyo's Shinkuju to La Défense in Paris to the Frankfurt Bankenviertel to the Chicago Loop. A delegation visited several European business districts for inspiration. McKinsey finally proposed that the Wuhan city planners use London's Canary Wharf as an example and advised them to not only follow a similar master plan, but also to use a comparable approach to private-sector, rather than government, development, with the idea that companies have shareholders and won't create "vanity projects" that will be vacant for years.

The mix of functions in the Chinese inner city—offices, restaurants, shops, hairdressers, hotels, and apartments, all stacked and crammed together—leads to an incredible liveliness. Contemporary Chinese urban planning, however, is strongly based on Modernist principles—the division of work, housing, recreation, and traffic. Proposed business districts follow this logic and are highly mono-functional: they are aimed at attracting office workers but not so much creating a mix of functions. This approach means these areas are deserted on nights and weekends, like Canary Wharf, La Défense, and Midtown Manhattan. The Chinese CBD is marked by a large icon on the planning map, with the aim of stimulating development around it. In Wuhan, a central tower expresses ambitions for the future: 428 meters of glass and steel, almost twice as high as One Canada Square in Canary Wharf.

The other great asset of Chinese cities is urban informality: street sellers, night markets, lively streets, and people of all sorts mixing in public space. This concept does not fit the image of a modern business center, and has no place in the new business districts. Real estate developers allow only shops selling top brands.

•••

Shanghai and Beijing make significant marks on global politics, economy, and culture and can justifiably call themselves global cities. As China strengthens its position in the world and develops its interior, a number of cities in central China also will make the list of world cities. This has not happened yet, but city authorities have huge ambitions. By attracting foreign companies and multinationals, they hope, first, to create jobs and money and, second, to raise their international profile. Administrators have a personal interest in success. China may not be a democracy in which politicians answer to their constituents in elections, but the ruling party does hold mayors and other senior officials to account based on

Chongqing 2020 is represented in this 900-square-meter model at the Chongqing Urban Planning Exhibition Hall, accompanied by a sound and light show and copious numerical superlatives attesting to the speed and scale of development.

performance. "Officials holding government posts, such as governor or mayor, are rated according to an impressively lengthy list of numerical indicators, which look like they were drawn up by management consultants," writes Richard McGregor in his revealing book *The Party*. "Economic growth, investment, the quality of the air and water in their localities, and public order all theoretically count in benchmarking performance." The most important criterion by far is that of economic growth. Directors able to show the highest levels of economic growth can count on promotions to larger cities or national politics. Cities compete in all sorts of ways for the favor of foreign investors, who are among the main drivers of economic growth.

Mayors increasingly turn to urban development and architecture to lure potential investors. This happens in their so-called urban planning centers, which depict the future global city in scale models. Every ambitious Chinese metropolis has such a specially designed arena for the seduction of foreign delegations. Visitors first pass photographs of senior officials, followed by panels exhibiting the history of the city and maps of the area. They then enter the holiest of holies: a hall with a giant model depicting the city in 2020. After taking seats on a special VIP balcony overlooking the model, the lights dim and a slick sound and light show commences, astonishing the visitors with the sheer expression of ambition. The spectators can observe with their own eyes that the city they are visiting is swiftly becoming a city of global importance, with all the investment opportunities that will provide. A physical model and a 3D animation say more than a thousand Excel spreadsheets. As the *pièce de résistance* of the presentation, the skyline of the future business district appears.

Many Chinese cities are developing plans for a CBD with the hope of attracting foreign companies. Zhengzhou, Chengdu, Chongqing, and Shijiazhuang all want their own skyline of office blocks. According to researchers Li and Chibamba of the University of Geosciences in Wuhan, the "megaproject" of the new CBD "must be seen as evidence of stiff competition between Chinese cities for foreign capital."

This is significant. In the struggle for the dollar and the yen, China is probably building more CBDs than it needs. In a lengthy and surprisingly open interview, the deputy director of the provincial planning institute in Guiyang city, Shan Xiaogang, told us he purposely avoids joining the craze. "A real CBD is a commercial area with headquarters, supported by financial institutions and consultancies," Shan lectured. "As a city planner, you might copy the buildings but not their content. Most Chinese cities have not yet reached that level of development. Let's put it this way: if you wanted to start a management consultancy firm, I would still advise you to do that in Shanghai."

The battle to establish the most successful banking district of the interior is reminiscent of the competition among the airports of Dubai, Doha, and Abu Dhabi to become the main hub on the Arabian Peninsula. It is clear there will be a winner. After completion, most office towers, hotels, and cultural centers of these new CBDs will stand empty. China builds prior to use, a result of the fact the government drives most developments. Seeing such new heavy infrastructure in a state of disuse evokes associations with the *grands travaux inutiles* of the former Soviet Union. Although the realities of Soviet Communism cannot be simply equated with present day state capitalist China, thirty years of abundant east-coast growth might have made officials and investors in other Chinese cities slightly too optimistic.

•••

To create a CBD of international appeal, cities seek advice from large international design companies. For their urban plans, they ask architecture firms such as SOM, Atkins, Obermeyer, or one of the big Chinese design institutes to submit proposals. This happens by what is known as "plan selection," a typical Chinese phenomenon in which several parties are paid to submit designs. The client then picks the elements it likes best and forges them into a single whole. This kind of pragmatism is completely absent from western urban development. In plan selection, the quality of the final master plan depends on the quality of the client.

During the development process, the city auctions large parcels of land to various property developers, which then design the buildings themselves. They have to abide by a limited number of preconditions prescribed in the master plan, such as maximum height, maximum density, and minimum amount of greenery. The consequences can be seen all over China. Huge roads separate individual blocks that don't have a relationship to each other, as in, for instance, Shanghai's Pudong business district. As a result, pedestrians avoid large parts of the neighborhood, giving it a gloomy and desolate aura.

Walking around the CBD you'll find wide roads, high towers, and a central square with an imposing new town hall, a cultural center, a five-star hotel, and a conference building. The designs of the towers evoke the feeling that you have seen them somewhere before, in another business district in a different large town, in Asia or somewhere else on the planet. The CBD has the same expensive offices, shops, hotels, and serviced apartments just like countless other business districts all over China and the rest of the world. Like everywhere else, the conference center and a large theater must attract the first visitors to the area. That local party functionaries intentionally encourage a copy-and-paste job is evident from the meaningless briefs they formulate for these areas: "High starting point, high standard, high efficiency and high level." The fact that the same global architects operate worldwide further produces conformity. SOM has made plans for CBDs in Beijing, Chicago, Tianjin and drafted the master plan for Canary Wharf, in London. It also developed the plan for Wuhan's new CBD.

All over China, authorities invite the same architects to submit designs, even for iconic buildings such as the highest tower, the museum, or the theater. The Frenchman Paul Andreu has made cultural buildings for business districts in Beijing, Shanghai, Jinan, Suzhou, Chengdu, and Taiyuan. As he consistently uses globes in his designs, Chinese architects say that Andreu "lays an egg in every Chinese city."

Chinese city governments are able to push this kind of development forward because they are able to transfer small rural plots into large-scale urban developments in a period of months. They are able to force villages to sell their land for redevelopment. This reality leads to a shift of land ownership and an incredible increase of plot size because it is easier for the city government to auction land in large parcels. This increase in size coincides with a shift from mixed use to mono-functional use of the land. Modernity washes away these possibilities for mixed use. What remains is a city consisting of islands, connected by wide roads.

If real estate developers and local governments respected land ownership at the fringes of Chinese cities, these areas would continue to develop into lively, mixed areas with a variety of architecture, just as in other Asian cities. By respecting landownership, plot sizes would remain small, which would lead to a highly permeable and walkable type of urban fabric. Entrepreneurs could build their own houses or small commercial blocks. Living, working, education, and shopping could be intermixed. Public space would be a place where people from various backgrounds could meet and mingle. The market would create a variety of housing types. Car traffic would be reduced because the proximity of functions would make it unnecessary to travel by car. The fringes of Chinese cities could have the same urban, architectural, and social qualities of those of Tokyo, Taipei, or Lower Manhattan.

In Chongqing, as in other Chinese megacities, authorities have not reached that conclusion, yet. Instead, they continue their investment-driven growth model, which engenders the construction of new architectural icons and office towers waiting to be filled with white-collar workers. One Central Business District has not even been finished before urban planners shift their attention to the next one.

•••

Two years later, we met Yu Yiding again. Construction in Wuhan's new business district had already started. The foundations for the Wuhan Tower were being poured. A line of billboards by the former airfield encapsulated the conformist dreams of the city government in a giant poster on which the skylines of New York, Paris, Hong Kong, and Shanghai smoothly assimilated into that of the future Wuhan.

The Wuhan Planning and Design Institute had moved to a new building. Yu received us in his new corner office, overlooking the city and the Yangtze River. Apart from the wooden globe, nothing resembled the crammed place where we met the first time. We moved to a meeting room of five by fifteen meters. There was no table, only a big red sofa surrounded by a cream colour carpet. The center of the carpet presented the logo of the institute.

"The plans for the CBD at the former airfield are still interesting," Yu explained, "but the government proceed too slowly. We've shifted our focus." His assistant handed him a small package, a gift for visitors of the institute. It contained a silk shawl that was inscribed with the urban plan of the city. He used the shawl to explain his ambitions. "We really need to develop a new area here," he said, pointing to the district of Wuchang, on the other side of the city. "This is where our new focus for future development is." The key project in the development? A 625-meter-tall tower.

The view from the observation deck of the Shanghai World Financial Center, with the neighboring Jin Mao Tower.

The new Chongqing Opera House looms across the river from the Chaotianmen plaza at the tip of the peninsula of central Chongqing.

PP.62/63 New towers are rapidly filling the areas surrounding the center of Chongqing.

P.64 The traditional low-rise residential urban fabric persists, for now, near Xintiandi in central Shanghai.

3. PRECEDENTS

3.1.0. Mixed-Use Typology

3.2.0. Xintiandi

3.1.0.

Mixed-Use Typology

3.1.1.

Jing An, Kohn Pedersen Fox Associates, Shanghai, under construction

CIRCULATION STRUCTURE

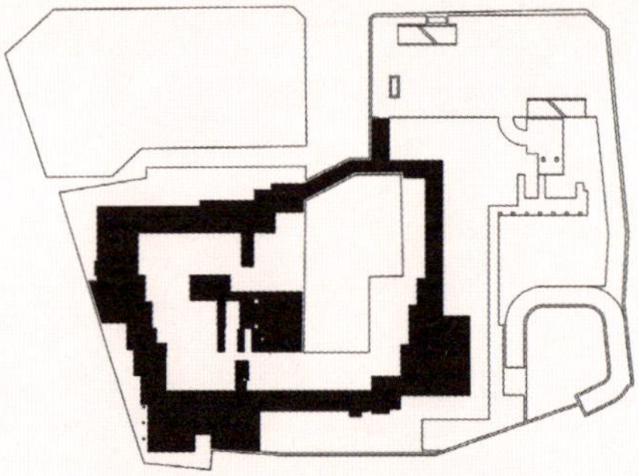

Level -1

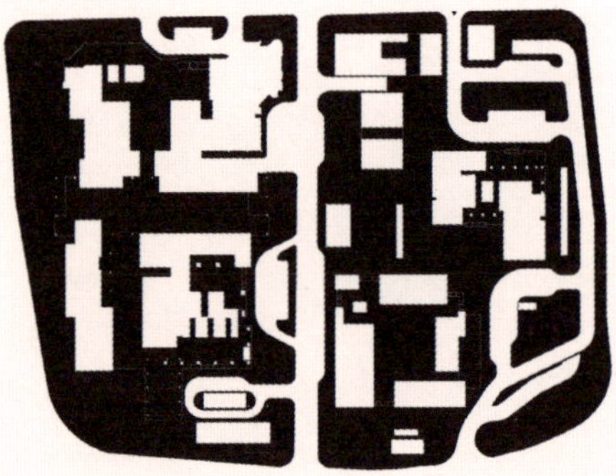

Level 0

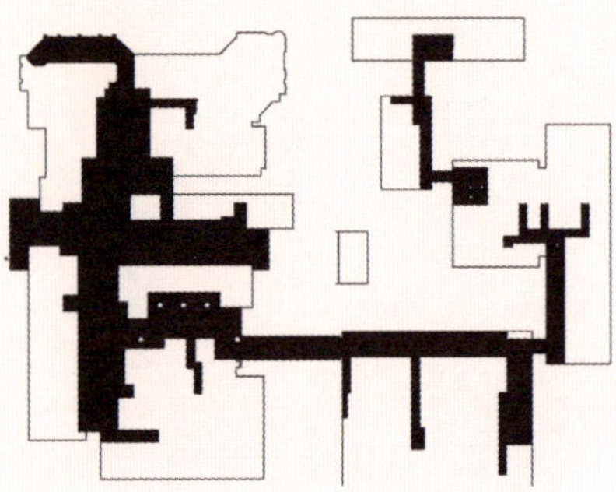

Level 2

PROGRAM DIAGRAM
Distribution

- Residential
- Hotel
- Office
- Retail
- Cultural

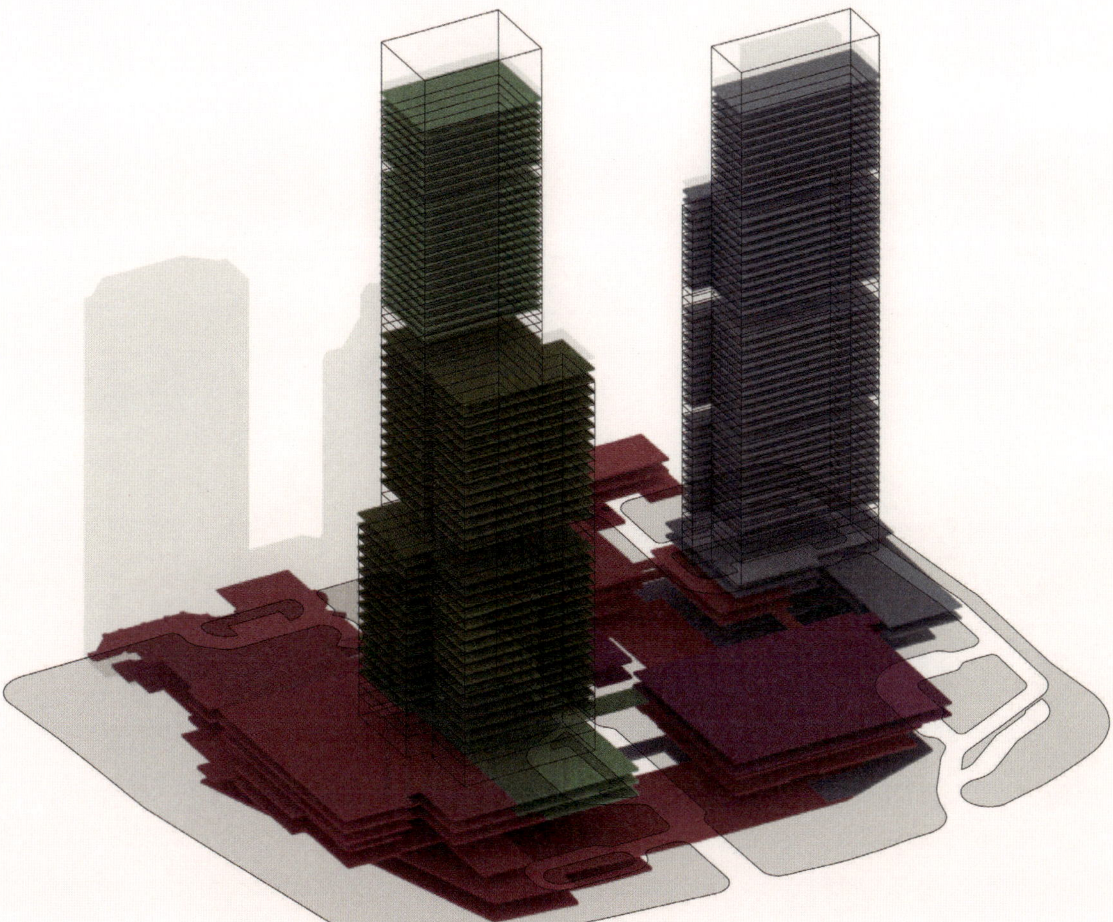

3.1.2.

Plaza 66, Kohn Pedersen Fox Associates, Shanghai, 2002–06

CORE/FLOOR AREA DIAGRAM
Core Area to Lettable Area and Core Elements Area Distribution

TOWER 1

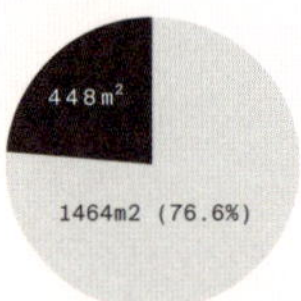

- Core Area
- Lettable Area

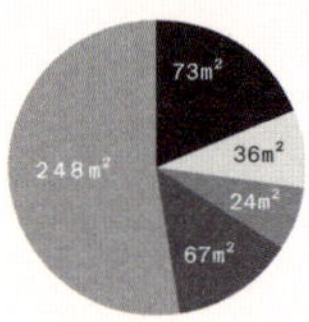

- Lift Area
- Stair Area
- Mech Area
- Wall Area
- Occupiable Area

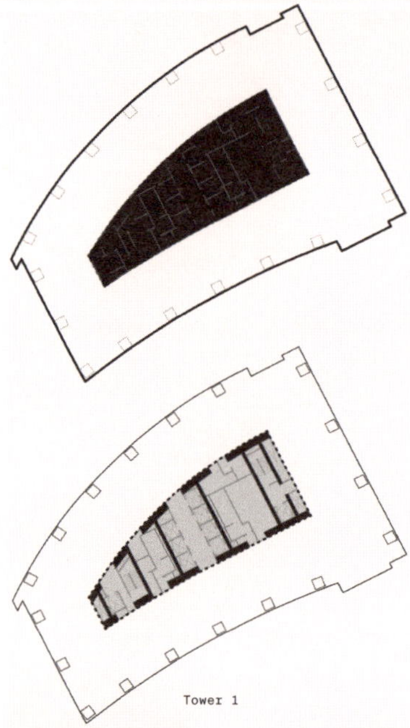

Tower 1

TOWER 2

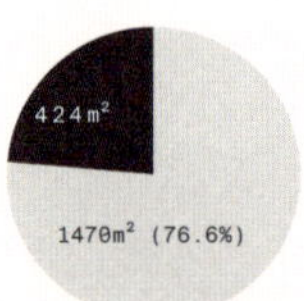

- Core Area
- Lettable Area

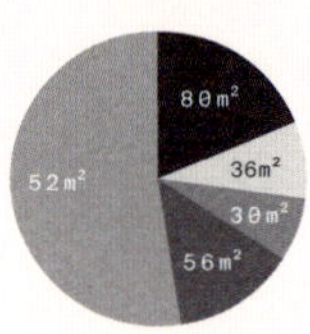

- Lift Area
- Stair Area
- Mech Area
- Wall Area
- Occupiable Area

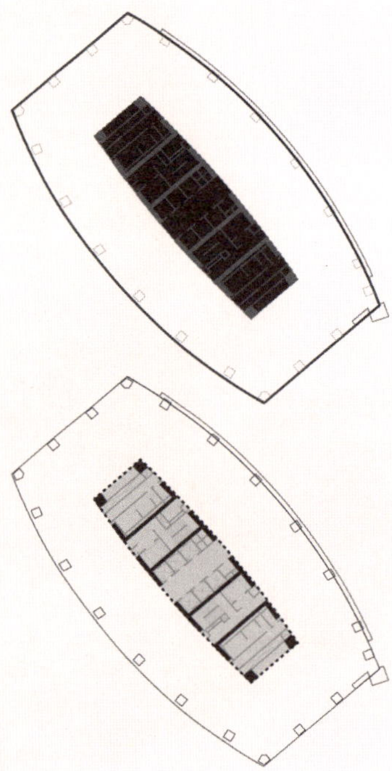

Tower 2

PROGRAM DIAGRAM
Distribution

- Residential
- Hotel
- Office
- Retail

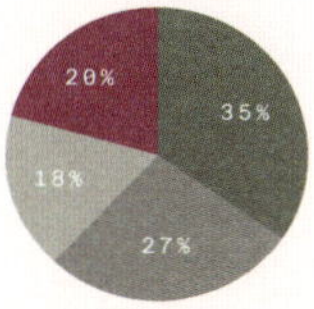

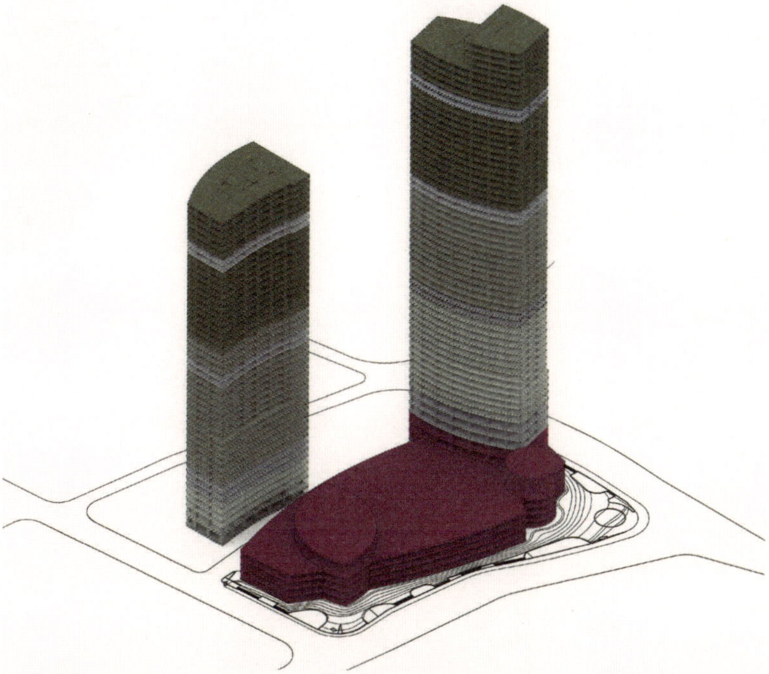

SECTION

- Retail
- Office 1
- Office 2
- Office 3

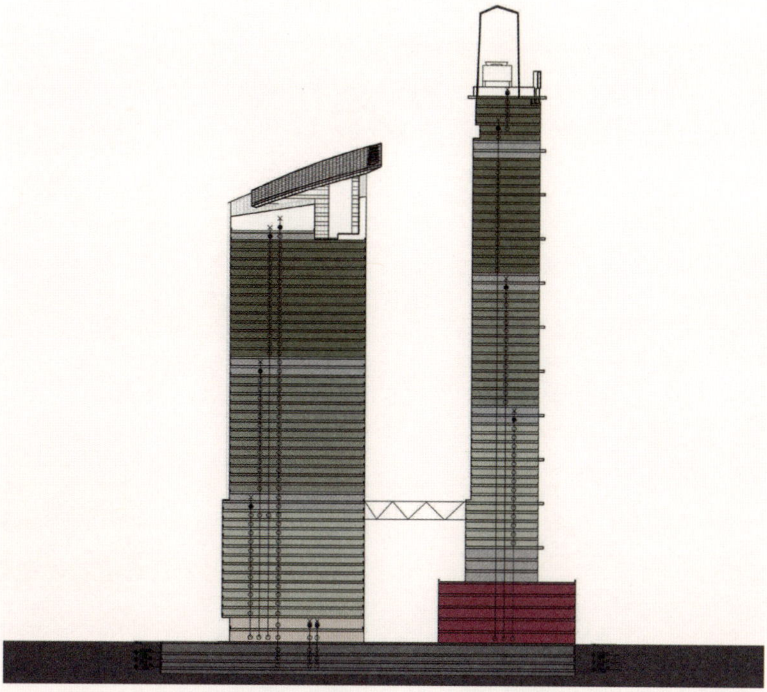

3.1.3.

People's Square, Shanghai

People's Square
Shanghai, China

Piazza Del Campidoglio
Rome, Italy

SCALE COMPARISON

Piazza San Marco
Venice, Italy

Red Square
Moscow, Russia

Tiananmen Square
Beijing, China

SITE PLAN

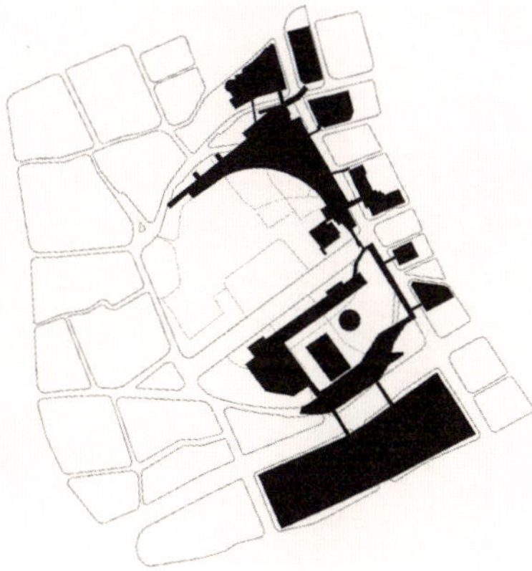

Underground-level 1

Ground Level

PROGRAM DIAGRAM

Site plans and
site section

- Residential
- Hotel
- Office
- Retail
- Cultural

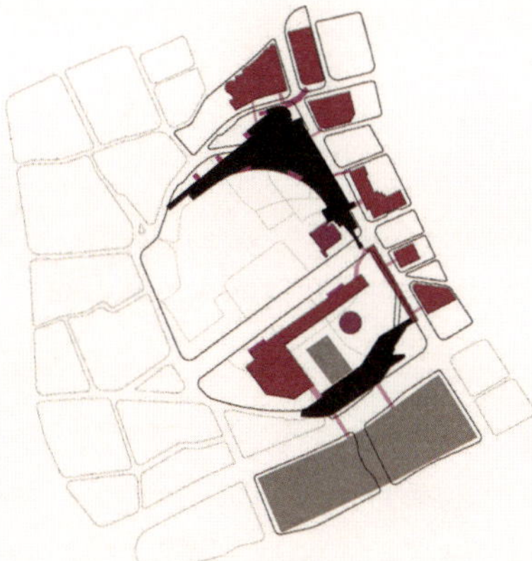

Underground-level 1

Ground Level

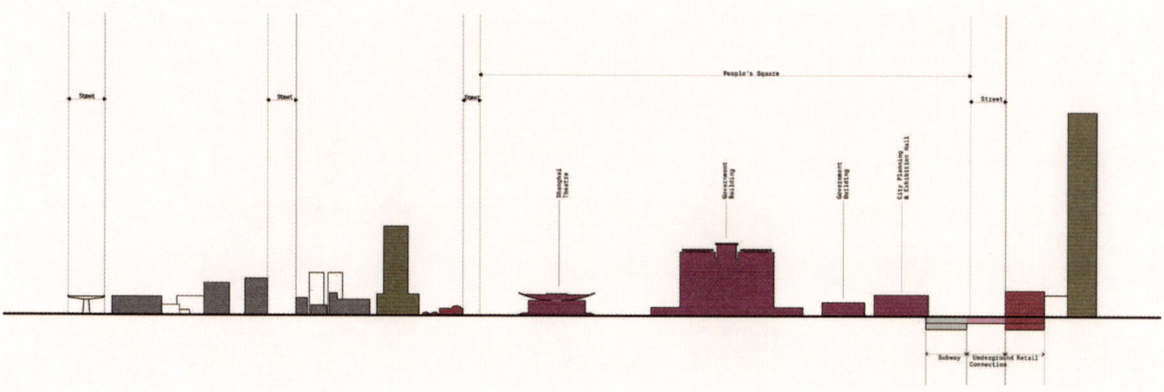

3.1.4.

Shanghai International Finance Center, Pelli Clarke Pelli, Pudong, Shanghai, 2011

CIRCULATION STRUCTURE

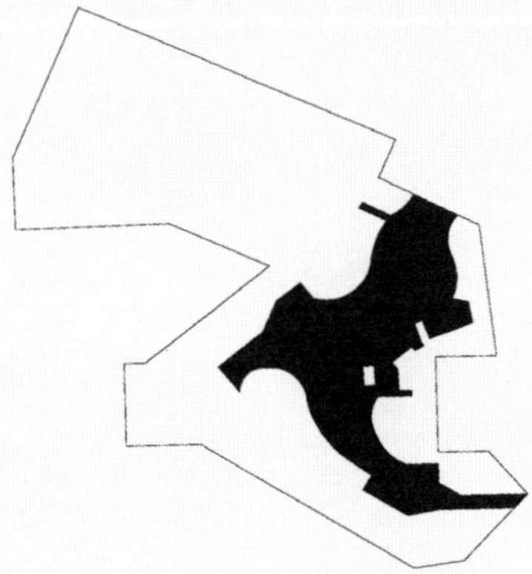

B2 Level

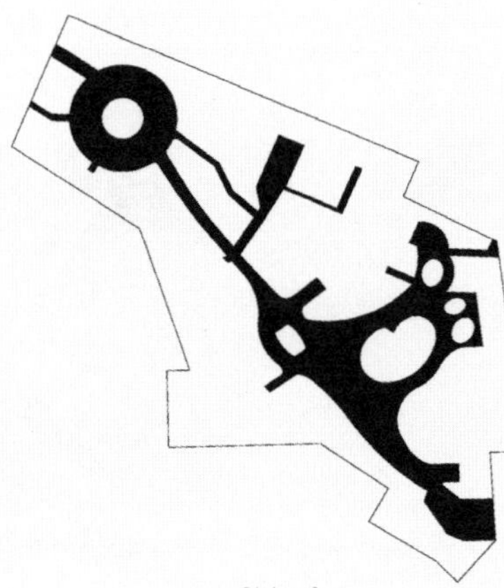

B1 Level

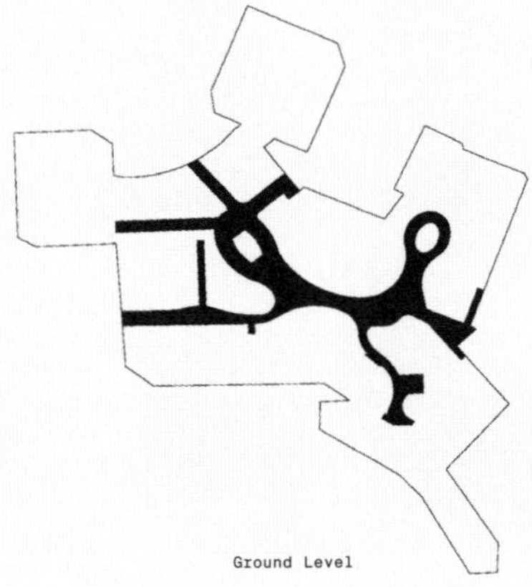

Ground Level

PROGRAM DIAGRAM
Distribution

- Residential
- Hotel
- Office
- Retail
- Cultural

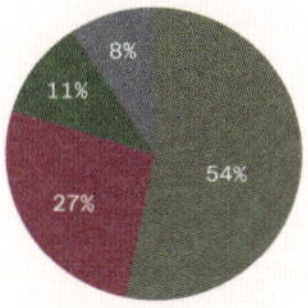

LOT Area: 76,950 m²
GRF: 370,000 m²
FAR: 4.8

PROGRAMS

Office: 200,000 m²
Retail: 100,000 m²
Hotel: 40,000 m²
Residence: 35,200 m²
Parking: 1,800 spaces

PROGRAM DIAGRAM
Section

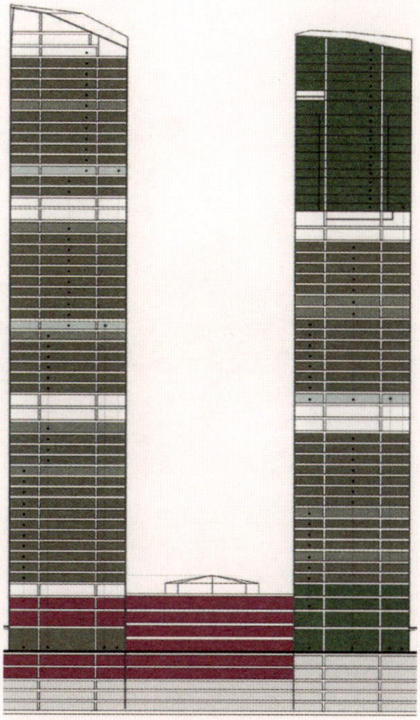

3.1.5.

Shanghai World Financial Center,
Kohn Pedersen Fox Associates,
Pudong, Shanghai, 2008

PROGRAM DISTRIBUTION
Ground Level Plan

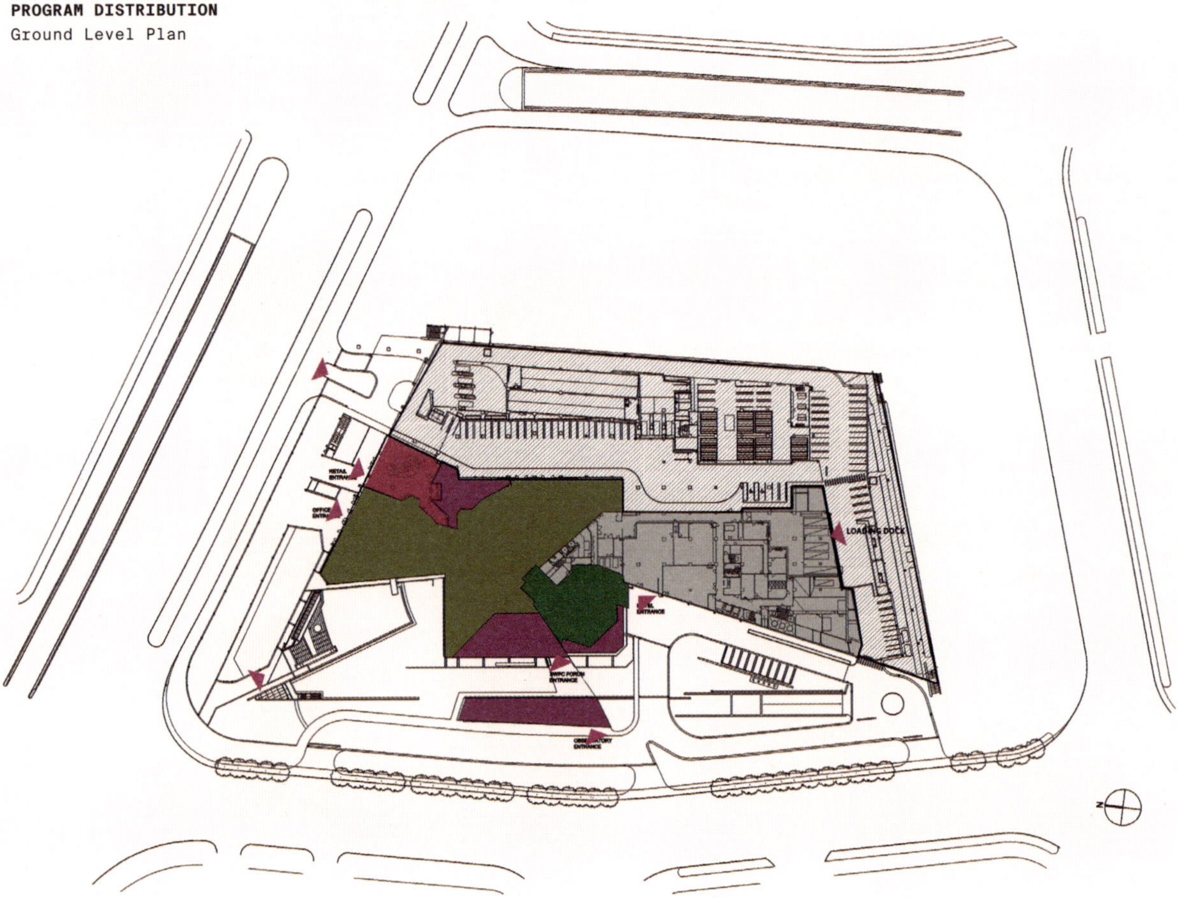

PROGRAM
Distribution and Section

- Residential
- Hotel
- Office
- Retail
- Cultural

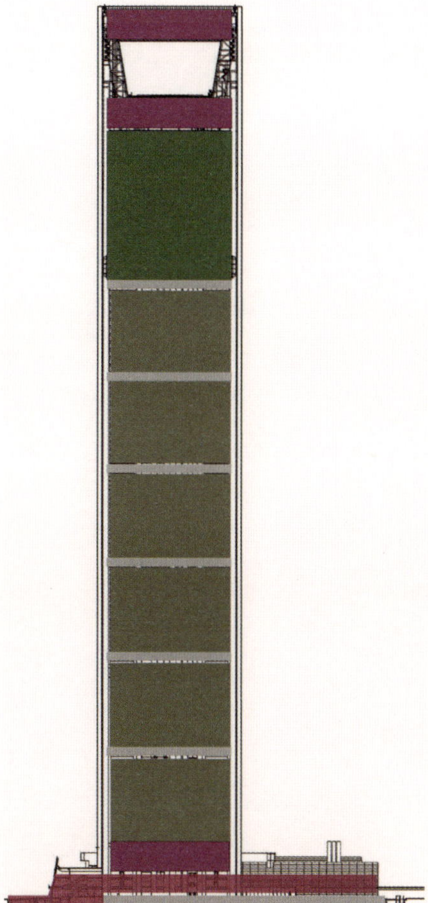

3.1.6.

Hong Kong IFC, Pelli Clarke Pelli, Hong Kong, 2003

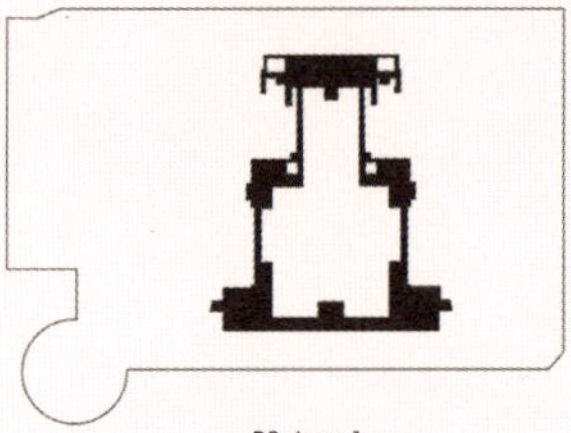

B2 Level
Transfer Zone

Ground Level
Airport Extension Rail Concorse

CIRCULATION STRUCTURE

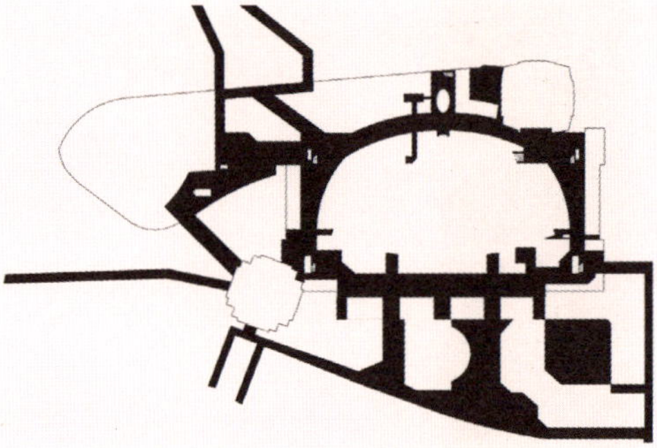

2F Level
Bridge Connections

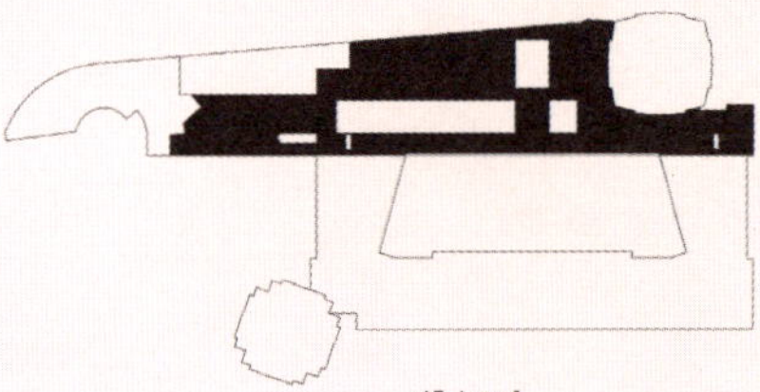

4F Level
Podium Garden

PROGRAM DIAGRAM
Distribution

- Station
- Residential
- Hotel
- Office
- Retail
- Cultural

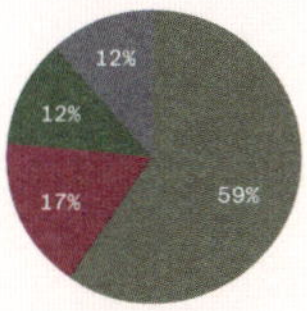

LOT Area: 91,150 m²
GRF: 437,000 m²
FAR: 4.8

PROGRAMS

Office: 260,000 m²
Retail: 75,000 m²
Hotel: 52,000 m²
Residence: 50,000 m²
Poidium Green: 13,000 m²
Parking: 1,800 spaces

PROGRAM DIAGRAM
Tower and Station Sections

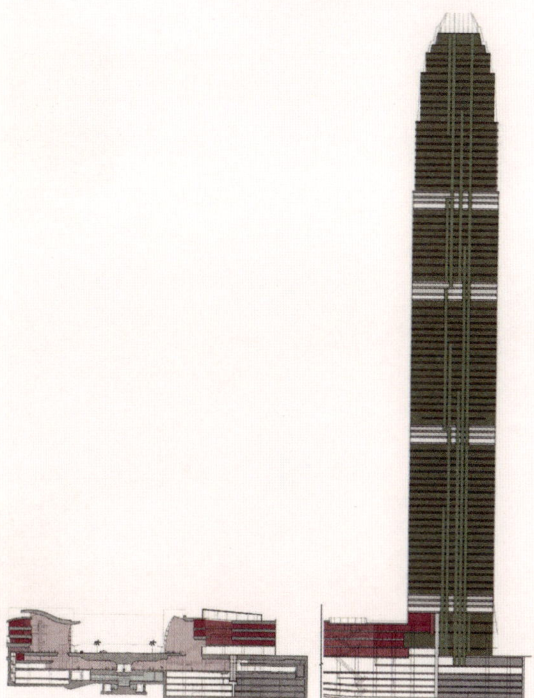

3.1.7.

Hong Kong ICC, Kohn Pedersen Fox Associates, Kowloon, Hong Kong, 2010

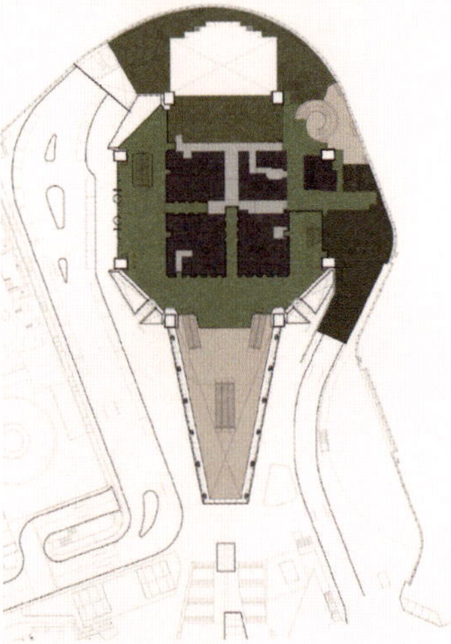

Lower Lobby

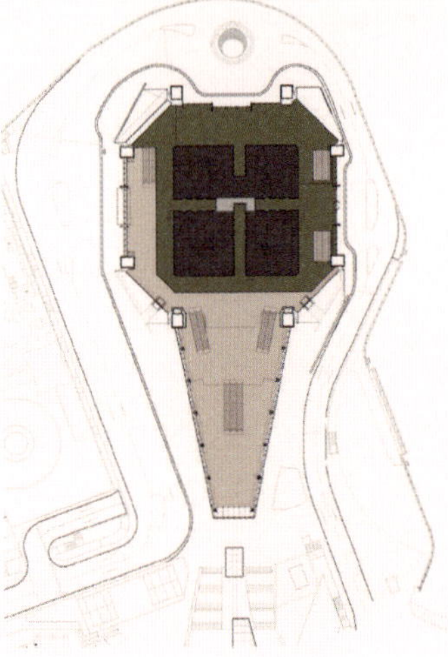

Upper Lobby

PROGRAM DIAGRAM
Floor Plans

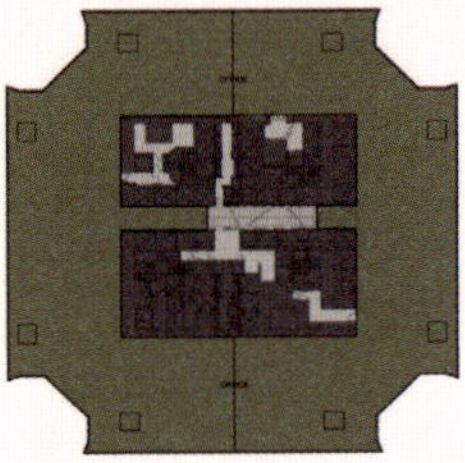

TYP Office

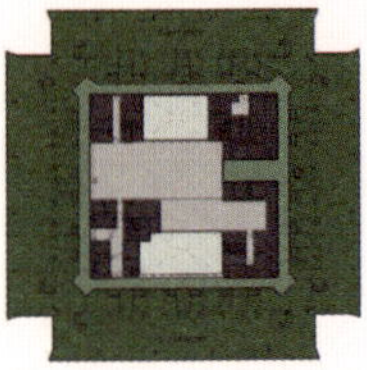

Hotel Room

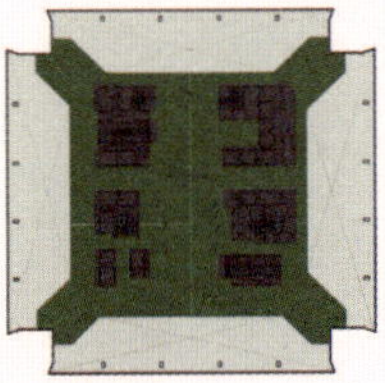

Hotel Reception

PROGRAM DIAGRAM
Section

- Residential
- Hotel
- Office
- Retail
- Cultural

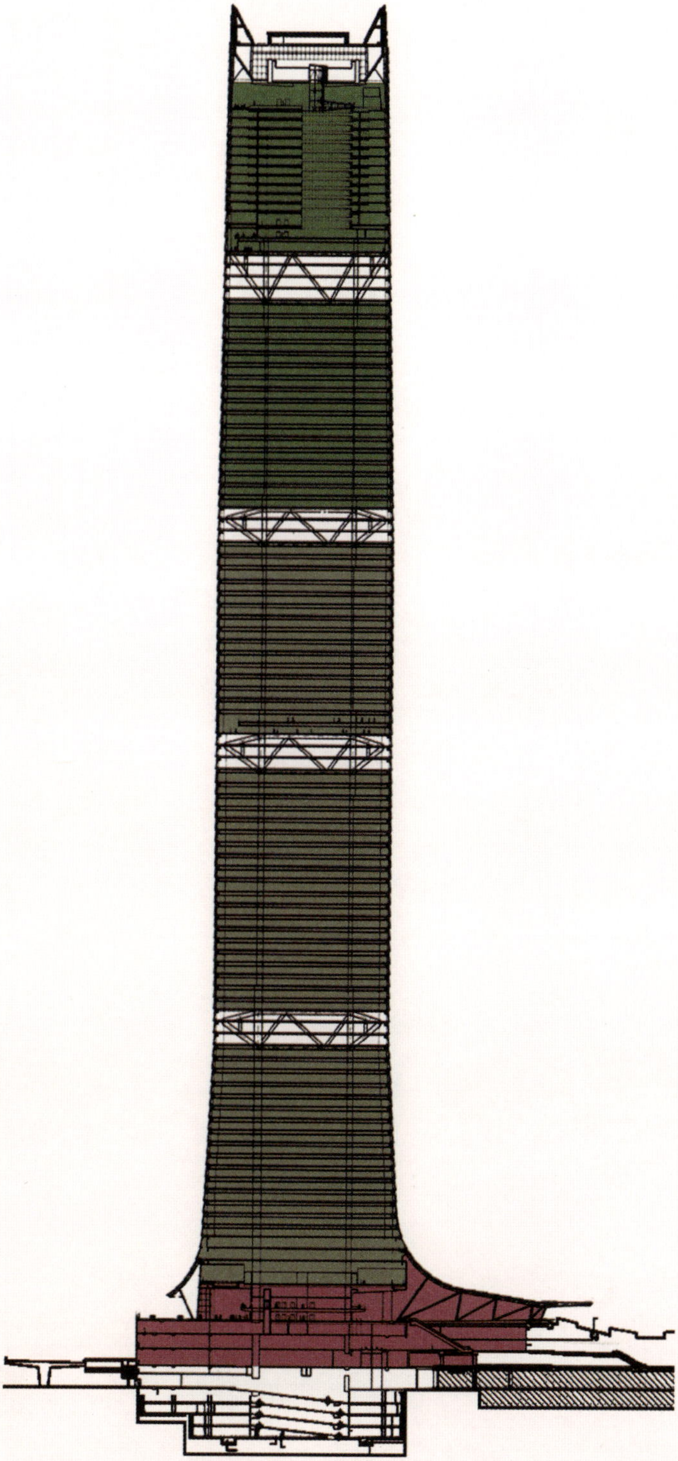

3.1.8.

Landmark, Kohn Pedersen Fox Associates, Hong Kong, 2003–06

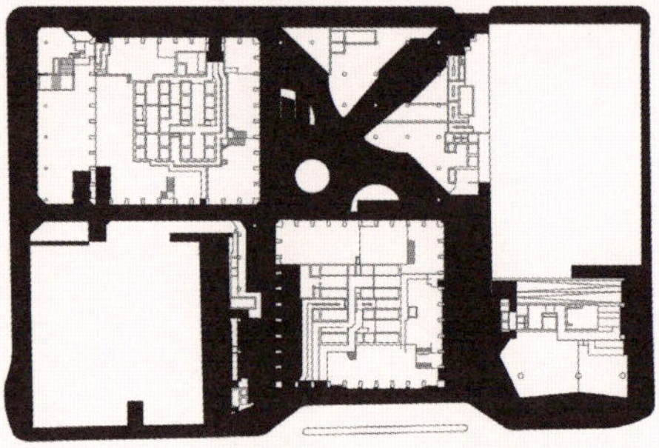

Level 1

CIRCULATION STRUCTURE

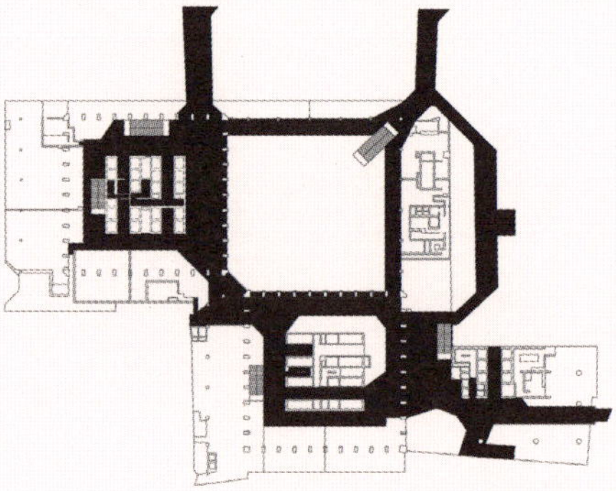

Level 3

PROGRAM DIAGRAM
Section

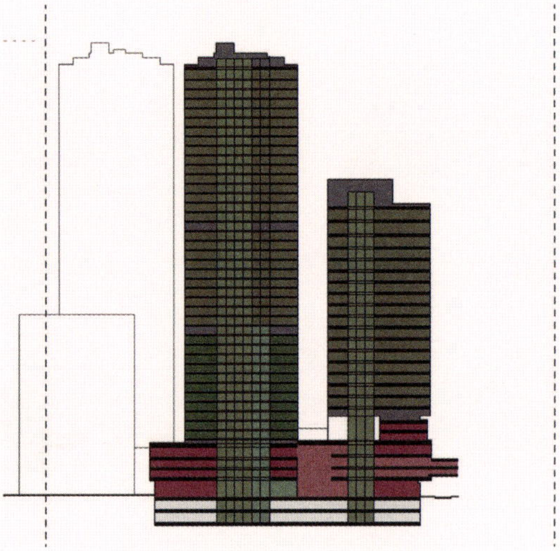

PROGRAM DIAGRAM
Distribution and Circulation

- Residential
- Hotel
- Office 1
- Retail
- Cultural

3.1.9.

Pacific Place, Hong Kong, 1989

PROGRAM DIAGRAM
Podium Level Plans

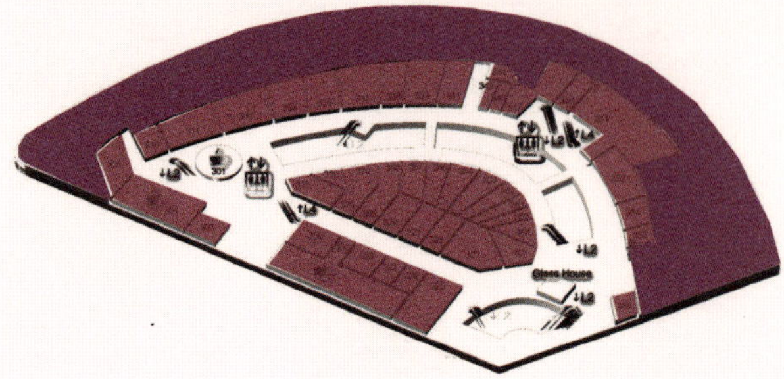

Level 3

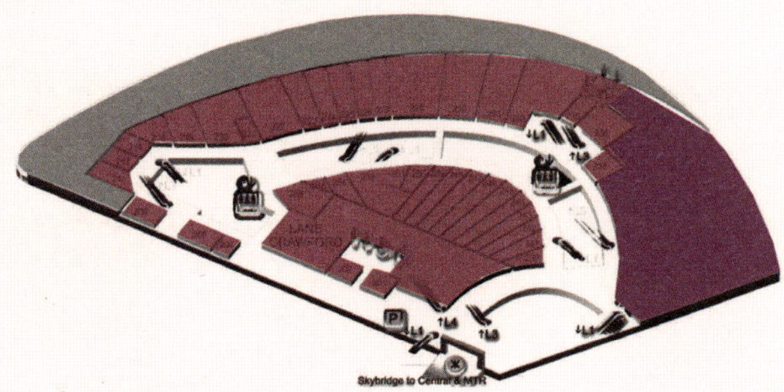

Level 2

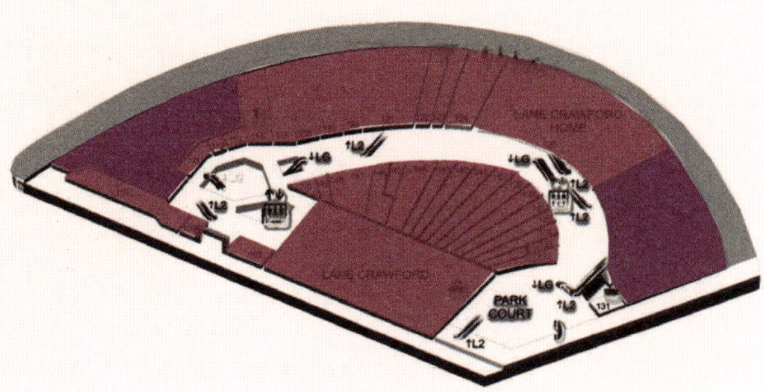

Level 1

PROGRAM DIAGRAM
Distribution

- Residential
- Hotel
- Office
- Retail
- Cultural

PROGRAM DIAGRAM
Section

3.1.10.

Shun Tak Center, Spence Robinson, Hong Kong, 1984–86

PROGRAM DIAGRAM
Retail-Level Plan

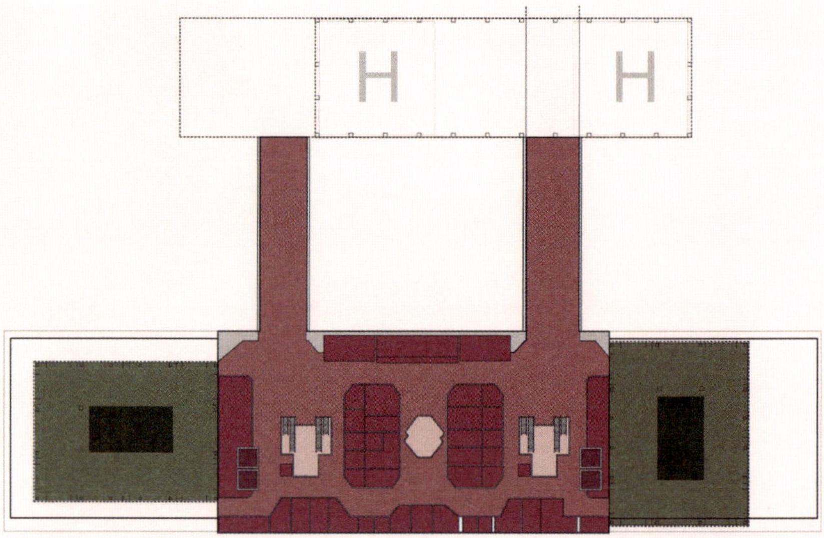

PROGRAM DIAGRAM
Section

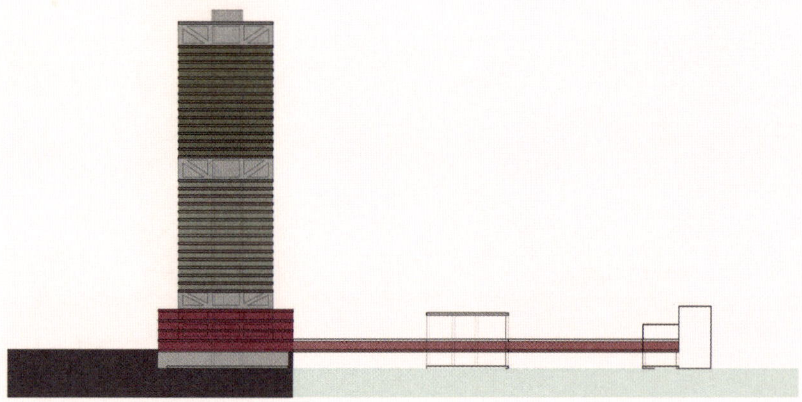

PROGRAM DIAGRAM

Distribution

- Residential
- Hotel
- Office 1
- Office 2
- Retail
- Cultural

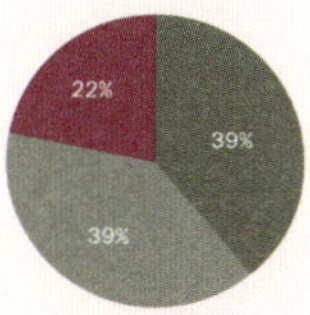

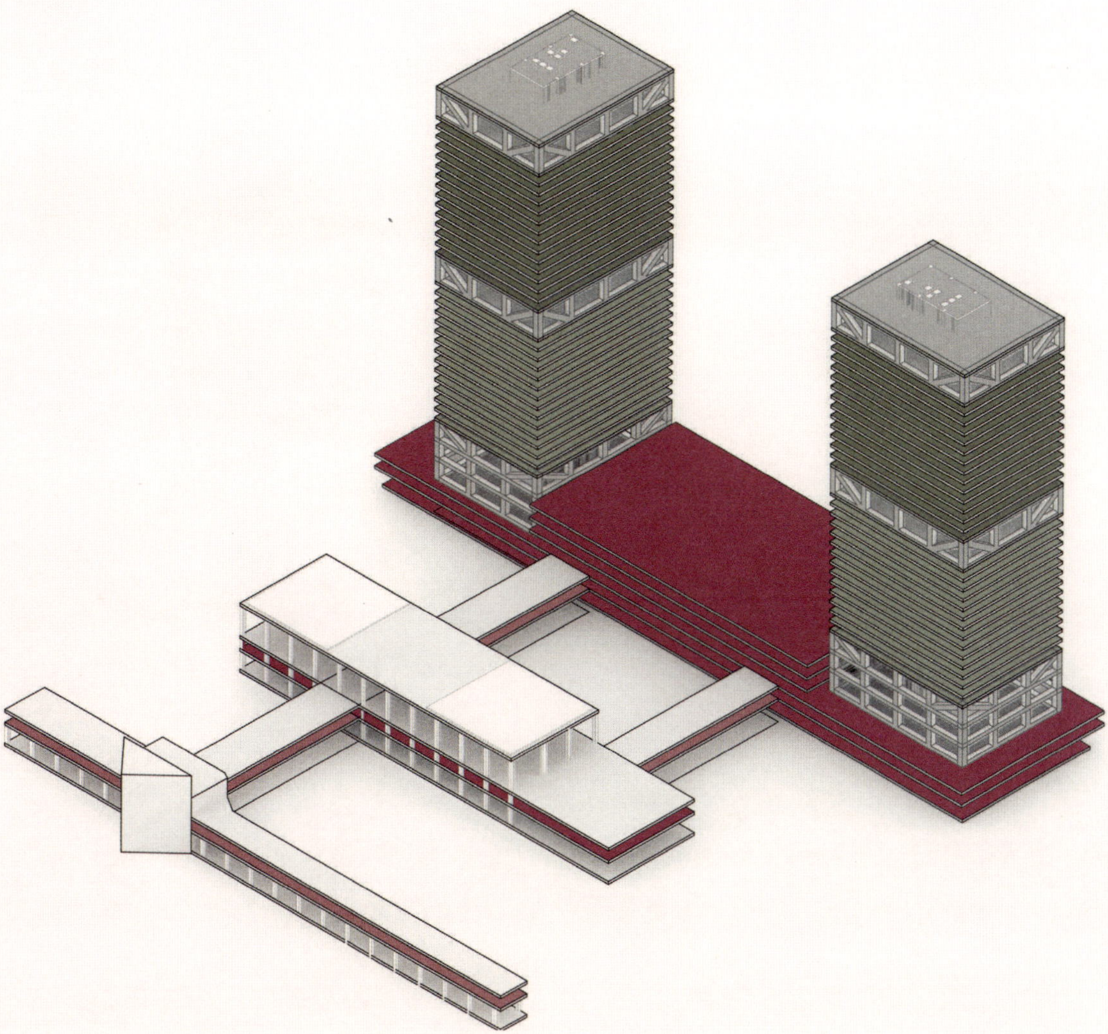

3.1.11.

Tokyo Midtown, Skidmore Owings & Merrill, Tokyo, 2007

PUBLIC STRUCTURE

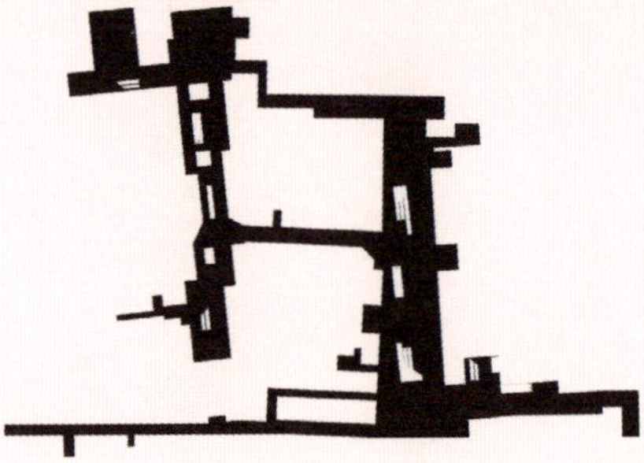

B2 Level
Subway Connections

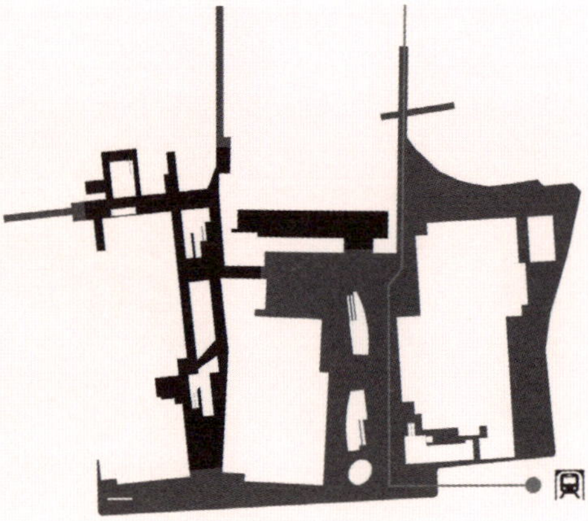

Ground Level

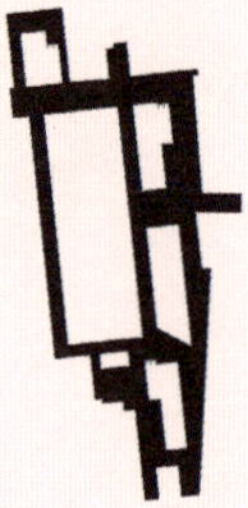

Level 2F (Galleria)

PROGRAM DIAGRAM
Distribution

- Station
- Residential
- Hotel
- Office
- Retail
- Cultural

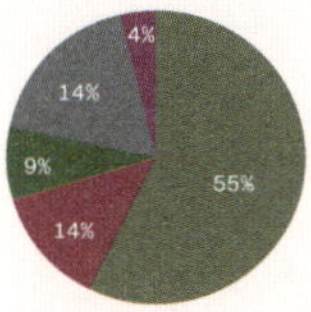

LOT Area: 68,900 m^2
GRF: 563,000 m^2
FAR: 8.1

PROGRAMS

Office: 311,000 m^2
Retail: 71,000 m^2
Hotel: 43,750 m^2
Residence: 96,500 m^2
Culture: 6,400 m^2
Halls: 14,000 m^2

Landscape: 40,000 m^2

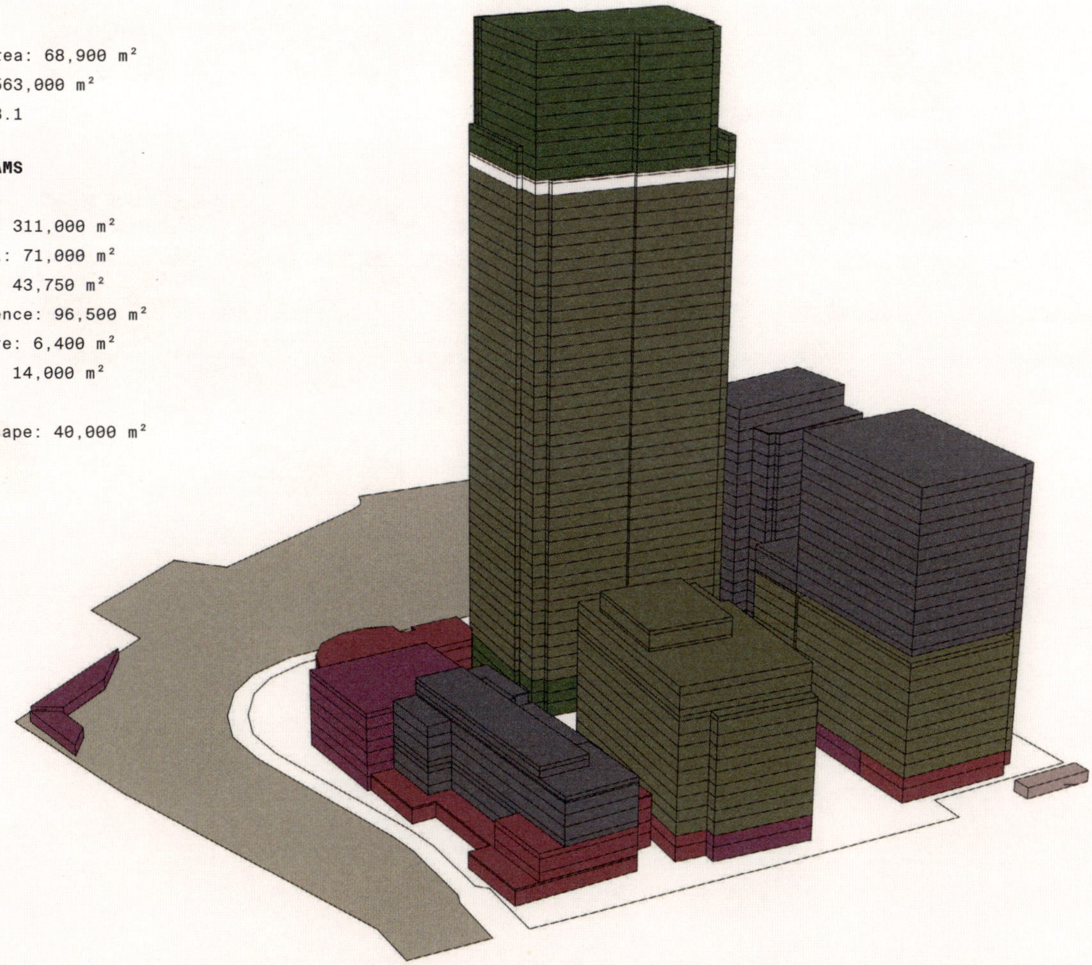

3.1.12.

Tokyo Station, Tokyo, original building 1914, continuously renovated and expanded

PROGRAM DIAGRAM
Entry-Level Plan

- Retail
- Transit

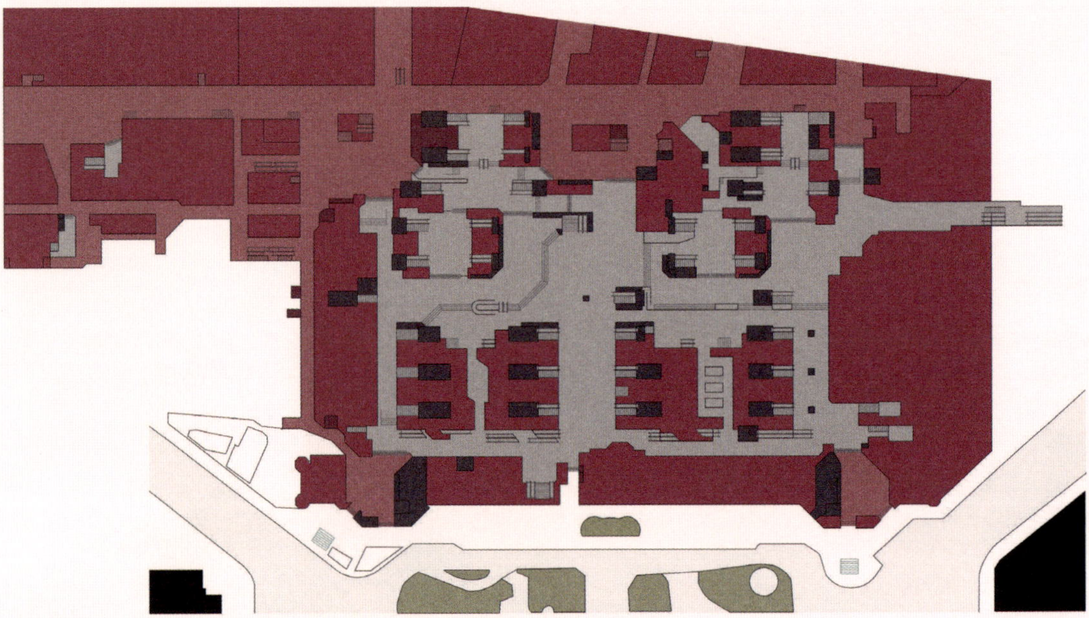

B1 PLAN

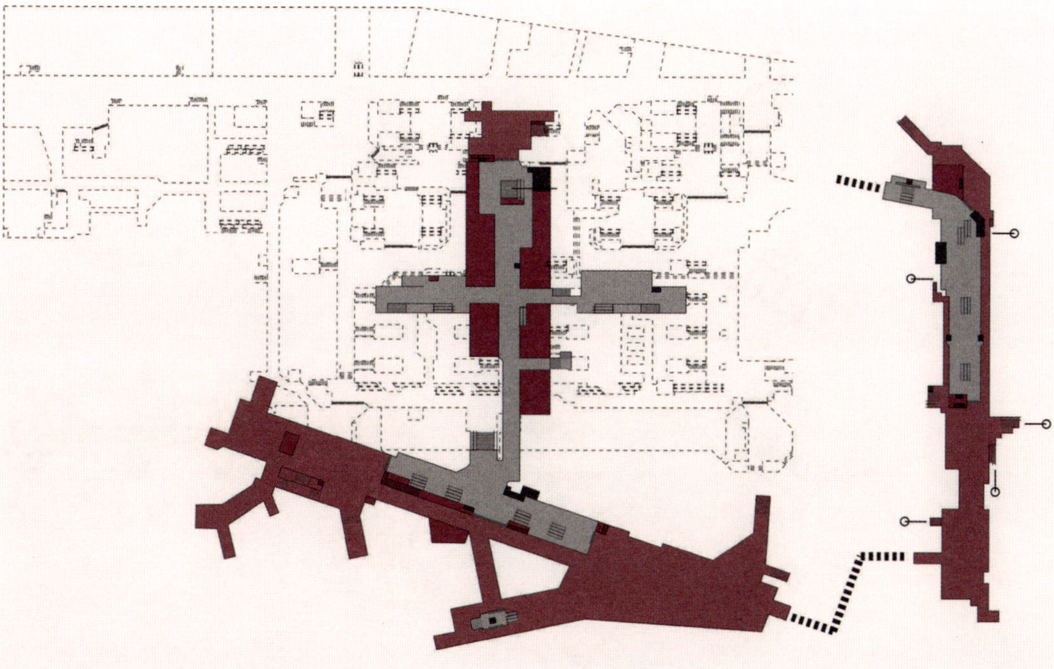

3.1.13.

Roppongi Hills, Kohn Pedersen Fox Associates, Tokyo, 2003

CIRCULATION STRUCTURE
Retail Level Plans

● Public Outdoor
● Public Indoor

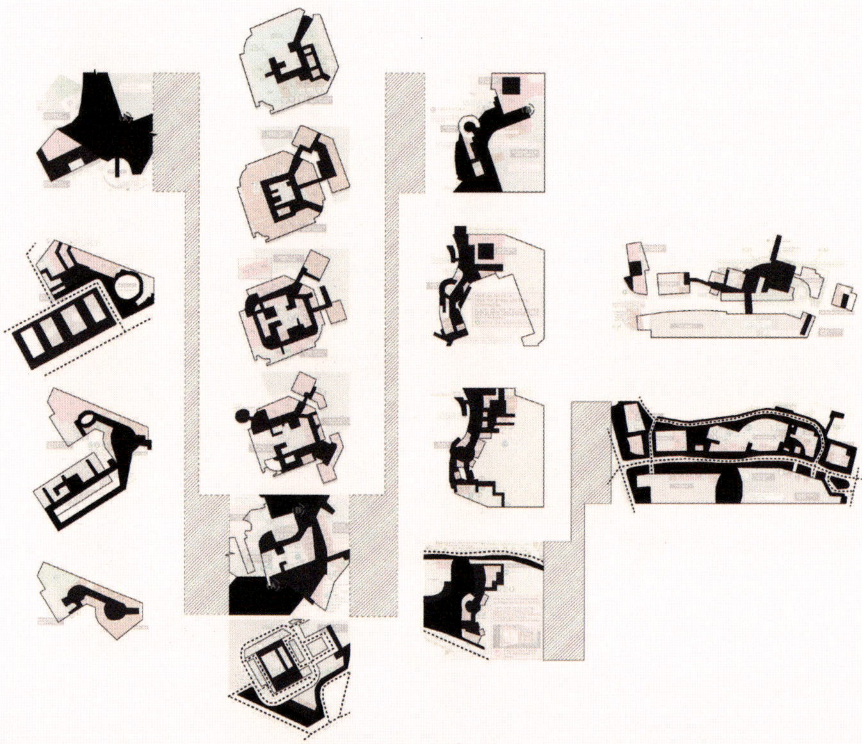

PROGRAM DIAGRAM
Distribution

- Residential
- Hotel
- Office
- Retail
- Cultural

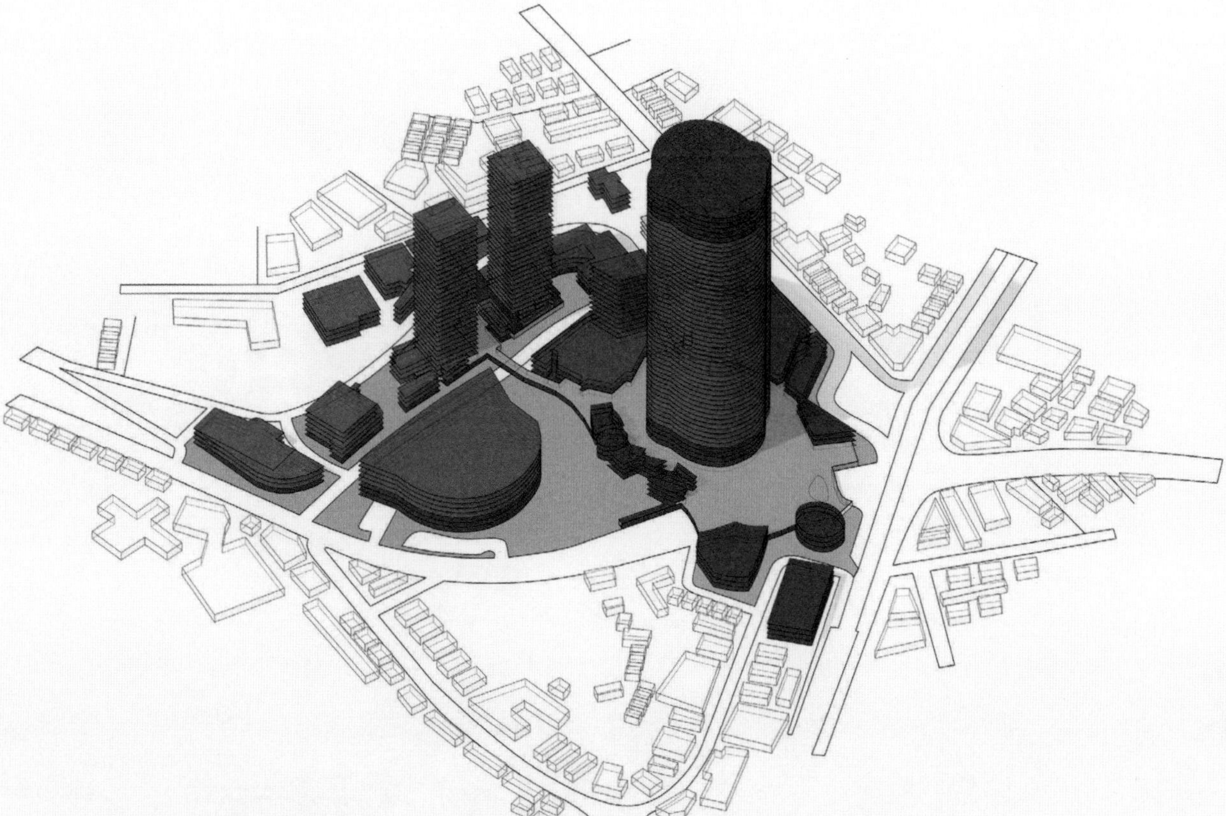

3.1.14.

Kyoto Station, Hiroshi Hara, Kyoto, 1991–97

CIRCULATION STRUCTURE

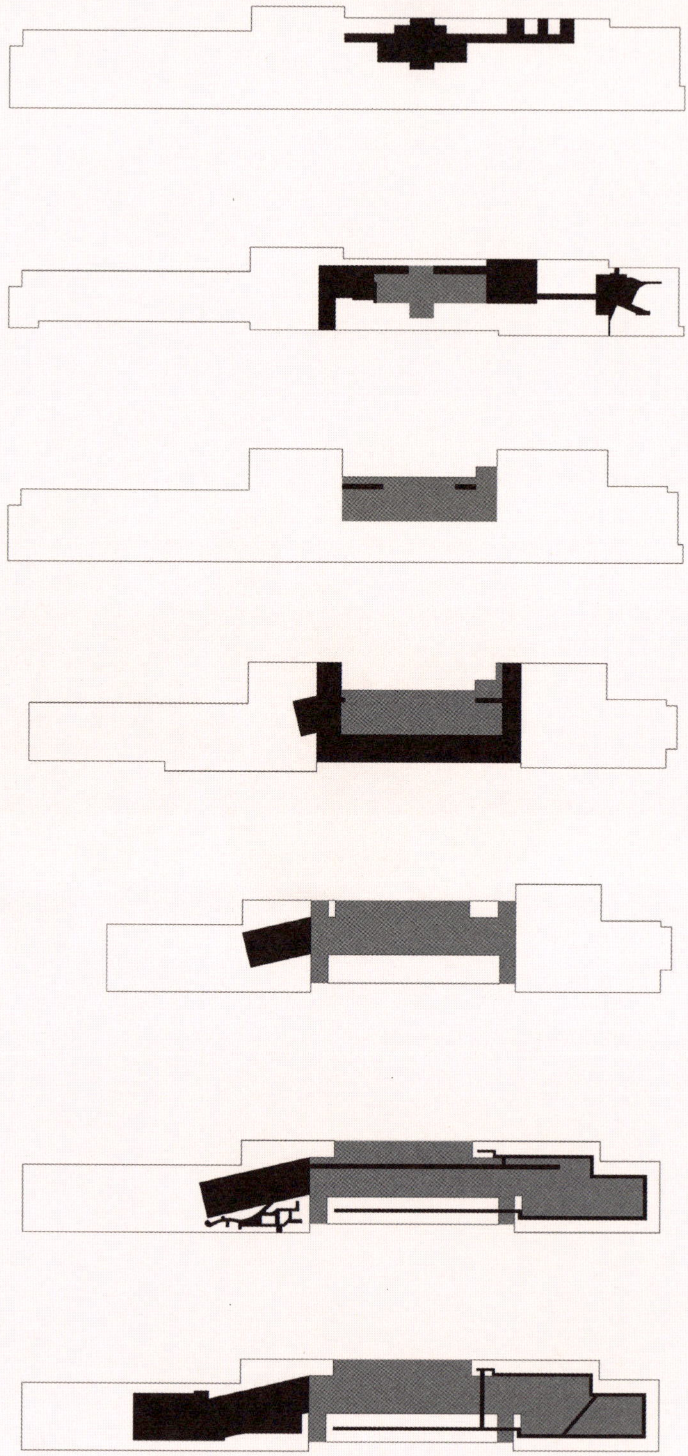

PORGRAM DIAGRAM
Section

- Residential
- Hotel
- Office
- Retail
- Cultural

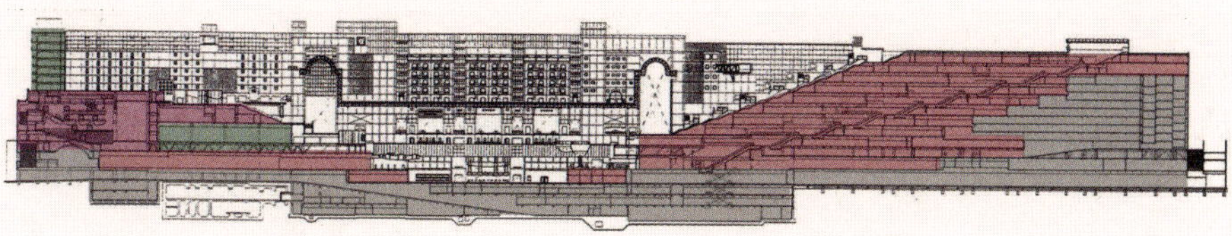

PROGRAM DIAGRAM
Distribution

- Hotel
- Retail
- Cultural
- Parking

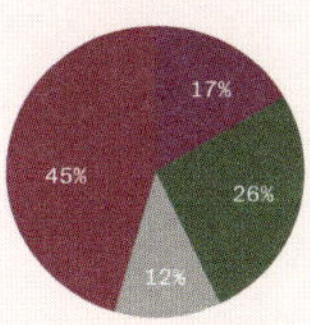

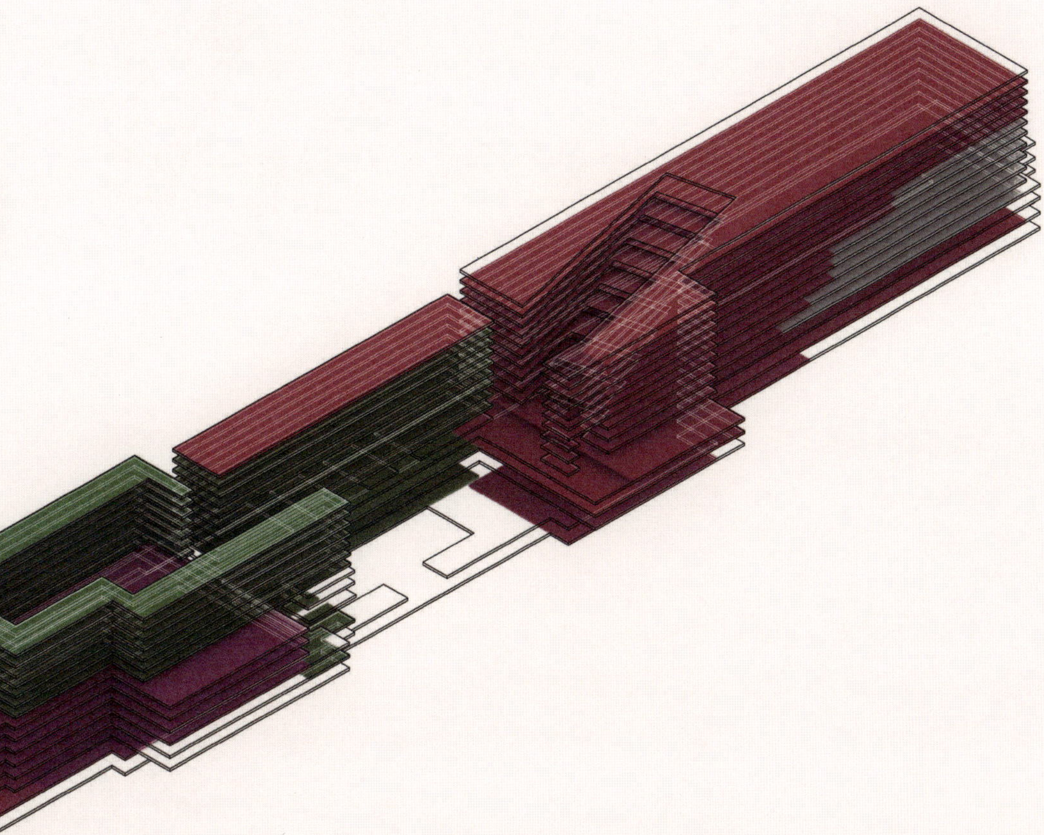

3.1.15.

JR Central Station, Kohn Pedersen Fox Associates, Nagoya, 2000

SITE DIAGRAM

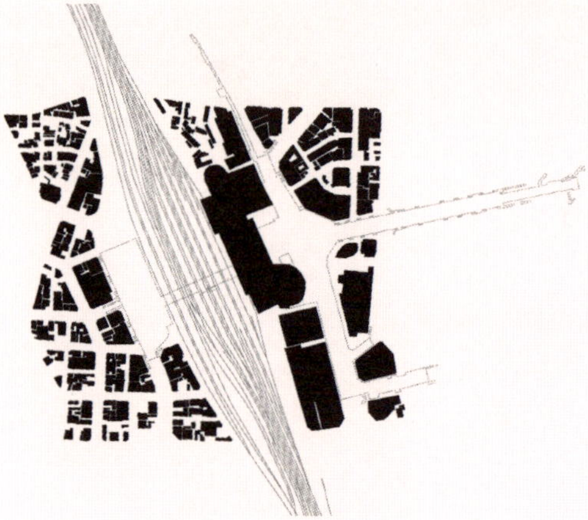

Figure-Ground

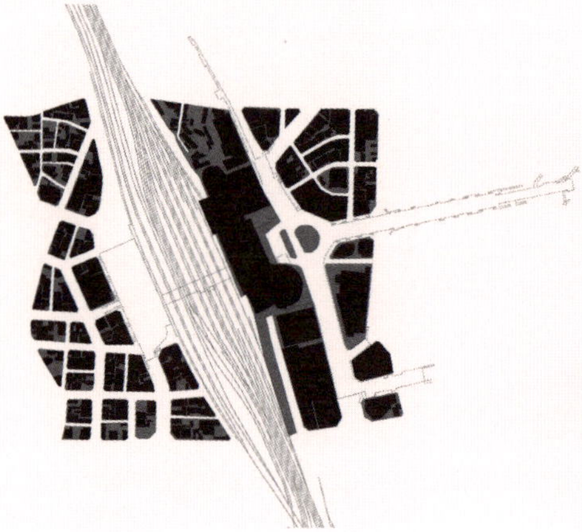

Figure-Ground and Public Space

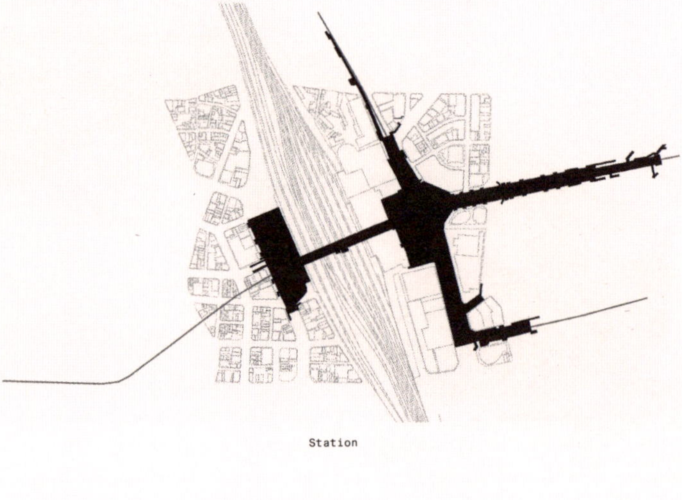

Station

PROGRAM DIAGRAM
Distribution

- Residential
- Hotel
- Office
- Retail
- Cultural

PROGRAM DIAGRAM
Section

3.2.0.

Xintiandi

3.2.1.

Open Space

TAIPINGQIAO DEVELOPMENT
Master Plan

TAIPINGQIAO DEVELOPMENT
Lot Coverage Ratios

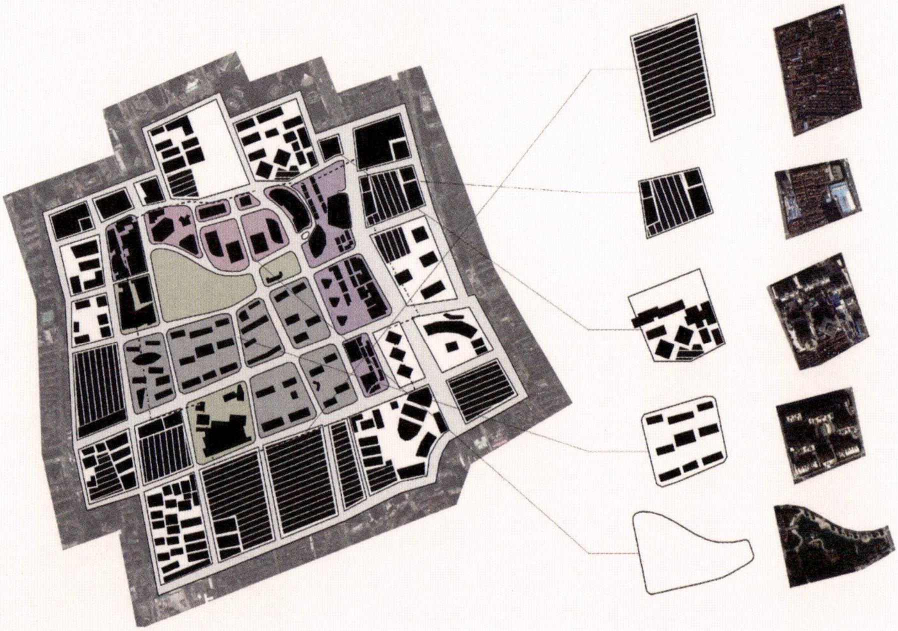

Historic Shikumen Network

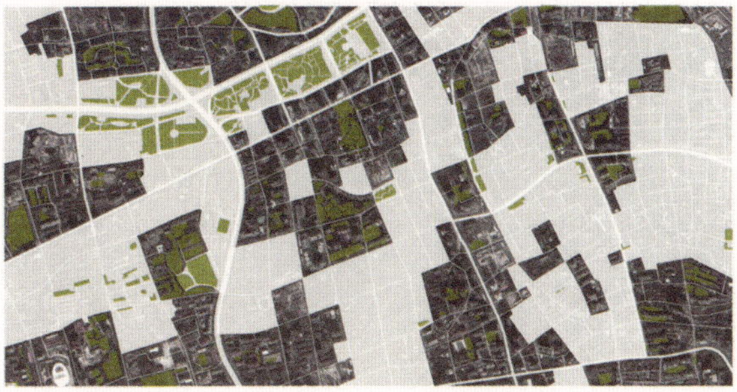

Redeveloped Urban Fabric

Scale Comparison

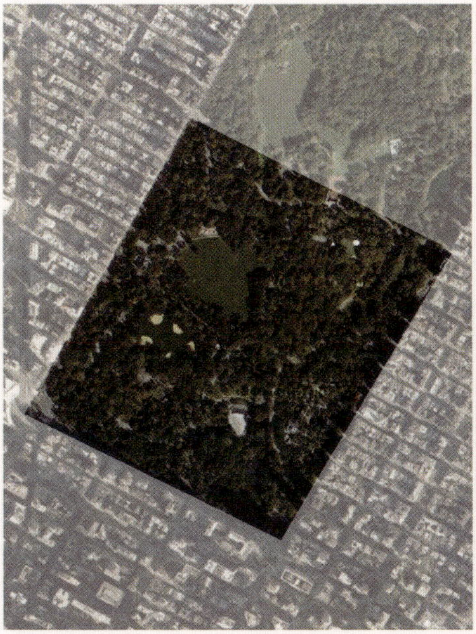

Central Park, New York City
929,000 SQM

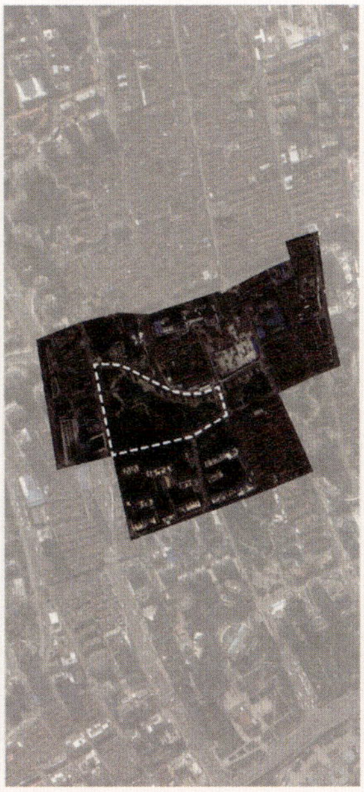

Xingtiandi, Shanghai
350,000 SQM

New Haven Green, Connecticut
65,000 SQM

Rockefeller Center, New York City
20,000 SQM

3.2.2.

Xintiandi Retail

CIRCULATION STRUCTURE

Daily Visitors: +30,000
Monthly Revenue: 100 M Yuan
(U.S. $14.65 meters)
Daily Revenue: U.S. $488,000
Monthly Per Person: U.S. $488

Total Site Area : 35,463 m2

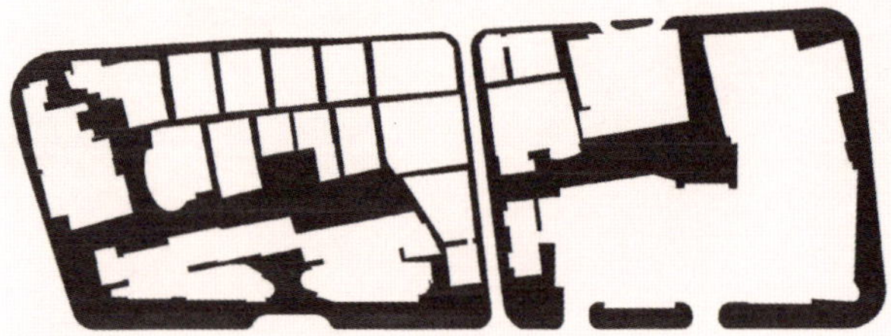

Total Built Retail Area : 21,644 m² (64 percent)

Open Public Space : 13,823 m² (36 percent)

SKYLINE WITH CONTEXT FROM EAST

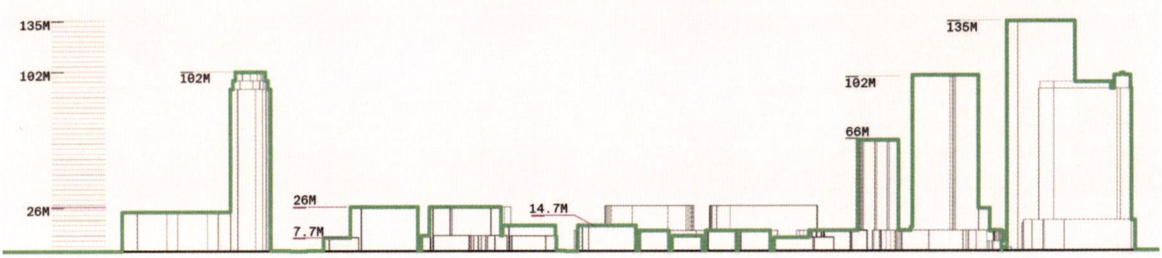

PROGRAM DIAGRAM
Ground-Level Plan

- Residential
- Hotel
- Office
- Retail
- Cultural

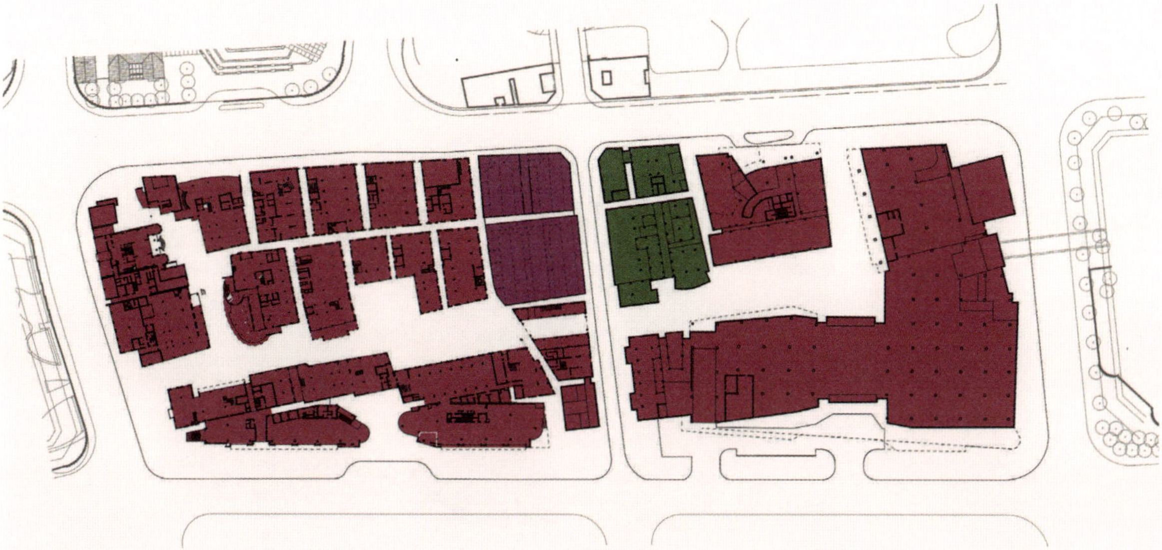

3.2.3.

Taipingqiao Residential

SITE-PLAN DIAGRAM
Figure Ground

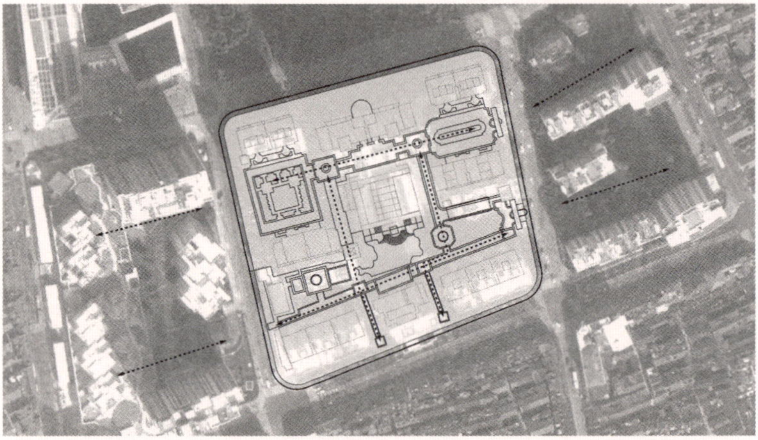

PHASE 2/LAKEVILLE REGENCY, Open-Space Network

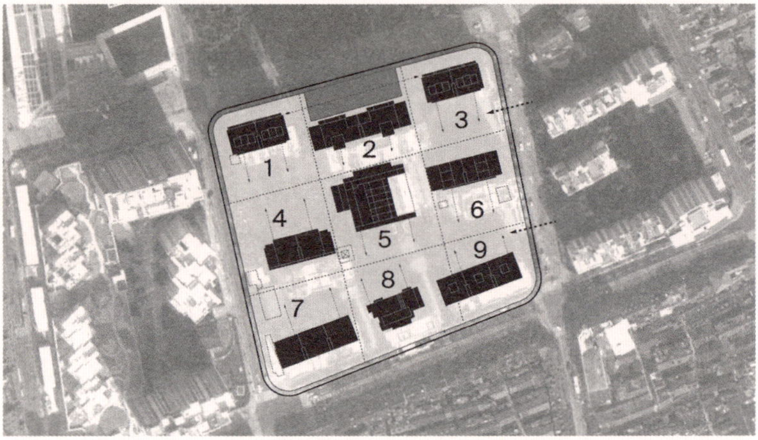

PHASE 2/LAKEVILLE REGENCY, nine-Square-Block Strategy

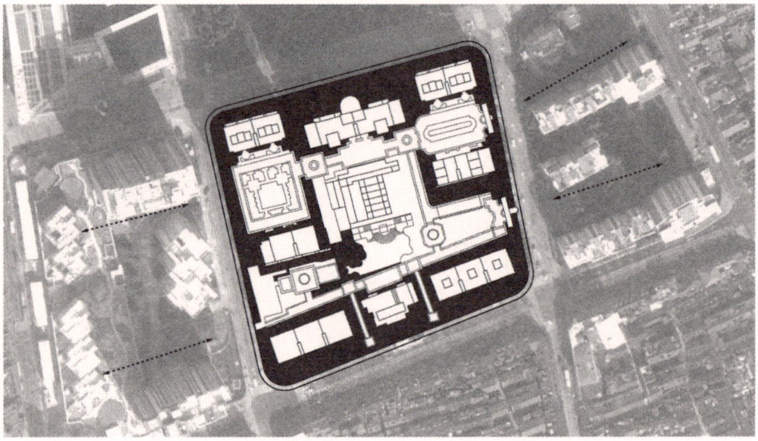

PHASE 2/LAKEVILL REGENCY, Inner Block Figure-Ground

SITE PLAN DIAGRAM
Project Phasing

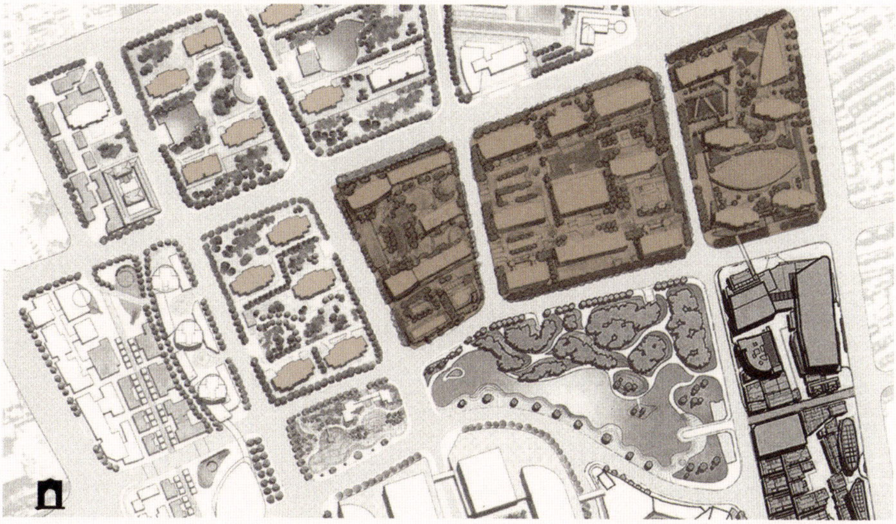

SITE PLAN DIAGRAM
Site Circulation and Connections

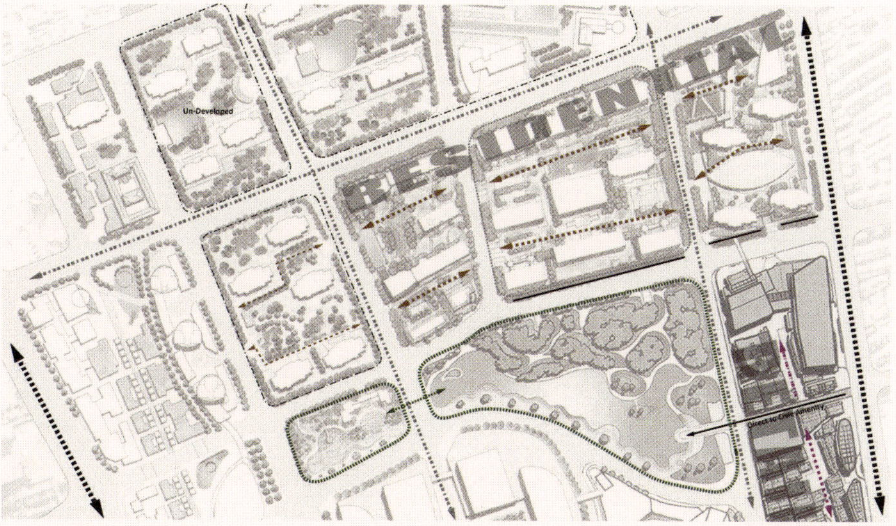

- Primary Bounding Street
- Xintiandi Secondary Street
- Retail Street(internalized)
- Residential Green Street(internalized)

3.2.4.

Taipingqiao Corporate Avenue Building

SITE PLAN

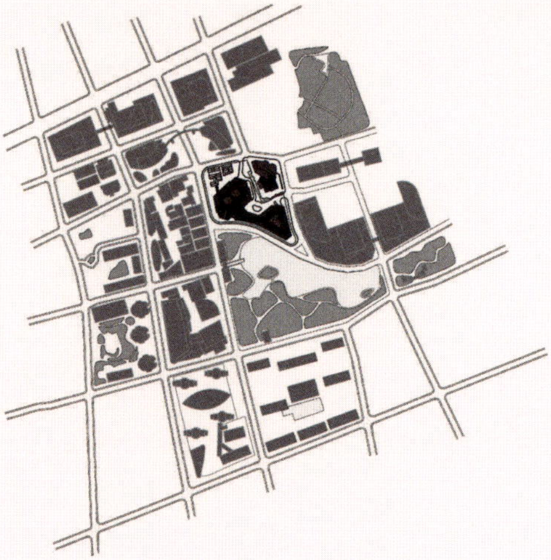

PROGRAM DIAGRAM
Ground Plans

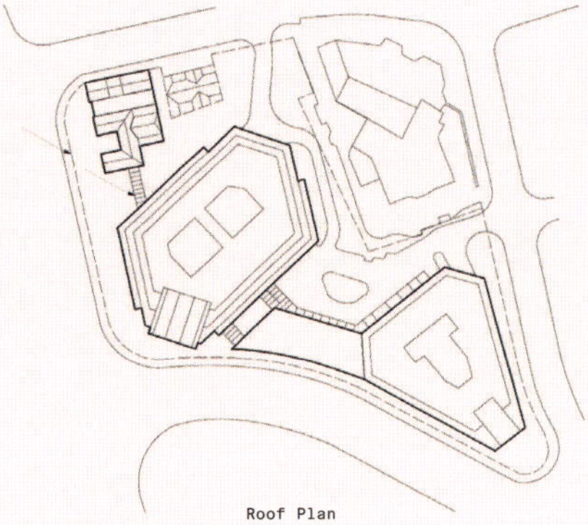

Roof Plan

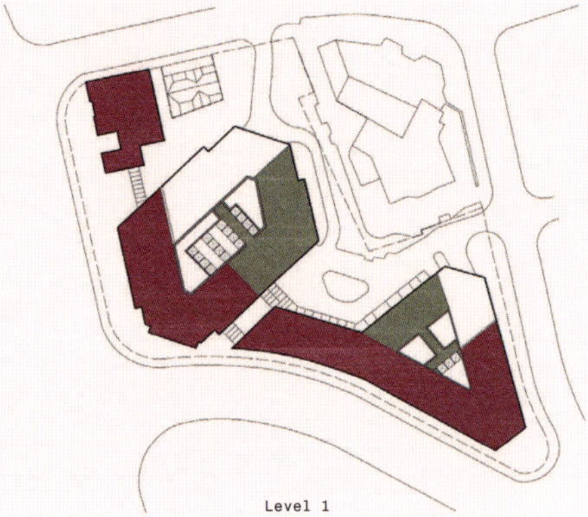

Level 1

PROGRAM DIAGRAM
Distribution

- Residential
- Hotel
- Office
- Retail
- Cultural

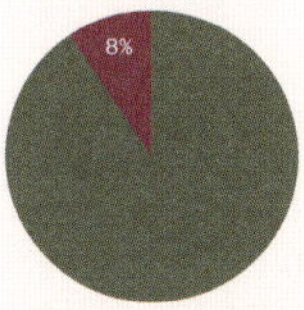

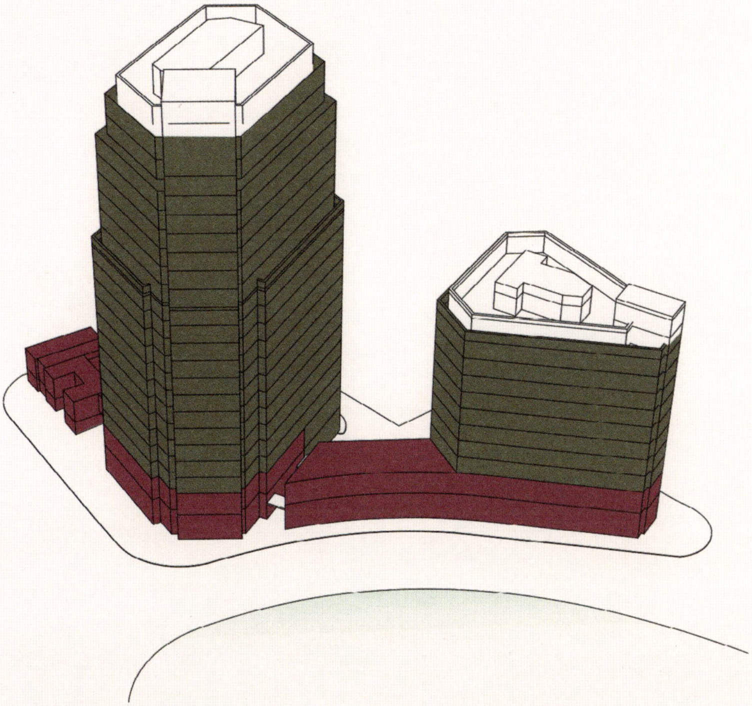

LOT Area: 5,610 m²
GRF: 38,000 m²
FAR: 6.8

PROGRAMS

Office: 35,990 m²
Retail: 3,140 m²

PROGRAM DIAGRAM
Section

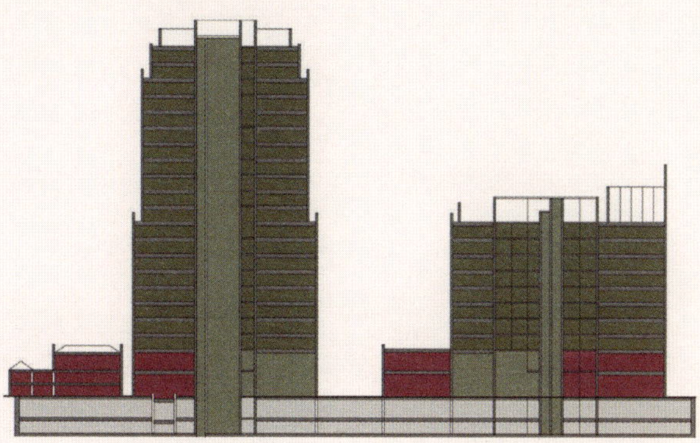

4. CHONGQING ON THE CUSP

4.1.0.

Meetings

—

Ling Yeuming, Vice Mayor of Chongqing

PP.104/105 Children walk on the bank of the Yangtze River in central Chongqing.

P.106 The remnants of an older residential area of central Chongqing.

Trained as an economist and engineer, Ling Yeuming has been vice mayor of Chongqing since 2008 and a member of the Chongqing Municipal Committee of the Communist Party of China since 2008. He met with students during their visit to discuss the city's recent development and strategic planning goals.

Chongqing is one of the four cities that has been appointed by the central government to be a directly controlled municipality; therefore, in recent years we have witnessed very rapid development.

Prior to this, our city planning and city building were confined to the downtown, the first ring of the city, which is no more than 230 square kilometers. Last year, we started a huge program to extend our city to two rings, to 2,200 square kilometers from 230 square kilometers. For the first ring, we have a highway of 78 kilometers, and, for the second ring, we have a highway of 186 kilometers.

In this new ring there are twenty-one building areas that will be our focus in the future. For each group area, we plan to have 200,000 to 250,000 people. Right now, in the center of Chongqing, we have a population of 6.5 million. We plan to build this area up to a core population of ten million. This rapid development and extension of the city is based on the rapid development of the economy of Chongqing. According to the latest government data, global economic growth was 4.3 percent last year. In Asia, economic growth was 7.8 percent in the same time period. However, in Chonqing, it was as high as 17.1 percent.

In the past year, the real estate industry in Chongqing has sold a total of 350 million square meters, which could equal the quantity of an entire European country.

In the past, Chongqing's main industries were motorcycles and cars. In the past year, we have started to develop the information-technology industry in Chongqing; we have a contract with Hewlett Packard from the United States as well as ACER from Taiwan, in addition to six other factories with total contracts for 100 million personal computers. I'm very confident that, in three or five years, of all of the friends who are in this hall today, one in two of your personal computers will have been built in Chongqing.

—

Shirong Li, Chongqing Foreign Trade and Economic Relations Commissioner

Shirong Li is deputy director of the Foreign Trade and Economic Relations Commission for Chongqing, where she is responsible for the promotion of foreign investments in the city and is professor of construction management at Chongqing University. She was formerly vice mayor of Chongqing overseeing urban development and construction. She spoke with Yale students about Chongqing's economic and development outlook.

I want to begin by describing Chongqing's features and how it attracts foreign business. We call Chongqing the biggest city in the world, but first you have to define "city." In China, you will find five different levels of city. Chongqing is the highest level of city, called a directly-controlled municipality. So, for instance, when people ask me to compare Chongqing and Chengdu, I say it's almost useless because they're very different types of cities. Chengdu is the capital city of Sichuan province, but as a directly-controlled municipality, Chongqing is like a province in itself. The municipality of Chongqing consists of almost forty districts and counties spread over 82,000 square kilometers, and more than half of these districts and counties have at least 800,000 people living in them, with a total population of 32 million. Many visitors to Chongqing see only the central core area, the most developed area, where the population right now is over five million. By 2020, that will double to ten million. At that point, half the urban population of Chongqing will live in the core area of the municipality; the other half of the urban population will be in these other districts and counties. In this way, Chongqing is also very different than Shanghai and the other direct-controlled municipalities because their populations are very concentrated in their core urban areas.

In terms of Chongqing's development strategy, urbanization is really the key—urbanization and industrialization. In 1998, 18 percent of the population was urban, and now it is 53 percent. By 2020, our urban population will reach 70 percent, or more than twenty million people. Four hundred thousand to 500,000 people will be urbanized each year. In fact, every year, Chongqing creates a small city, and that means we have to create the infrastructure, the buildings, and the municipal functions to serve this new urban population.

Let's look briefly at the development of infrastructure in Chongqing. As we planned expanded road networks, we set targets, including the ability to access neighboring cities within eight hours and all of Chong qing within four hours. In the past ten years, we've built two thousand kilometers of expressways, and, in the following five years, we will build a thousand more. In planning for our railways, we set the target of reaching the majority of Chinese cities from Chongqing within eight hours, including Beijing in seven hours, Shanghai in eight hours, and Guangzhou in five hours. Guangzhou is also along a planned rail route that will be used for trade with Europe. And, of course, the port is also developing very fast. We will soon become the biggest inland port in China, and our airports and river ports are, combined, an advantage over other Chinese free-trade zones. Our airport also is growing very fast: we already have sixteen million passengers per year.

When people in China say "Go west," they are often referring to the potential of the domestic market in inland China, but in Chongqing this is only one factor in our growth. If you look at Hewlett Packard coming to Chongqing recently, 90 percent of its products in the future will be exports, and that is because Chongqing is very different from other interior cities. In my opinion, Chongqing is even more attractive from a foreign-trade standpoint than the free-trade zones along the coast. For example, in 2010, there were $12 billion U.S. dollars in foreign trade in Chongqing. In 2015, that number will be $100 billion. The distance to the coastal areas is short; with air travel, there is little difference accessing coastal areas versus, Chongqing. In terms of the railways, we're in a better position than the coastal cities. If you think of traveling to Beijing, Shanghai, Hong Kong, or Guandong, Chongqing is in the center.

Along with urbanization, we have industrialization. We have key industries that are developing very quickly. Our biggest industries are machinery, chemicals, and information technology, in that order. Today, machinery is still the largest industry because of automobile and motorcycle production. Our chemical industry is growing very fast because we have natural gas in Chongqing, and this industry will be our largest within a year. But, in 2009, we decided that information technology should be our largest industry in the future, and the recent agreements with Hewlett Packard and others are a result of that decision. In addition, we have strong growth in agriculture—we even have some American companies moving here to grow oranges!

In terms of foreign business in Chongqing, in the early 1970s, there was nothing. It has taken many years to reach the point that we are at now, but—in 2008, 2009, and 2010—there were big jumps. Foreign investment is growing faster than Chongqing's GDP or total investment. In 2007, foreign investment was a lower percentage than China's average, and, in 2009, it was higher than China's average. So, foreign investment will play a larger role in our total investment as Chongqing grows. Right now, we're entering our twelfth five-year-plan period. At the end of this five-year plan, our GDP will have doubled.

4.2.0.

Site Documentation

The existing station plaza is vast and often empty, sized to accommodate crowds of travelers that mob the rail station during the spring festival, when many urban migrants travel home to their villages to be with family.

Aerial View of Municipality. Chongqing Municipality, consisting of nineteen districts, fifteen counties, and four autonomous counties, covering 82,403 square kilometers–slightly larger than the U.S. state of Maine.

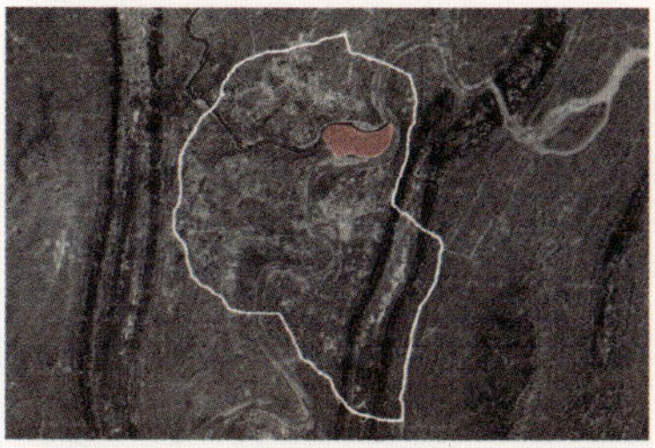

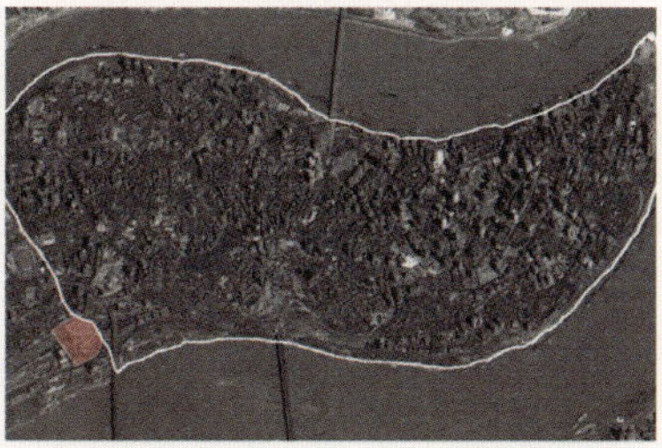

Aerial View of Urbanized Area. The urbaized area of Chongqing lies in south-western portion of the municipality.

Aerial View of City Center. The city center occupies a peninsula between the two rivers.

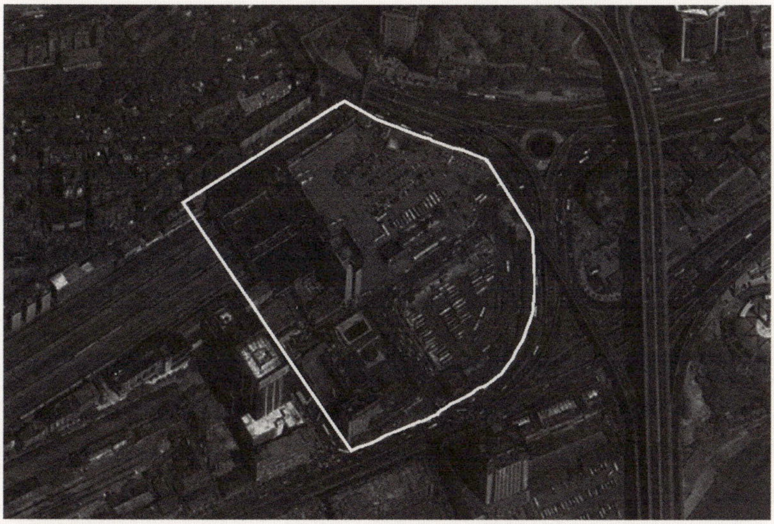

Aerial View of Site. The site sits at the edge of Chongqing's central area, wedged between steep topography rising to the north and major roads, elevated highways, and railroad tracks to the south.

Low-end convenience retail fronts at the station plaza.

Due to the congested infrastructure around the site, some of the major pedestrian routes into the station plaza are partially subterranean. These passages are lined with vendors selling food and other convenience goods.

P.113 North of the site, a pedestrianized, reconstructed historic street ascends the steep slope, connecting the station plaza up to a market and the new central business district (CBD) currently under construction at the top of the hill.

向陽隧道

P.114 Tunnel for cars and trucks connects the station area to the north side of the peninsula.

Elevated highways dominate the edge of the Yangtze River.

Economically marginal developments surround the existing station plaza. Some are in a derelict state.

A pedestrian bridge connects the station plaza to the reconstructed historic street to the north of the site.

P.117 Just east of the site, elevated highways connect the city center to the south bank of the Yangtze but do not connect easily to the site because of the difference in elevation.

During peak holiday travel times, temporary shelters are erected in the station plaza to accommodate passengers who sometimes wait in the plaza for days to buy tickets and board trains.

P.118 Laundry hangs from the power lines outside of residences in central Shanghai.

5. STUDENT PROJECTS

5.1.0.

Linked Towers

5.1.1.

De-Congested Density

—

William Gridley

01 Site plan

02 Ground-level plan. Connections to local streets and parking are made at the lowest level.

03 Retail-level plan. Retail along the waterfront connects through a new, open-space network north to the train-station plaza and then up the hill to the existing historic shopping street.

04 Sky bridge-level plan. Continuous retail space occupies the sky bridges, providing a comfortable indoor connection among the water-front, train station, and the Central Business District to the north.

The Chongqing high-speed rail station, centrally located within local, regional, and national geographic and infrastructural networks, is poised to become a critical Chinese hub for global commerce and consumption in the twenty-first century. Embracing the developer's demand for density and profitability, as well as the municipal government's efforts to avoid urban congestion, this project introduces a new urban condition for Chongqing: De-Congested Density. In examining the seemingly contradictory project demands, De-Congested Density blends principles of physical and visual networking with those of programmatic layering and overlapping to achieve a dynamic typology that offers a solution to the challenges of social and economic growth and urban and cultural sustainability.

The project first proposes to build over the existing infrastructural knot around the site, thereby establishing levels for traffic, parking, and service below a new ground plane that connects to the adjacent urban fabric. These physical links expand the site beyond its existing island condition, blending it within the adjacent context, which includes a historic cliff-side bazaar, a future central business district, metro and ferry stations, and a waterfront park. Next, one million square meters of new program is disposed vertically within towers and bridges across the site to link these disparate features through multiple layers of activity and circulation, resulting in a decongested but super-dense network that expands beyond the limits of the proposed site itself.

The high-speed-rail station is at the heart of the site, acting as a primary connection point as well as an architectural centerpiece that attracts pedestrians along carefully constructed axial sight lines while dispersing rail commuters into the surrounding plaza. Three distinct retail typologies are used to both absorb density and facilitate decongestion across the site's vast office, residential, and hotel program. First, flagship megastores located at the base of each tower pull visitors across the plaza and function as vertical circulation points to access the towers and bridges. Second, an intimate retail village along the waterfront activates the park space, links to the future ferry terminal, and provides an expansive vista across the river. Third, a raised shopping mall contained within a continuous, stepped sky bridge connects the entire site from the northern central business district to the southern waterfront. The sky bridge provides an efficient means of circulation for commuters and visitors, stimulates retail exposure and consumption, offers an observatory for the city, and spans dramatic terrain, while echoing the historic cliff-side steps of Chongqing to establish an iconic architectural identity for the project. Crowning this striated groundscape are the towers themselves, which collectively achieve a distinctive sculptural composition that is both functionally and aesthetically innovative. Taking into account the planning requirements of various programmatic functions, the floor plates within each high-rise shift relative to the building cores to create

01

02

03

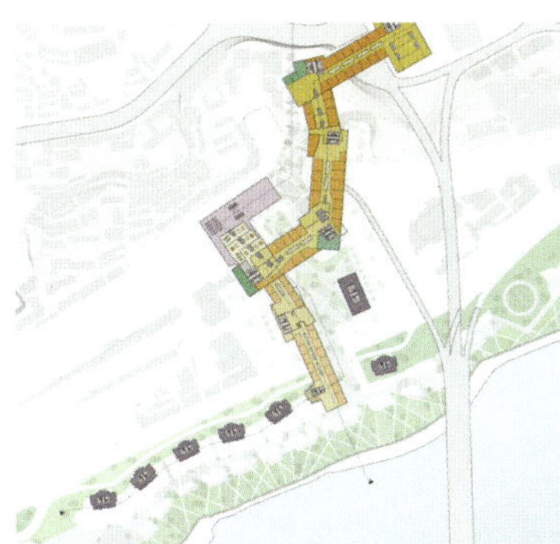

04

05

06

05 Section perspective. Sky bridges step up as they ascend the steep hill.

06 Section perspective.

07 Currently disconnected areas of the site are relinked through the intervention.

08 Point towers linked by sky bridges produce the project's characteristic density, without congestion.

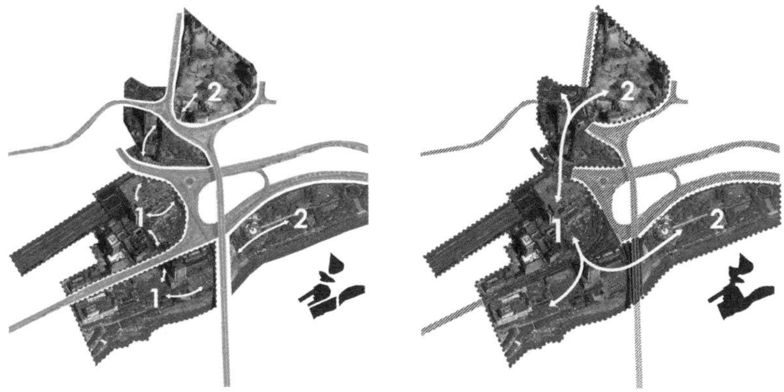

07

08

08 Program Distribution

09 The train station and office towers are organized around a new, grand public space.

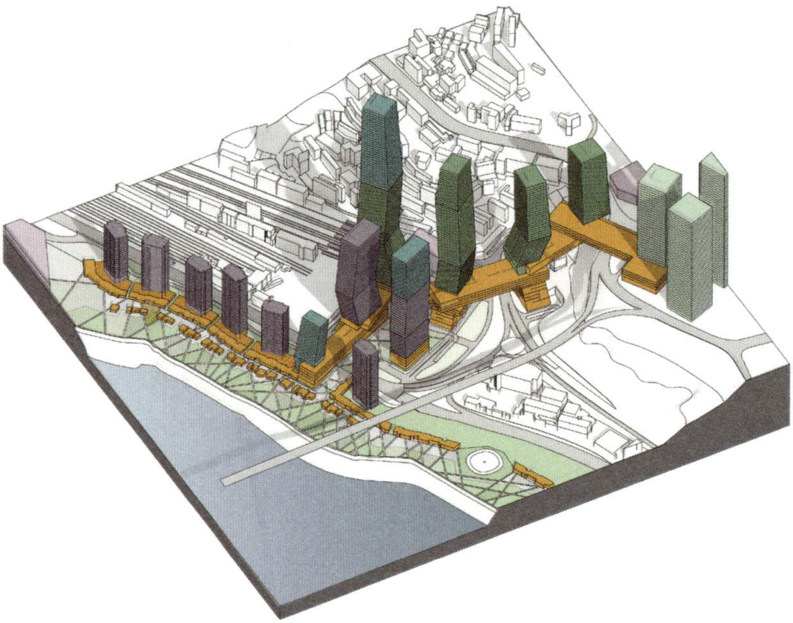

08

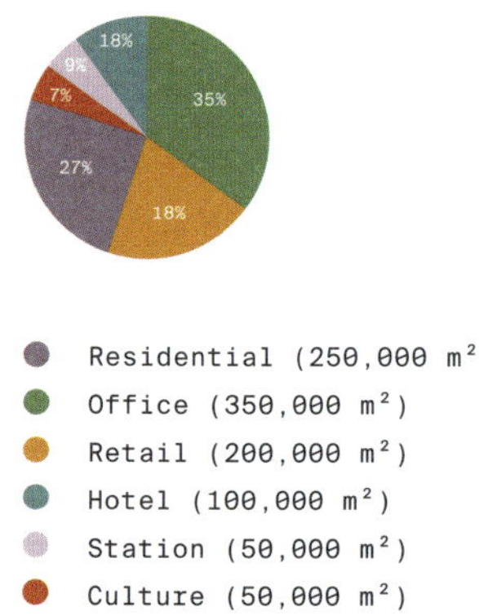

Virgin

10 The lowest levels of the towers contain retail, which provides public connections up to the sky bridge.

11 The towers oscillate in plan,producing an iconic image for the project.

11

ideal spatial conditions at critical points, such as lobbies, bridge atria, trading floors, and high-capacity event spaces.

Once combined within the context of this development, the architectural, infrastructural, and urban components provide density without congestion. The result is a new model for Chongqing that is both iconic and symbolic in nature; it embraces the full spectrum of an evolving, global society's demands and generates productive, sustainable urban space for the stimulation, growth, and exchange of twenty-first-century society, culture, and commerce.

5.1.2.

Chongqing Express

—

Kee Lew

This project reasserts the relationship between the economic identity of the city and its realization in architecture, which is achieved through strategic vertical programming and hybridization between building and urban infrastructure. The typological organization for high-density, high-rise planning and architecture is reconfigured in response to the topographical arrangement of the surrounding context and adjacent infrastructure, emphasizing new conditions and opportunities for the internal programming and architectural form of the project.

The city of Chongqing is undergoing unprecedented growth, which will result in an increasing demand for transportation, retail, and housing in its central districts. While the automobile market still has a large influence on the overall manufacturing industry and image of the city, the goal of the project is to provide a high-density complex for high-end automobile retail and business, along with ancillary high-end residential and hotel functions needed to support these uses.

In order to organize the large amount of program within the site, two major issues had to be solved: the congestion caused by disorganized automobile parking on the ground and the limited amount of foot traffic supporting retail. Although the existing plaza provides enough space for occasional crowds throughout the year, it does not relate to any other public activity. Meanwhile, the area suffers from heavy traffic congestion due to its multiple intersecting roads and inadequate parking and inadequate vehicular circulation around the block. There is too much traffic congestion, while the congestion of everyday public activity is not sufficient for sustainable retail business.

01 Ground-level plan. A retail loop and rail station surround a new central public space.

02 Site plan. The project links directly into the elevated highway system through new flyovers.

03 Instead of parking on the ground plane, parking reservoirs are located in the upper stories of the building to provide access from the adjacent elevated roads.

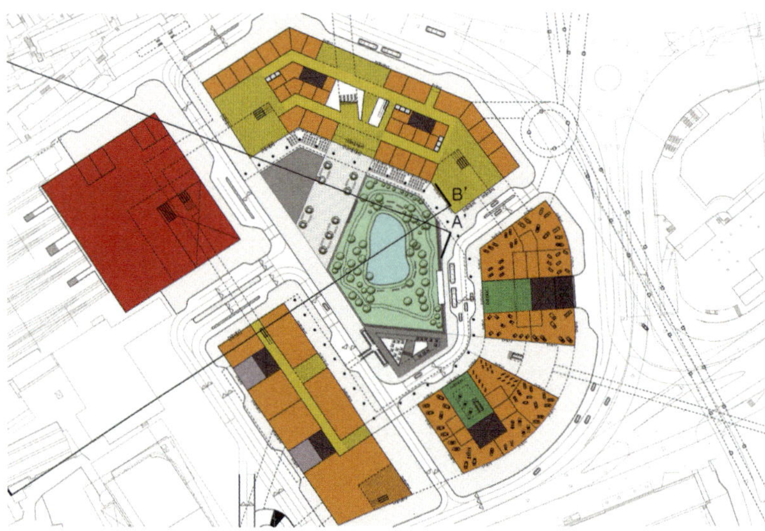

01

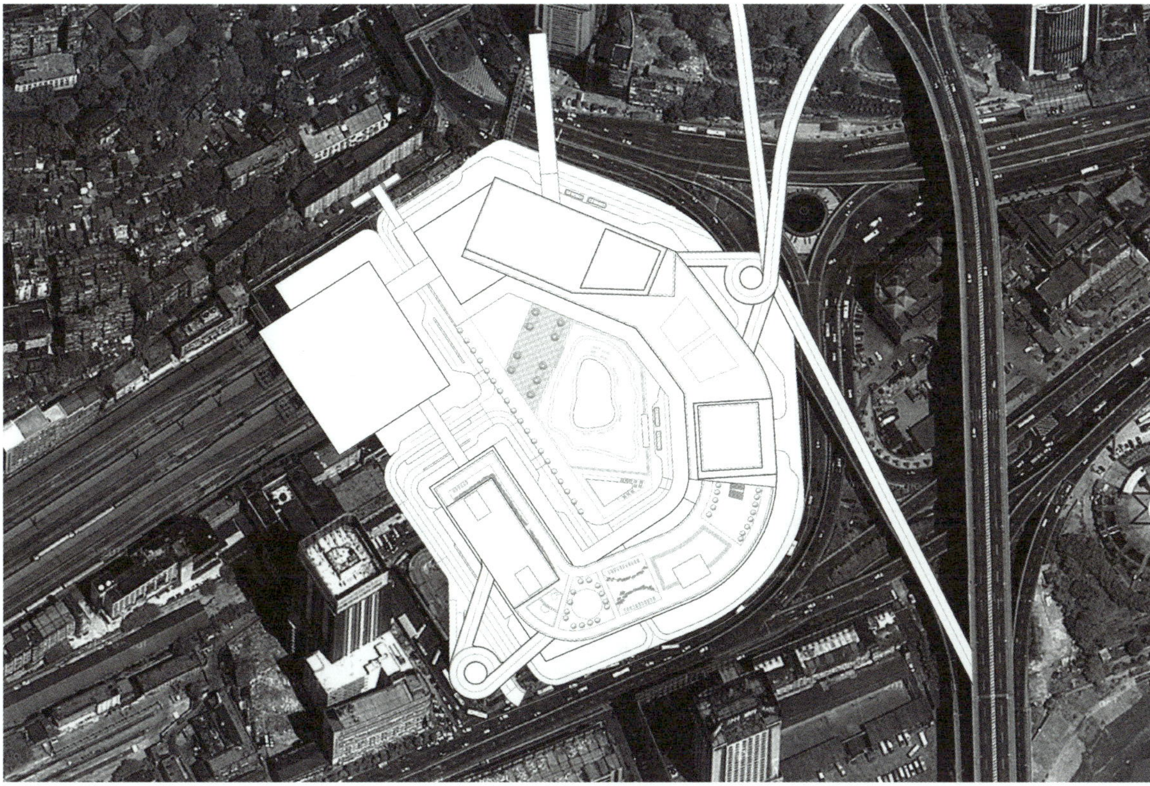

02

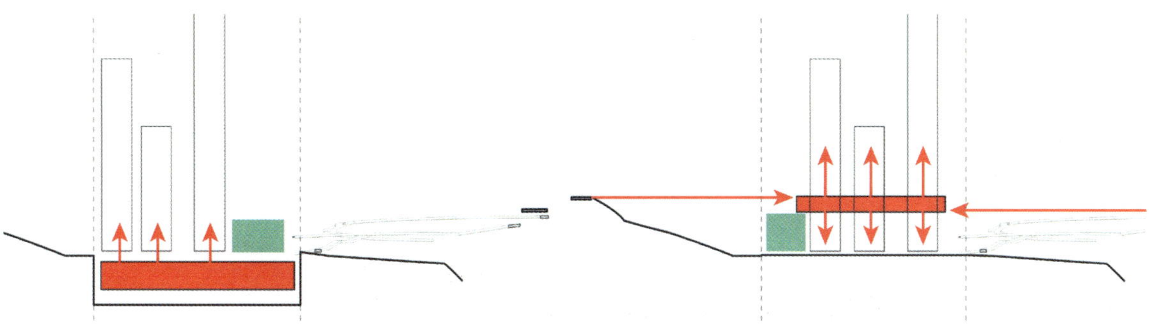

03

04 Section. The parking bridge spans between the towers.

05 Section.

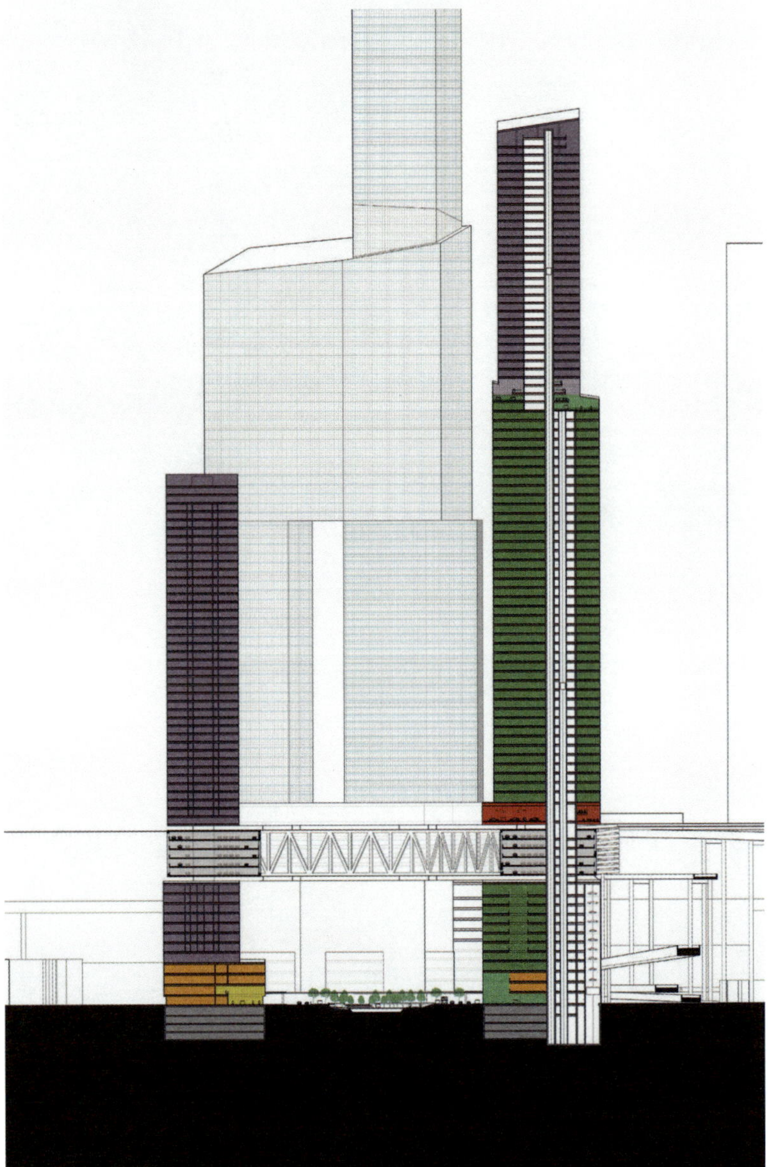

04

05

Rather than subdividing the site with traffic circulation and evenly distributing public space by each block, a variety of retail typologies—including large-scale department stores, a hyper-market, and automobile retailers—form a larger complex surrounding an open space, which will be dedicated to a public park. The retail types, which comprise busier and faster public circulation, such as the department store and hyper-market, are located closer to the train station, while the high-end car retailers are located closer to the highways.

The second strategy is to elevate the parking structure above the retail levels, bringing the distinctive surrounding elevated roads of Chongqing to the project. Since the project is surrounded by hills, there are a series of sloped highways and tunnels passing through the site. The site marks an entry point from the southern area of Chongqing into the peninsula and thus has the potential to serve as a link for those entering and exiting the city. Since vehicle traffic and parking function very inefficiently due to the drastic slope of the landscape and since building right above or below the ground plane would create more congestion, a five-story parking bridge is elevated to provide a direct connection from these high roadways.

By raising the parking to a significant elevation, the project is liberated from ground congestion yet gains more connectivity to the city. The vehicular traffic can enter the parking bridge without driving through the

07

06 The central public space is ringed by parking, towers, and the rail station.

07 The parking level separates the lower base elements from the towers of various heights.

tunnels and down the hill. Visitors for retail descend from the parking level on escalators, passing through luxury retail sections with a panoramic view of the city and the central park.

Meanwhile, visitors and users of the automobile headquarters enjoy the elevated lobby as a new entry to the business sector, a series of skyscrapers that stagger and rotate as they ascend. Within the towers, programs that require a larger footprint and proximity to the lobby, such as the automotive company headquarters and convention hotels, are located on the lower part, while the more exclusive and private programs, such as the boutique hotel and luxury apartments, occupy the higher towers. At each transition level between two different towers, a multi-story garden and atrium serve as a grand lobby for the private program, which allows a view down to the city and the open lounges of the headquarters.

5.1.3.

Chongqing Urban Refuge
—
Brian Spring

Chongqing Urban Refuge is located at the nexus of several areas of influence within the city. It serves as the connective tissue between the tech developments to the west, the old central business district to the east, the new Central Business District to the north, and the cultural convention center to the south. This development proposal attempts to leverage these connections while addressing Chongqing's ambition to move from a manufacturing-based economy to a service-based economy. This proposal aims to maximize density on the site and provides an expansive civic amenity that serves as a counter to the post-industrial, gritty residue of the surrounding context.

Focusing largely on future demand for office space, the program distribution is 55 percent office, 24 percent retail, 8 percent hotel, 5 percent residential, 5 percent multi-modal station, and 3 percent convention. The primary built components are orchestrated in such a way as to imply a porous, yet semi-contained enclave that retains connections to local infrastructure in the adjacent context. Three towers are strategically arranged on the site, across the river along Caiyuan Road, to address the entry sequence and frame a vision of the project upon arrival via rail at the multi-modal station. Towers punctuate the development, rising to 210 meters, 260 meters, and, at the southern edge of the site, a super tall 600 meters. Locally maximizing the floor-area ratio within the tower footprints and consolidating as much gross floor area as possible, this strategy allows for a liberated ground plane and as well as green

01 Program distribution.

02 Site plan. Landscape bridges connect the project south to the waterfront and north to the Central Business District.

03 Circulation routes.

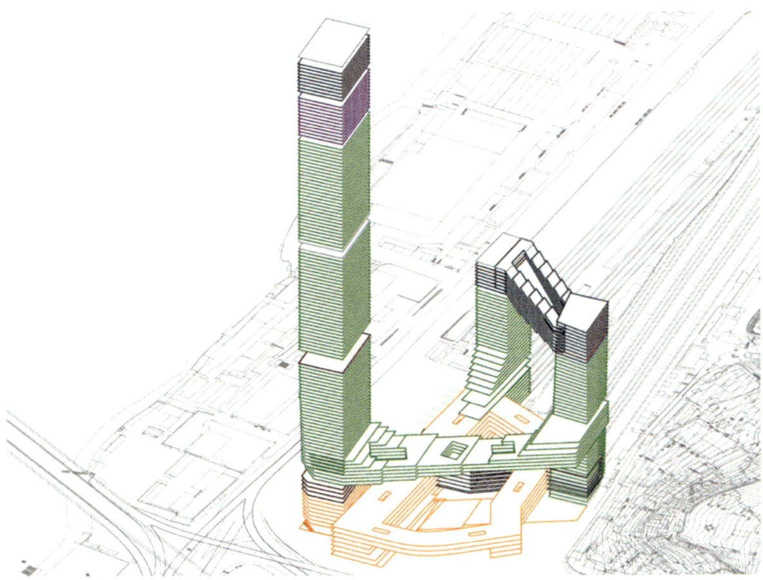

01

02

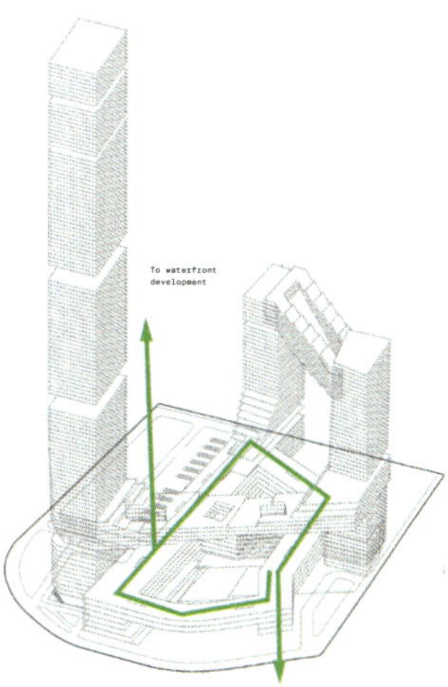

The CBD and Metro Station

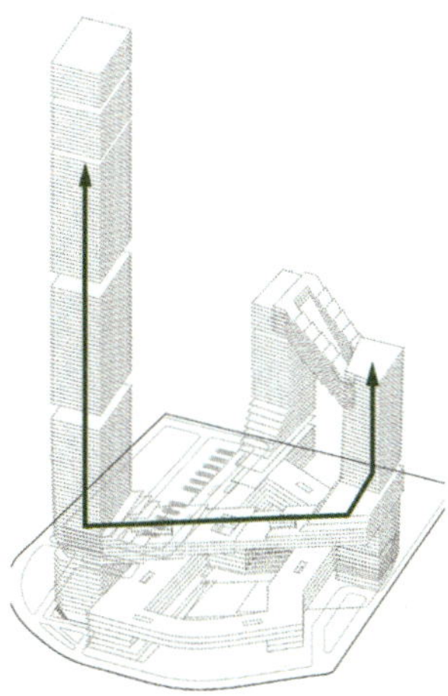

Office Bank Cantilevered Landscape

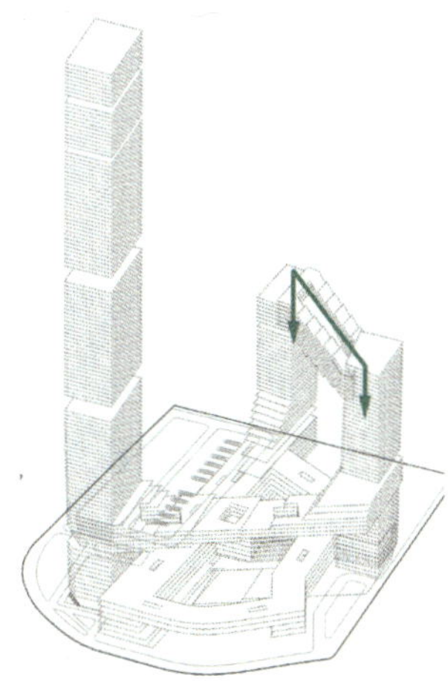

Hotel Circuit and Architectural Arrival

03

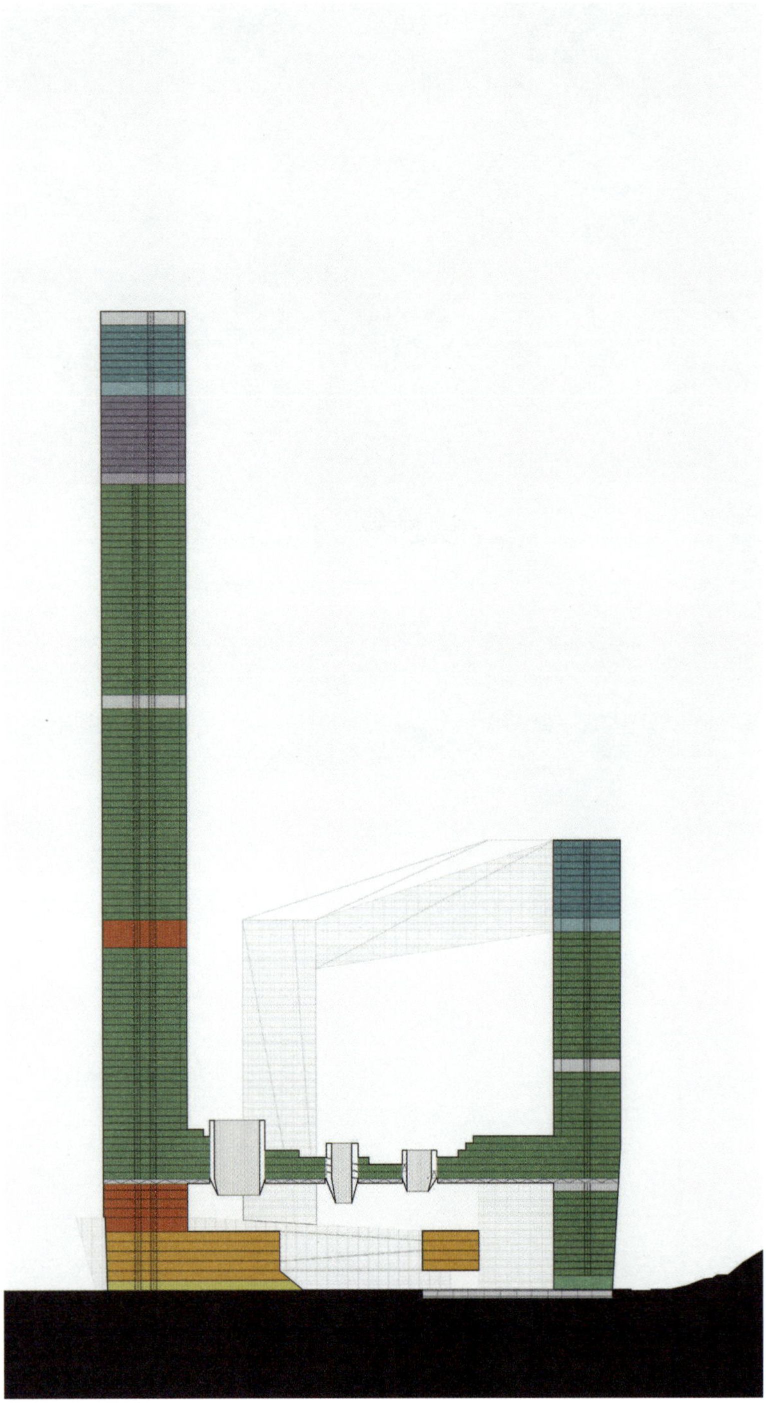

04

04 Section

05 Level-three plan. A continuous loop of retail connects the train station with the towers and other project elements.

06 Ground-level plan. Lobbies are adjacent to drop-off areas and connect to existing surface streets.

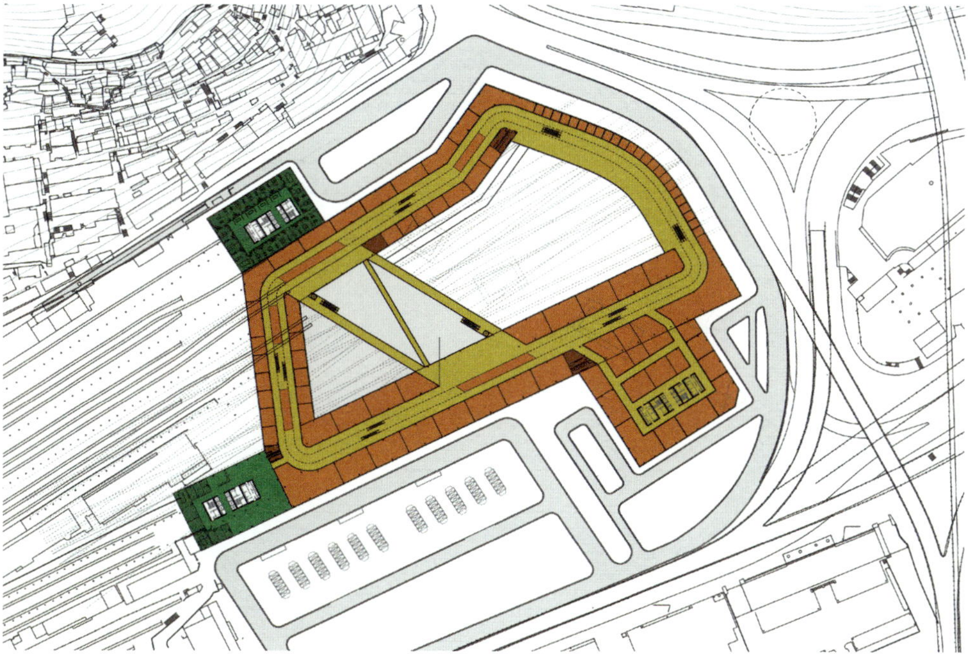

05

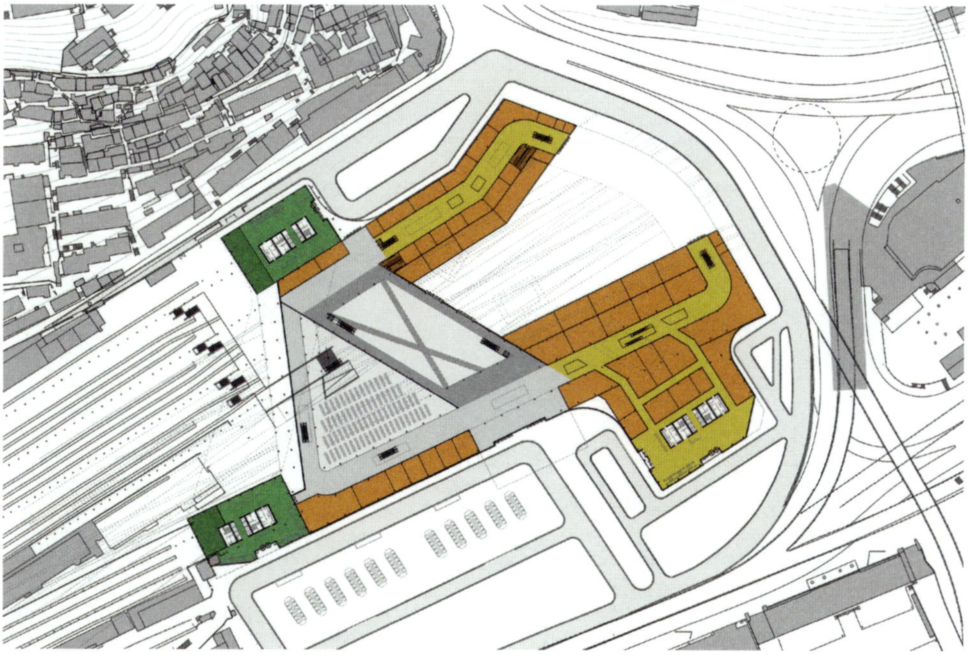

06

07

08

07 Bridges connect at multiple levels.

08 A super tall tower provides an identity for the project and can be seen from afar.

infrastructure to manage various systems of pedestrian circulation and access. This infrastructural greenscape operates at multiple sectional strata throughout the project, serving as an expansive public amenity but also operating above the public realm through cantilevered, bridging elements. The bridging creates a linkage between the three towers so as to further reinforce this localized infrastructure as the connective tissue of the project. This connective tissue is striated and terraced as a means to provide a heavily differentiated experience, oscillating between patterned hardscape and deliberately overgrown foliage. The terracing and ramping from level to level allow direct access from the various office floors, providing tenants with an uninterrupted park experience that is cantilevered fifty meters in the air. The retail podium is organized around a loop (viable for retail efficiency and shop exposure) and voids the center to address the population demands of the intersecting station. The podium green roof is accessible by retail users but also interfaces with the adjacent office floors, strengthening the connection between tower and podium. Chongqing Urban Refuge is a model of development that mitigates the congestion of super-density by consolidating gross floor area in a series of point towers to capitalize on the implementation of a localized, multi-level greenscape that serves as an urban refuge from the post-industrial contextual detritus.

5.2.0.

Megastructures

5.2.1.

Chongqing Megabridge

—

Katsunori Shigemi

01 Site plan. The megabridge not only connects the rail station to the Central Business District but also provides a large public space beneath the structure.

02 Project concept.

This design proposal integrates architecture and infrastructure in the form of a megabridge, which connects the rail station to the Yangtze River and the Central Business District. The project becomes an armature for superdense development to support the city of Chongqing, which faces a severe infrastructure crisis and land shortage due to mass migration from surrounding towns. The megabridge provides three distinct, yet interrelated, architectural features: a new ground for dense development, a programmed space within the bridge itself, and a roof for the rail station. This new infrastructure transforms the station and the surrounding area into a place that is attractive for business, housing, and travel while solving the urban issues with which the site is currently struggling.

A New Ground

The megabridge serves as a new ground for the site with direct vehicular and pedestrian circulation between the station, the Yangtze River, and the Central Business District, which is located 75 meters above, atop an adjacent steep hill. At the same time, it provides an entirely new platform, along which seven tall towers rise up to face the river. This new elevated street on the megabridge, which bypasses the streets on the top and bottom of the hill, enables business people and travelers to move between the business district and the station in less time, easing the now heavy traffic around the station. High-end offices, residences, and a luxury hotel are able to have their own drop-offs separated from the station level, avoiding conflict with the majority of station users.

A New Programmed Space

The space beneath the megabridge is programmed with boutique offices and research laboratories, such as the Chongqing Institute of Technology, generating mutually beneficial relationships with manufacturing enterprises and supporting the growth of the city's economy in the booming high-tech industry. The office and lab spaces within the megabridge are highly visible from the concourse level and, around the site, the adjacent highways. This plan presents a new and distinct architectural image that represents Chongqing's new identity as a high-tech industrial city while responding to the inherent high density of the existing city fabric.

A New Roof

Given the structural depth required for the bridge to span across the station concourse, the interior of the megabridge becomes programmed space. The concourse has a column-free space beneath a glazed roof that is suspended from the megastructure. The megabridge becomes an enclosure to protect the station users from the harsh climate of

01

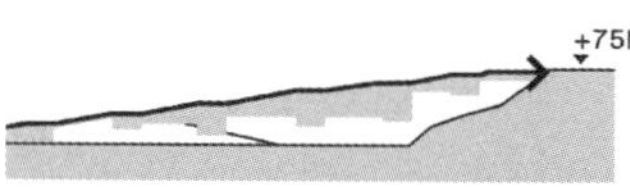

New ground connecting station to CBD.

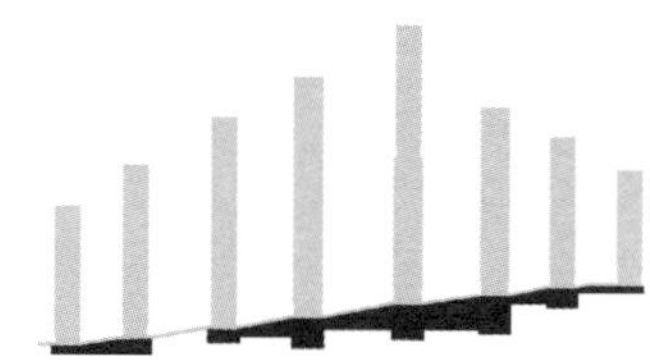

New programmed space.

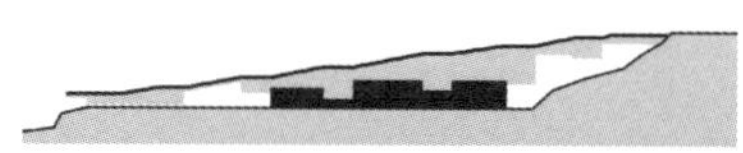

New roof and column-free space
For station concourse below.

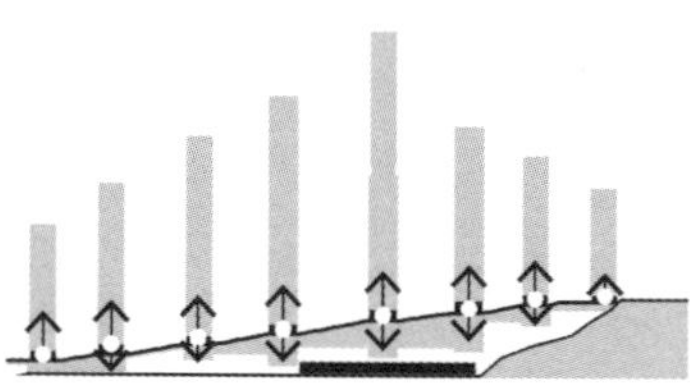

Seraration of drop-offs from crowd.

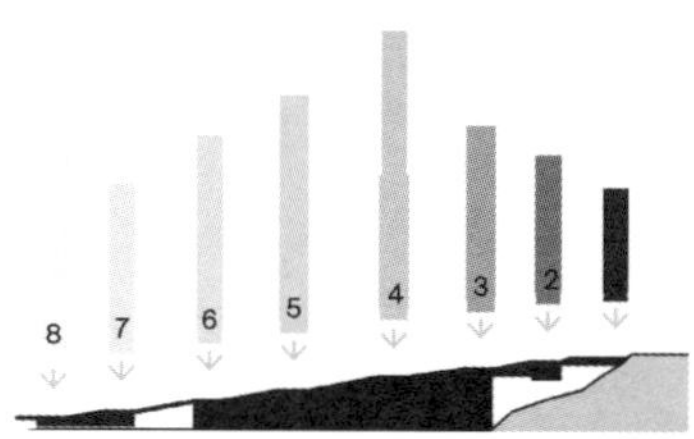

Phasable.

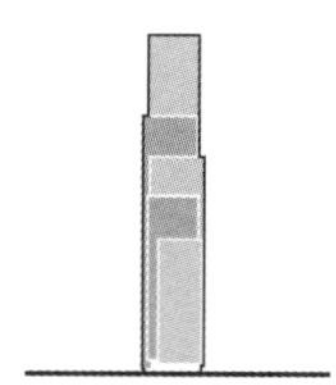

Less impact to existing and
future development.

02

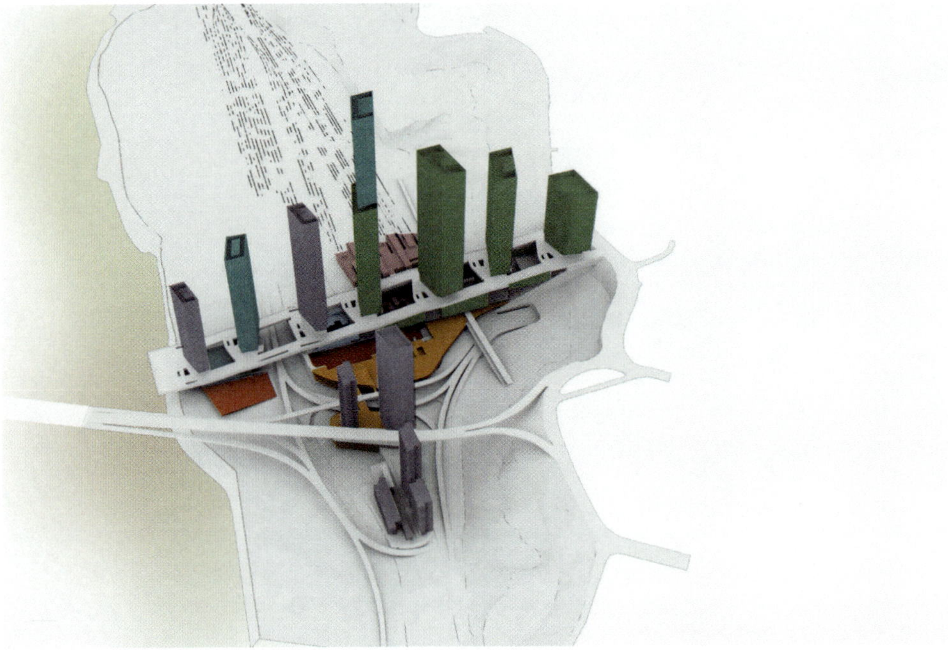

03

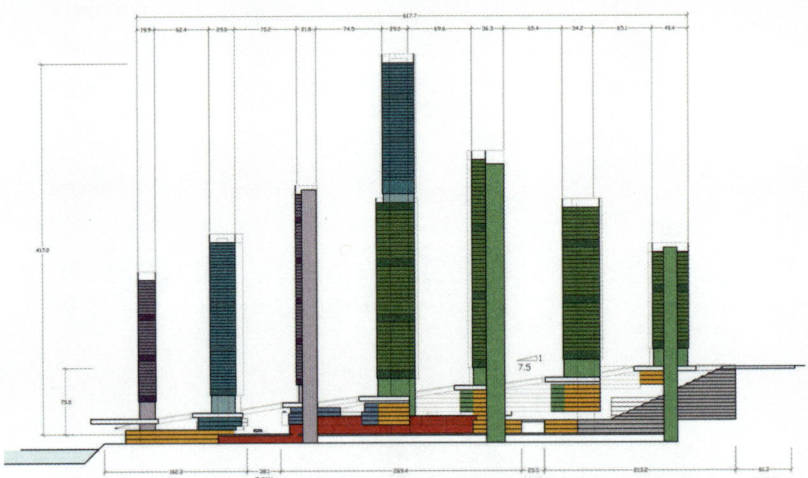

04

03 Program distribution.

04 Section. The megabridge connects the top and bottom of the 75-meter-high hill while providing a new street, programmed space, and a roof for the station.

05 The megabridge mediates between seven towers and the podium.

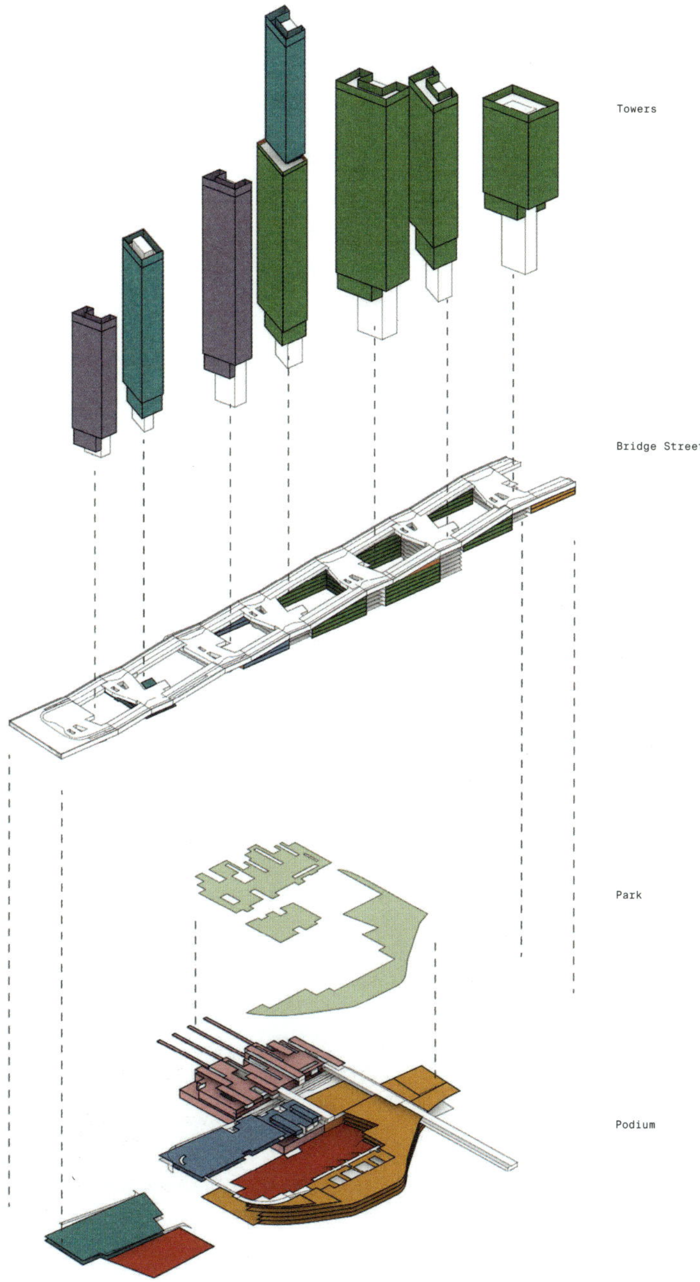

05

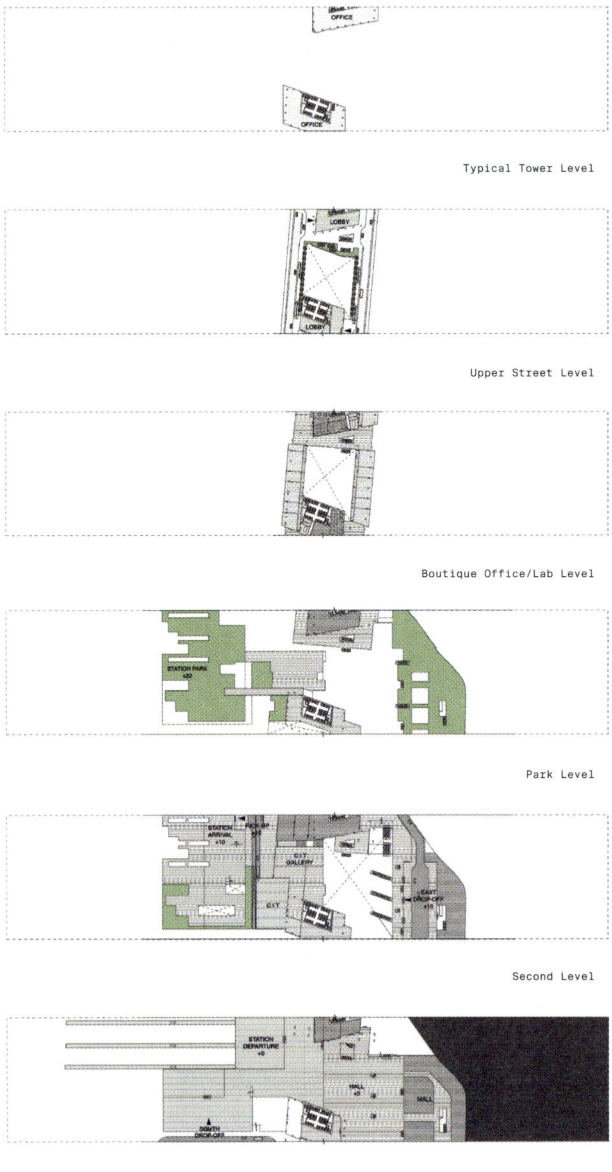

06

06 Plan vignettes.

07 Site plan. The introduction of the megabridge eases the gap between the Central Business District and the Yangtze River resulting from the topography.

08 The major space of the rail station sites below the megabridge and towers.

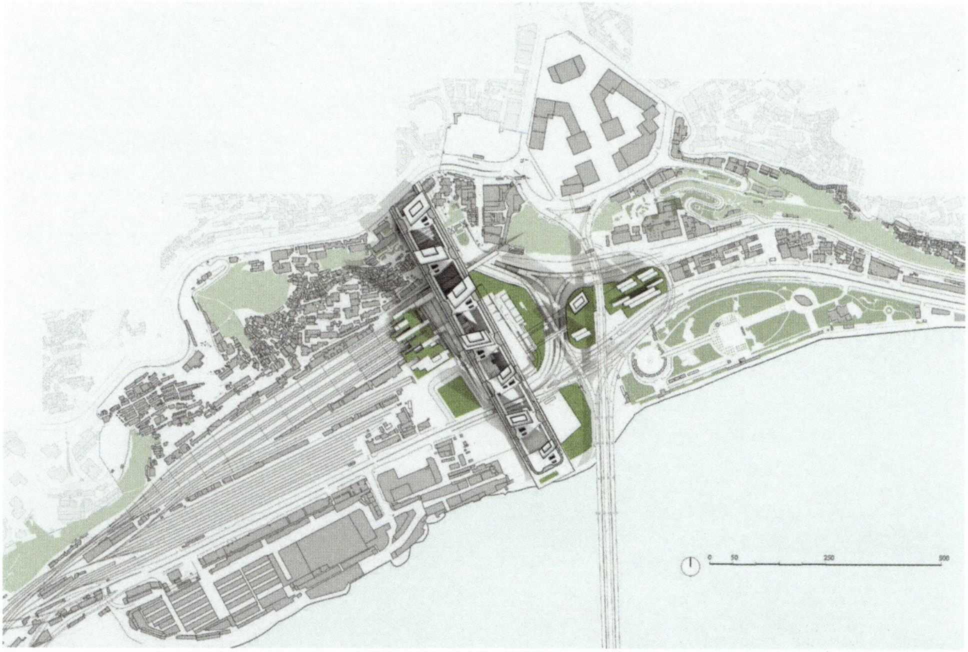

07

08

10

09 The megabridge serves as a structure for the roof to enclose the station concourse below.

10 The project presents an iconic image to the visitors arriving in Chongqing by high-speed rail.

Chongqing; in addition, its grid-like geometry allows sunlight to penetrate into the concourse area below, providing further comfort. At the concourse level, the station users can gaze at the unobstructed, open sky as well as the variety of office and retail programs within the megabridge. This unique, three-dimensional experience is produced by inserting this megastructure between the towers and podium levels, activating both the public realm and the commercial spaces in the development.

The introduction of the megabridge into the site is beneficial because it combines a rich mix of programs and comfortable urban space within superdense Chongqing. By enabling this trio of functions, the megabridge provides an organizational structure to the complex site as well as a rich spatial experience and character that the public can appreciate and share. Coupling superdense development with large-scale infrastructure, this new development becomes a vital gateway district for Chongqing today and in the future.

5.2.2.

Projecting Chongqing
—
Keith Johns

Often the superdense project's physical manifestation is as a point tower. Despite the proliferation and success of the tower as a form of urban development, the resulting tall buildings' fleeting iconicity, insatiable one-upmanship, and lack of connection threaten the sustainability of the urban realm. If architecture is to continue to accommodate the largest migration in the history of civilization—now occurring in China's cities—it must seek out other super-dense typologies that can perform in multiple ways. This project explores an alternative to going up.

Acknowledging the site's drastic elevation change, the project consists of two primary pieces. The first element is a slab that extends over the site at the 75-meter elevation of the Central Business District to the northeast. Establishing a new datum, the projecting slab allows a continuation of the commercial fabric of the CBD and introduces a horizontal strategy for growth. Contained within the belly of the slab is the second piece, a grand boulevard. While providing vehicular access down the length of the building, the boulevard datum is populated with office lobbies and entries and unites the slab above with the shops and retail hanging just below it. Not dissimilar in concept from the New York City viaduct that freed Park Avenue from the gritty rails below, the boulevard allows new commercial addresses at the elevation of the Central Business District. Office slabs are removed from the tangled mess of the street and highway infrastructure that currently plagues the site's ground level.

01 West elevation.

02 Typical upper-level plan. Large green courtyards act as light wells, allowing light to filter through the glass slab and down to the road level.

03 Circulation. Links and user groups.

01

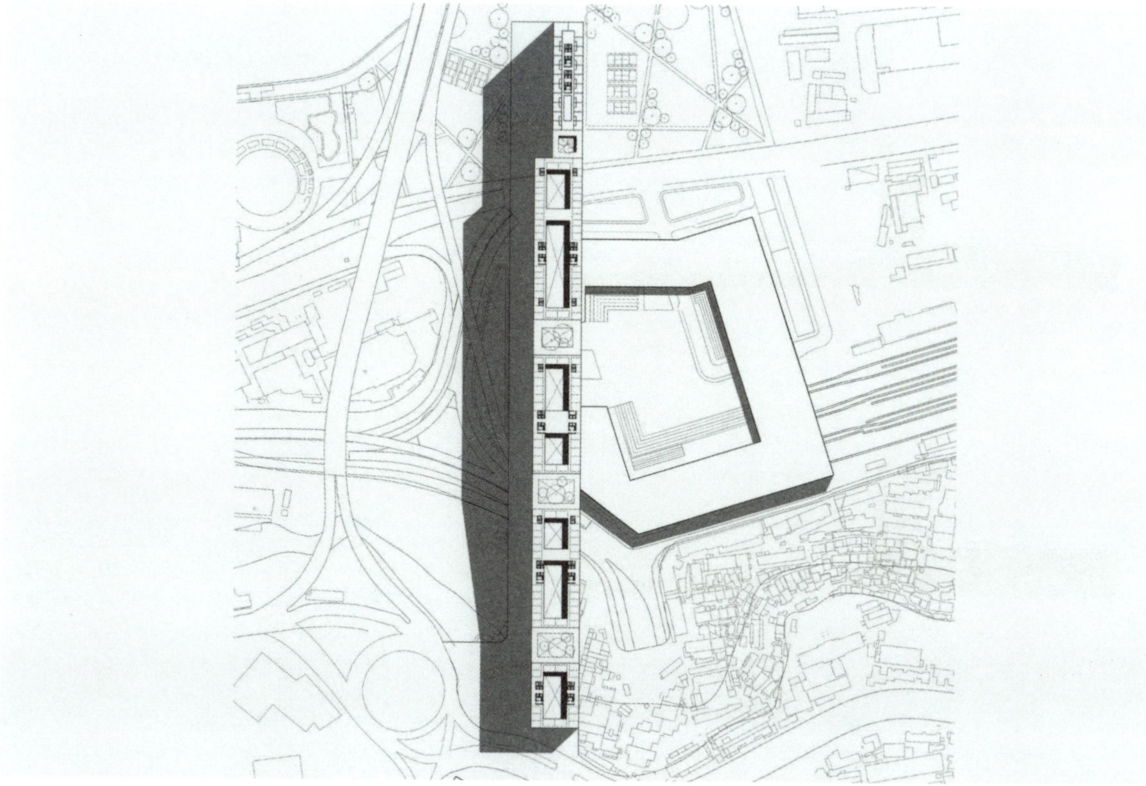

02

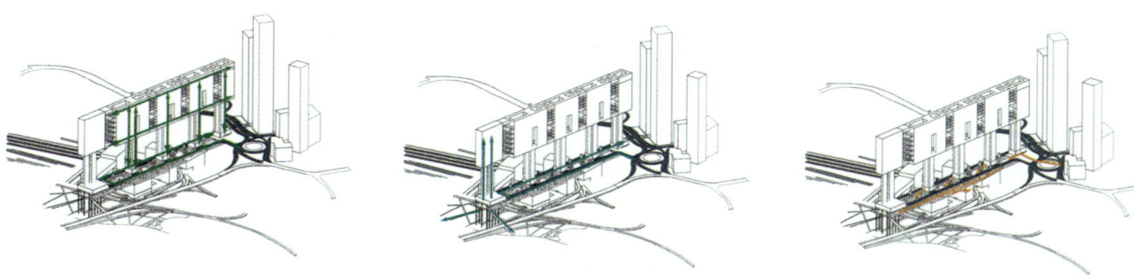

03

04 Project concept.

05 Program distribution.

06 The slab projects from the top of the hillside down toward the river.

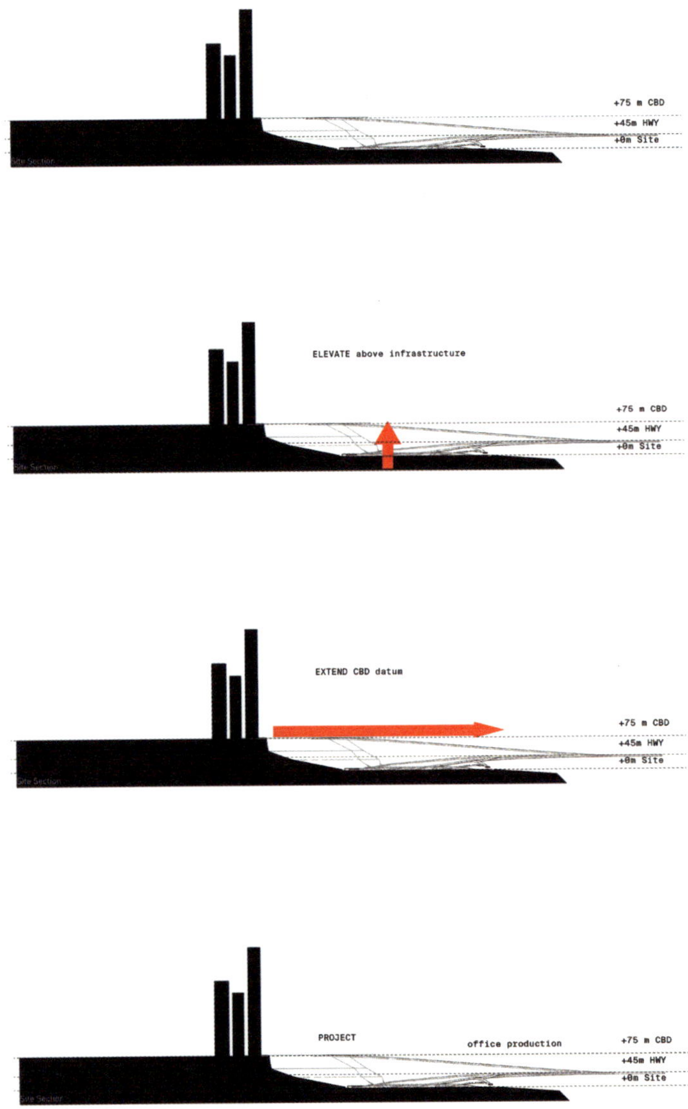

04

05

06

07

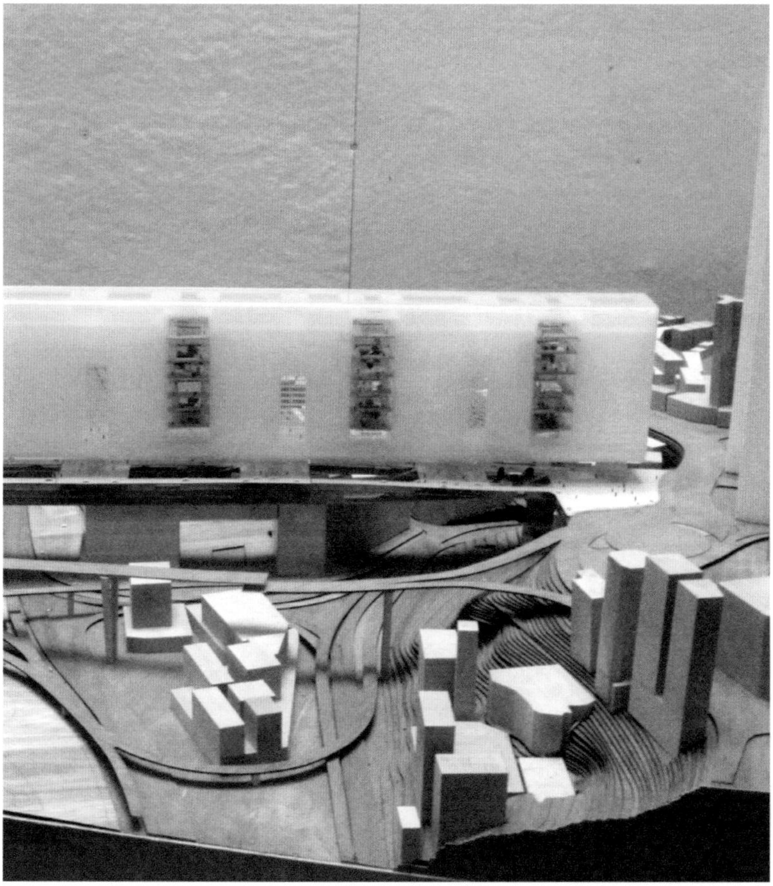

08

07 Detail of vertical courtyards and elevated grand boulevard.

08 Deep, verdant courtyards produce variation in the façade of the slab.

Progressing downward from the elevated datum, the program is predominantly retail and formed as a loop. Anchoring the northwest corner of the retail loop is the train station, where travelers can seamlessly enter retail or exit through the large, central plaza—a space that accommodates tens of thousands of waiting travelers. While the loop establishes strictly internalized space that promotes more conventional retail consumption, the offices above exemplify outward-looking space, projecting the new value of Chongqing's burgeoning creative economy. Exuberant in its blankness, the glass slab acts as a billboard for the city, a terminus for the train station, and a repository for the new medium of production.

5.2.3.

Total Retail

—

Alfie Koetter

This proposal engages Chongqing's aspirations to evolve from an economy heavily reliant on production to a consumer economy. Chongqing's inland location, which is far from export transportation networks, encouraged it to develop a manufacturing economy oriented toward producing goods for the local and domestic market, including food, cars, textiles, and electronics. These sectors have thrived even without the strong export sector that characterizes much of Chinese manufacturing. Today, Chongqing is China's third-largest producer of motor vehicles and one of the country's largest producers of iron, steel, and aluminum. Despite its industrial success, Chongqing hopes to transform itself into a consumer society over the next ten years. In this light, Total Retail embraces consumerism in the form of an economically and socially diverse retail hub that is also a civic, regional, national, and international destination.

The proposed retail program comprises 400,000 square meters of space. This central element is complemented by office and hotel programs, which contain 250,000 square meters each. The office program relates directly to the operations of the retail development and provides space for the manufacturers, brands, and labels sold there. The hotel program provides lodging for short- or long-term visits to Chongqing's Total Retail environment.

Equally important to this proposal is, within the city, a significant new public space, which draws together many of the disparate demographics of Chongqing's population. With Kyoto Station and Shanghai's Plaza 66 as precedents, this proposal mediates the large scale of the Chinese superblock typology by introducing internalized, open-air public spaces.

At nearly 60,000 square meters, Plaza 66's superblock is massive compared to blocks in most Western cities: for example, a typical New York City block is a 16,000 square meters and a Chicago block is a mere 13,500 square meters. Plaza 66 mediates the large scale of the Chinese block in the same manner as many larger American blocks—through subdivision. Through the introduction of a series of pedestrian pathways, the individual superblock is effectively broken down into a set of manageable blocks.

Kyoto Station provided a model for both programmatic distribution and framing of public urban space within a single building. As a train station, Kyoto Station has an incredible diversity of program, including a large amount of retail as well as various civic and cultural programs. The semi-conditioned cavity in the core of the building provides a large public space that is used not just by commuters but also by the city at large. Formally, Total Retail pinches and pulls the dimensions of Kyoto Station to produce a larger square-courtyard typology.

The courtyard typology of Total Retail allows different retail demographics, which are usually understood to be incompatible, to be united through a loop; rather than being at two ends of a line, high-end and low-end retail are linked together by the train station itself. Through this

01 Site plan. Multiple retail typologies are arrayed along the retail loop and surround ground-level public spaces.

02 Transformation of Kyoto Station into Total Retail.

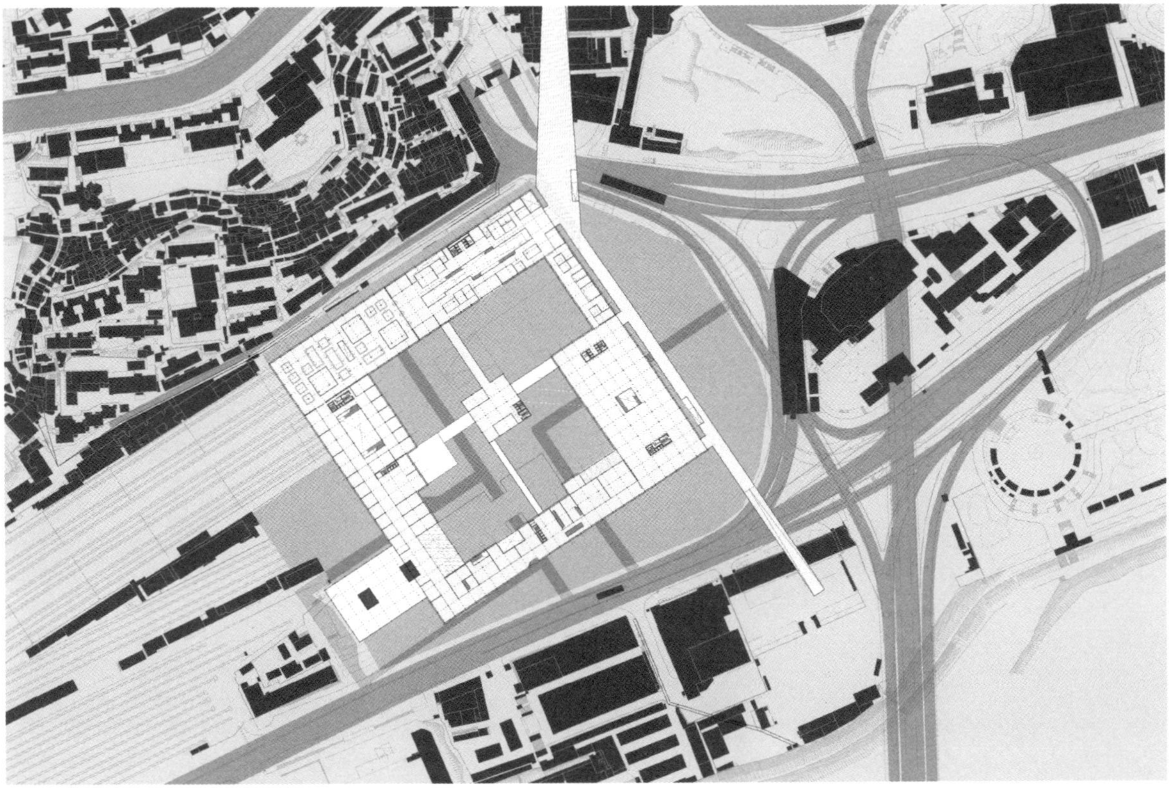

01

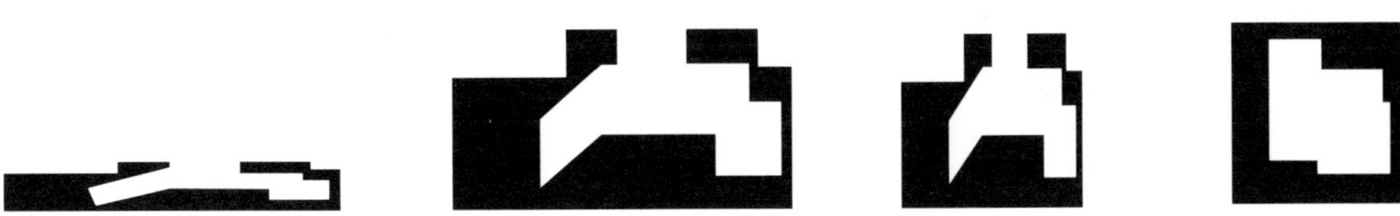

02

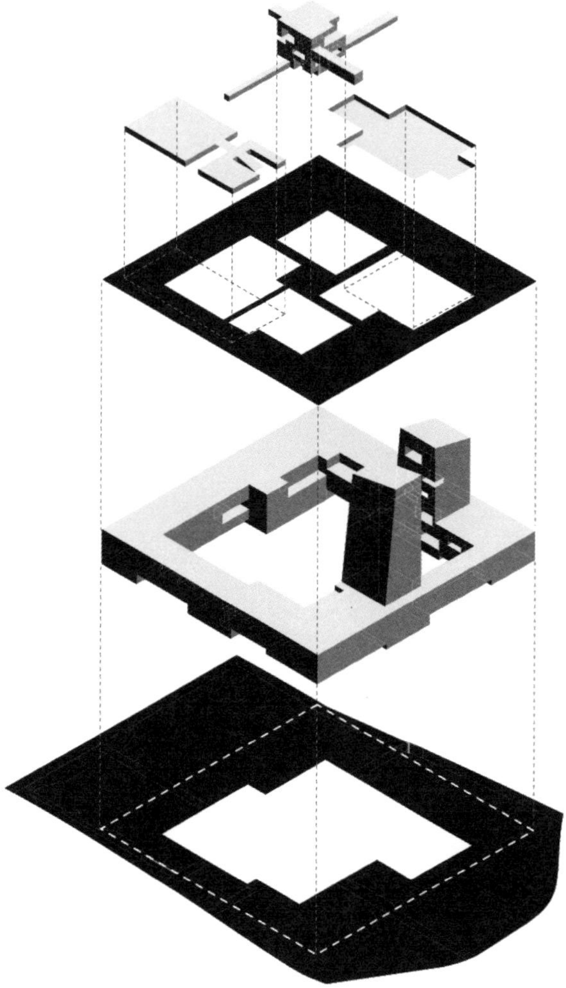

03

03 The overall retail ring defines a larger public space that is then subdivided into four distinct spaces by the central hub building and the sky bridges. While each of these spaces caters to different consumer demographics, the circulation invites and pulls in all visitors.

04 Sectional model taken through the high-end "district" of the Total Retail loop. Luxury-brand stores occupy larger, double-height retail spaces.

04

05

06

05 The central public space is open at its edges for the free flow of visitors, but it is defined by the central core, sky bridges, and the retail loop.

06 Section model taken through the low-end "district" of the Total Retail loop. Off-brand and knockoff vendor occupy small, informally organized spaces that accumulate into a retail tower.

tactic, similarities emerge between low-market and high-market brands; in effect, demographics previously segregated by brand are allowed to bleed into one another. As visitors move through the Total Retail loop, the scale, organization, and brands of the stores change. For example, as a shopper lingers around a series of open-air storefronts in one section, another shopper walks through a more typical, single-loaded retail corridor in a different section. Though the retail courtyard may be diagrammatically understood as a four square in which each square corresponds to a specific demographic, this proposal does not intend to segregate; rather, through the formal use of a continuous loop, this retail model erases previously assumed distinctions between the various demographics.

5.3.0.

Monumental Spaces

5.3.1.

Chongqing Plaza
—
Qiwei Liang

This proposal investigates architectural density in relation to the issue of urban crowding in China, particularly focusing on rail stations and using Chongqing station as a case study. While overcrowding at rail stations is a serious problem during the holidays, it has the potential to drive consumption. This project examines the possibility of creating a vibrant urban condition by, drawing the crowd and its purchasing power to the site.

Two Chinese building types are relevant precedents. One is the podium type, in which enormous retail levels occupy the lowest floors and support relatively small, extruded towers at their centers. This type of development occupies a lot of land without offering enough density to handle the scales of crowds that are drawn to the Chongqing site. Another conventional type in China is the formal inverse: the large public square, which is built to absorb crowds during special occasions but is otherwise deserted because it is not supported by an appropriate density of surrounding programs.

In terms of the train station, there are three challenges. The first is related to the crowds of travelers and visitors, which must be not only accommodated but enticed to shop at the retail development. The second is related to the site, which must create sustainable, open, green space—one of Chongqing's ambitions. The third is related to program, which must provide a comfortable, smooth transit experience and facilitate connections across the mountainous topography.

In response to these three issues, this proposal combines the formal types of the podium and the plaza. The heart of the project is a massive podium, which is too big to be understood as an architectural piece; instead, it becomes an infrastructural element that offers connectivity and public space. Different building types are sited upon this podium, producing a density that is different from both the bounded density of

01 Section.

02 Site plan.

03 Circulation.

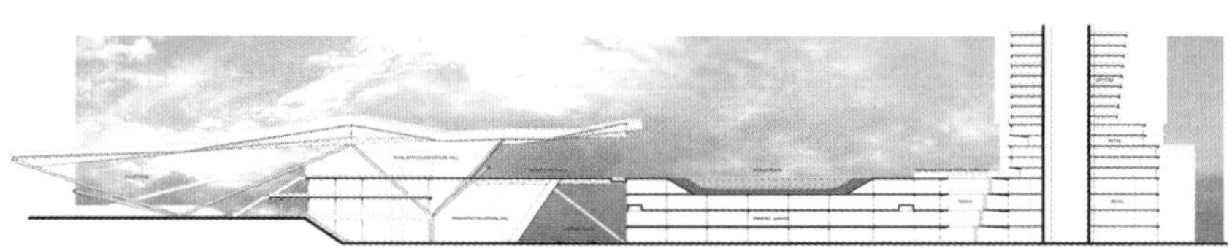

01

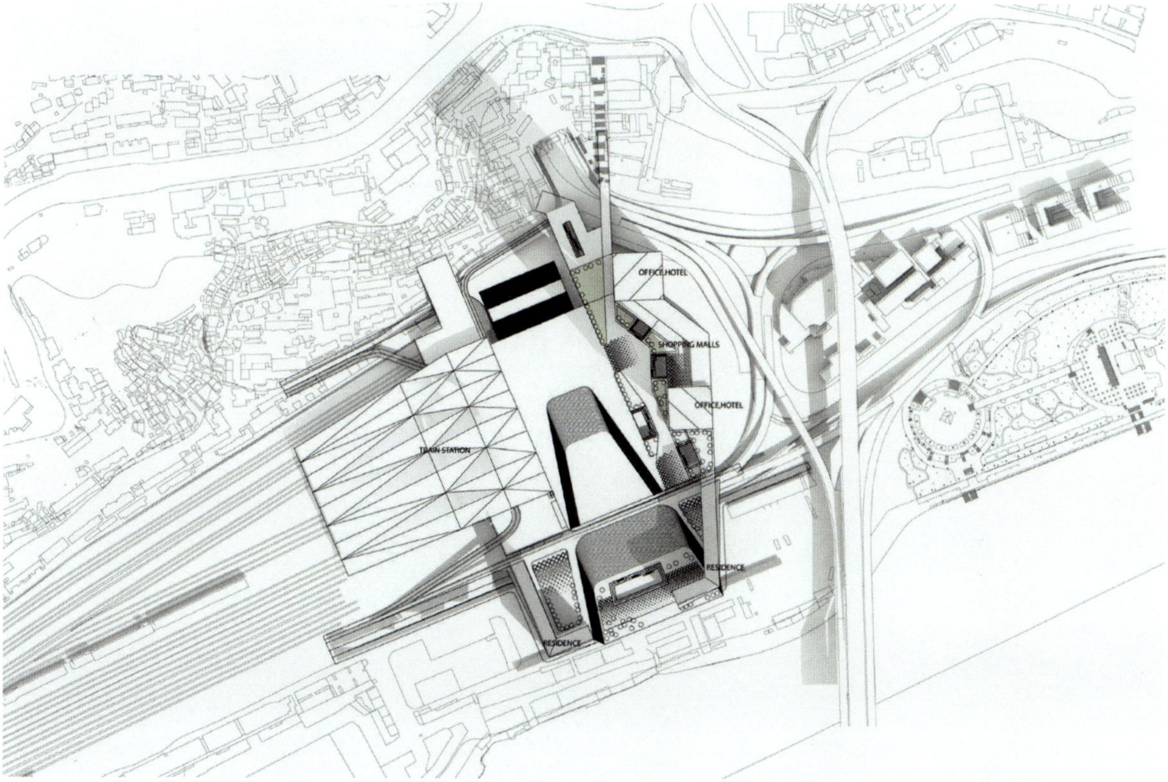
OFFICE,HOTEL
SHOPPING MALLS
OFFICE,HOTEL
TRAIN STATION
RESIDENCE
RESIDENCE

02

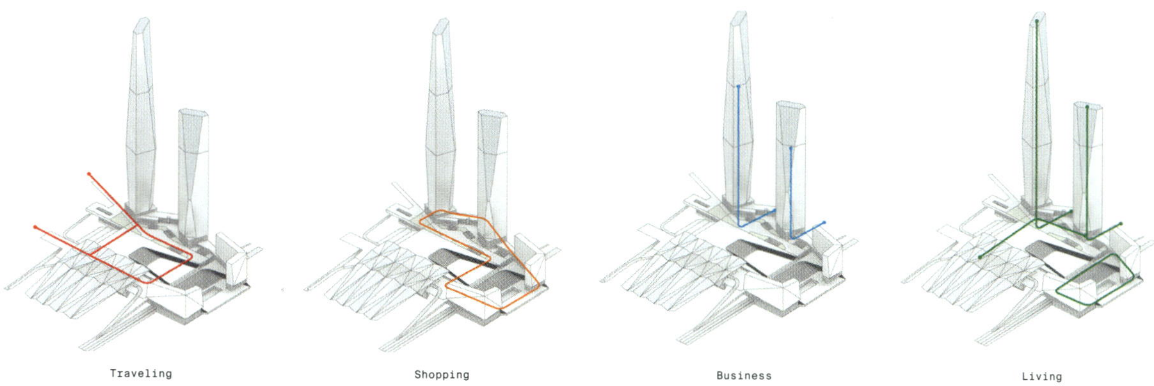
Traveling
Shopping
Business
Living

03

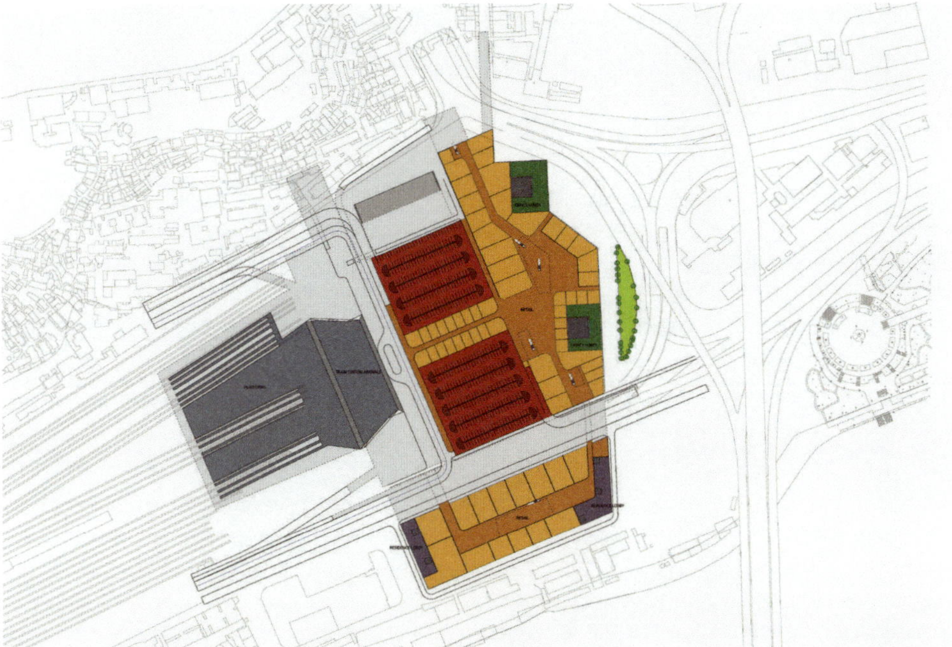

04

05

04 Ground-level plan. A large bank of parking is buried within the retail podium.

05 Podium-level plan.

06 Program distribution.

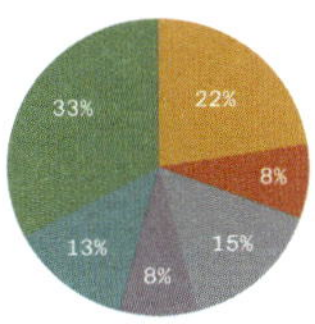

- Station (150,000 sqm)
- Residential (82,300 sqm)
- Hotel (126,500 sqm)
- Office (320,000 sqm)
- Retail (220,500 sqm)
- Parking Garage (80,200 sqm)

06

07/08 Concept diagram.

09 The large plaza is divided into smaller zones through surface treatments, elevation variations, and program along the edges.

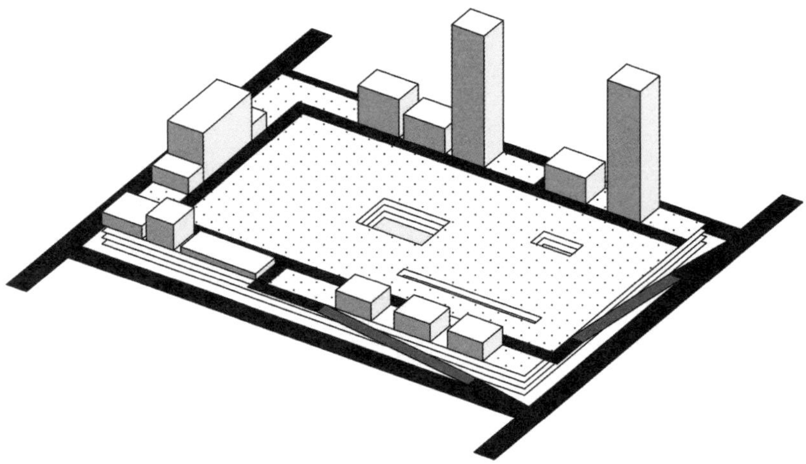

07

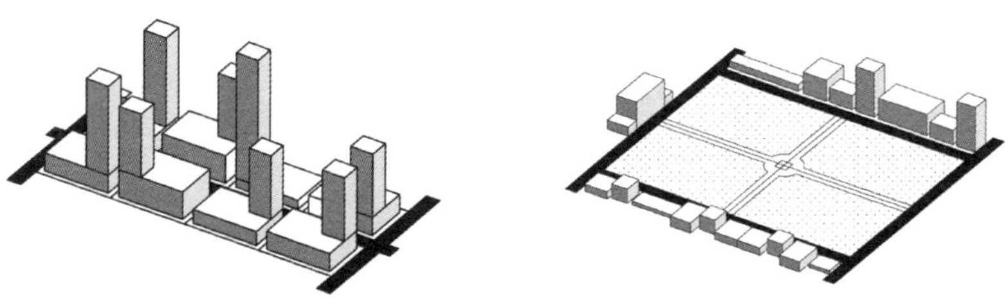

Podium-tower buildings

Iconic Plazas

08

11

10 Iconic towers can be seen from afar.

11 Openings in the podium allow light to penetrate the deep floorplates below.

the podium building and the unbounded density of the plaza. This crowd density becomes semi-concentrated: visitors are attracted by retail and entertainment programs, but they are not necessarily bounded by walls. This huge podium plaza is somewhat homogeneous: It is a free surface, but when the different building types plug in, they create different zones of intensity and program in this surface, without adding boundaries. After inserting these building types, a second layer of landscape devides this enormous plaza into seven different sub-plazas. The landscape is sloped to emphasize the fluidity and gradients between the spaces. While the central plaza is iconic and symmetrical, there is also a sunken plaza for gatherings and events, a station plaza, a commercial plaza, residential plazas, and a green plaza, which faces the river, and is sloped to act as a balcony overlooking the city. The boundaries between these zones are soft and implied so that, for special occasions such as the Spring Festival, they become fluid, and the crowds can be absorbed. In this way, the project achieves the value and intensity of a commercial development while, like a piece of public infrastructure, accommodating unusually large crowds.

5.3.2.

Chongqing Station and Exposition Center

—

Danh Thai

This proposal acknowledges China's inter-urban rail-network plan and addresses the increasing, dynamic population of Chongqing. It accommodates the demand for a larger railway station in order to sustain a superdense population but also lends a special theme, centered on the automobile and motorcycle industry, to the development. That theme is expressed through a specific, iconic program: an exposition center that celebrates the success of the automobile and motorcycle economy in Chongqing.

The new urban condition that is created at the site is articulated by five main elements: a reformulated rail station, including an intermodal exchange; a new exposition center; mixed-use business; high-end residential housing, which is stacked and terraced; and a sky street that creates a more efficient circulation route around the site. The design does not consist of just a super-expressway and a massive central hub; rather, it is a completely integrated world in which the flow of cars exists in tandem with life in the development above and below. The design aims to create a unified urban structure in which diverse infrastructural and public elements merge to form one conglomeration. Chongqing Station is currently a terminal, but future expansion might extend the train tracks to the city center; in the meantime, the exposition center serves as a hub promoting the auto and motorcycle industry in an innovative and high-quality environment.

01 Section. Residential units terrace back over the rail tracks.

02 Ground-level plan. A central promenade is framed by retail and the Chongqing Station and Exposition Center.

03 Upper-level plan.

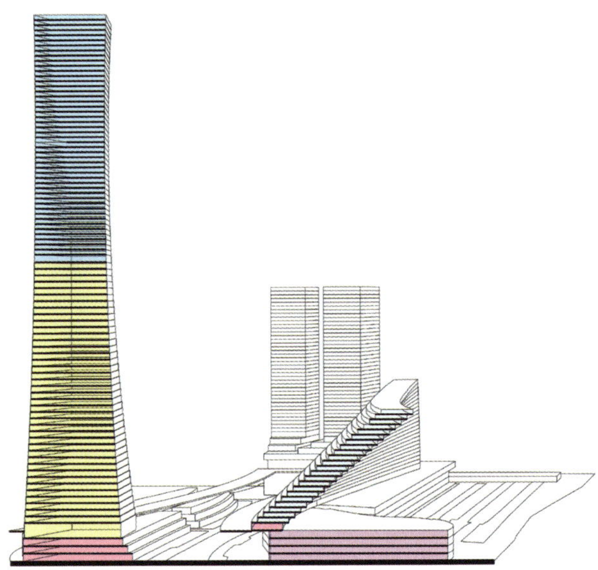

01

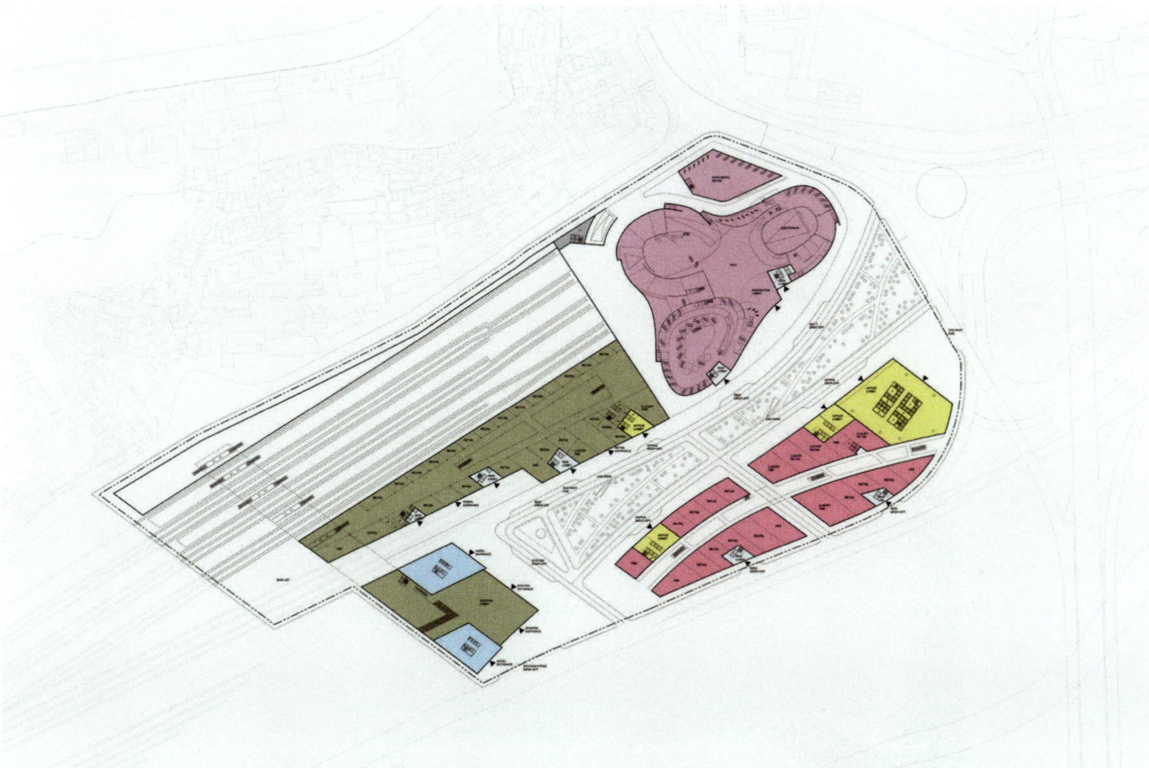

02

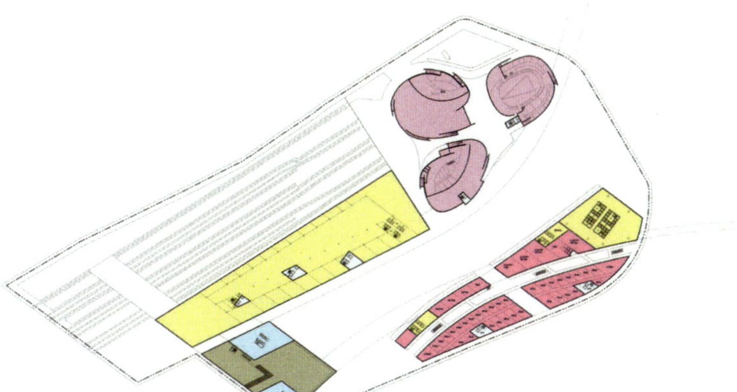

03

04 A new roadway allows vehicle access into the core of the project.

05 Program distribution.

04

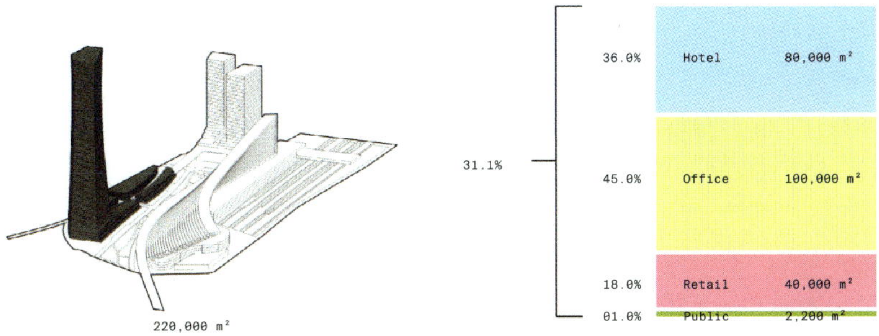
220,000 m²
31.1%
36.0% Hotel 80,000 m²
45.0% Office 100,000 m²
18.0% Retail 40,000 m²
01.0% Public 2,200 m²

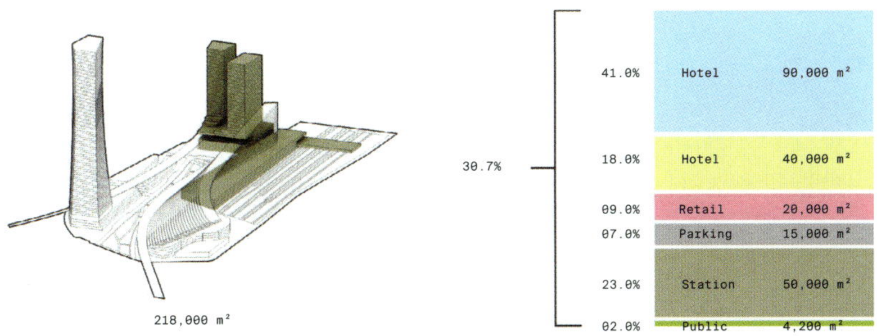
218,000 m²
30.7%
41.0% Hotel 90,000 m²
18.0% Hotel 40,000 m²
09.0% Retail 20,000 m²
07.0% Parking 15,000 m²
23.0% Station 50,000 m²
02.0% Public 4,200 m²

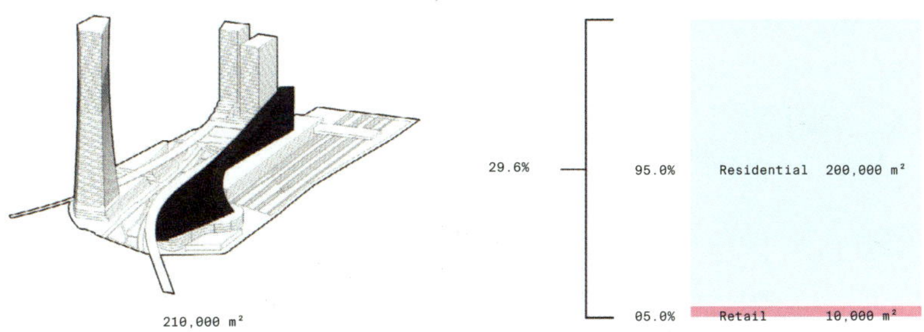
210,000 m²
29.6%
95.0% Residential 200,000 m²
05.0% Retail 10,000 m²

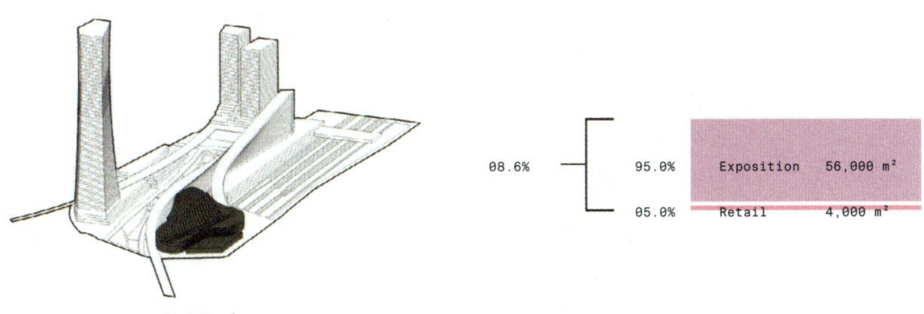
60,000 m²
08.6%
95.0% Exposition 56,000 m²
05.0% Retail 4,000 m²

05

06

07

06 The central promenade is an active public space framed by new buildings.

07 Terraced housing over the rail tracks provides an iconic image to those arriving by high-speed rail.

Program is composed strategically to take advantage of every critical node on the site. The design consists of one mass on the western end and two more on the eastern end. Visitors and users move between these points of interest. The rail station is sited farther west, allowing it to be larger than the existing station and providing space for complementary programs between it and the new Central Business District, just north of the site. The northeastern area of the site is occupied by the exposition center, which frames the edge at which heavy traffic from the north pours down toward the Yangtze River. Just opposite of the exposition center is the mixed-use office development, which functions as an extension of the existing retail and business zones. Above, on the northern portion of the site, is the high-end residential development. Spread horizontally and conforming with the natural topography of the mountain, it takes advantage of the riverfront views. This new urban node centers on modes of movement.

A thriving business and cultural center, the Chongqing Station and Exposition Center will be capable of housing the high-end exhibitions and events that a city of Chongqing's caliber should attract. The complex's easily accessible central location will not only make it the natural choice for holding large events but also create an influx of new activity and opportunity.

5.4.0.

Urban Fabrics

5.4.1.

Chongqing Village

—

Yijie Dang

This project aims to expand Chongqing's urban life and city identity. By connecting the riverfront to the hillside and creating a retail-culture village in the center, Chongqing Village will be able to not only distinguish itself from new urban developments in other Chinese cities but also exhibit a new model of city life to visitors arriving at the train station.

Taking full advantage of access to transportation and dramatic views of the river, high-rise residential and office buildings are situated along the hillside with direct connections to the existing elevated arterial road and future subway stop. The low-rise retail-entertainment village emerges from the base of the towers. Cascading downhill toward the waterfront, the form of the village will echo the local vernacular architecture typology.

A new train station separates two major types of users: commuters using local or ordinary rail service and intercity or regional travelers using high-speed rail. Though housed in the same building, each group enjoys their own lobby and waiting area with a separate drop-off zone and outdoor plaza.

The retail village is plugged into the train station on the west end, absorbing the massive flow of passengers while separating them based on their retail demographics. From the lowest level up, the village is sectionally differentiated by increasing purchasing power and exclusive accessibility. The bottom level, housing mostly food and beverage establishments, is directly connected to the local train station, serving general domestic passengers, while high-end retail stores and clubhouses

01 Buildable area versus open area. Areas that are well integrated with public transportation are indicated as more appropriate zones for building. Open areas are left for public recreational use.

02 Site plan. Multiple entrances and cross-circulation paths connect and weave through the site, setting the optimum flow for a retail complex.

03 Retail planning diagram. The zig-zag strategy maximizes shop-front exposure and visitors' time spent inside the shopping center.

04 Integration with topography. Overlaying the zig-zag strategy with the current hilly condition of the site produces a cascading retail landscape.

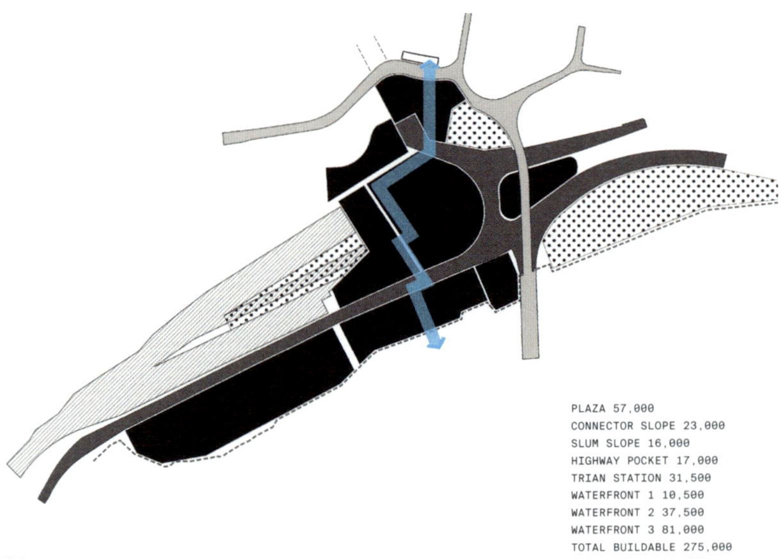

01

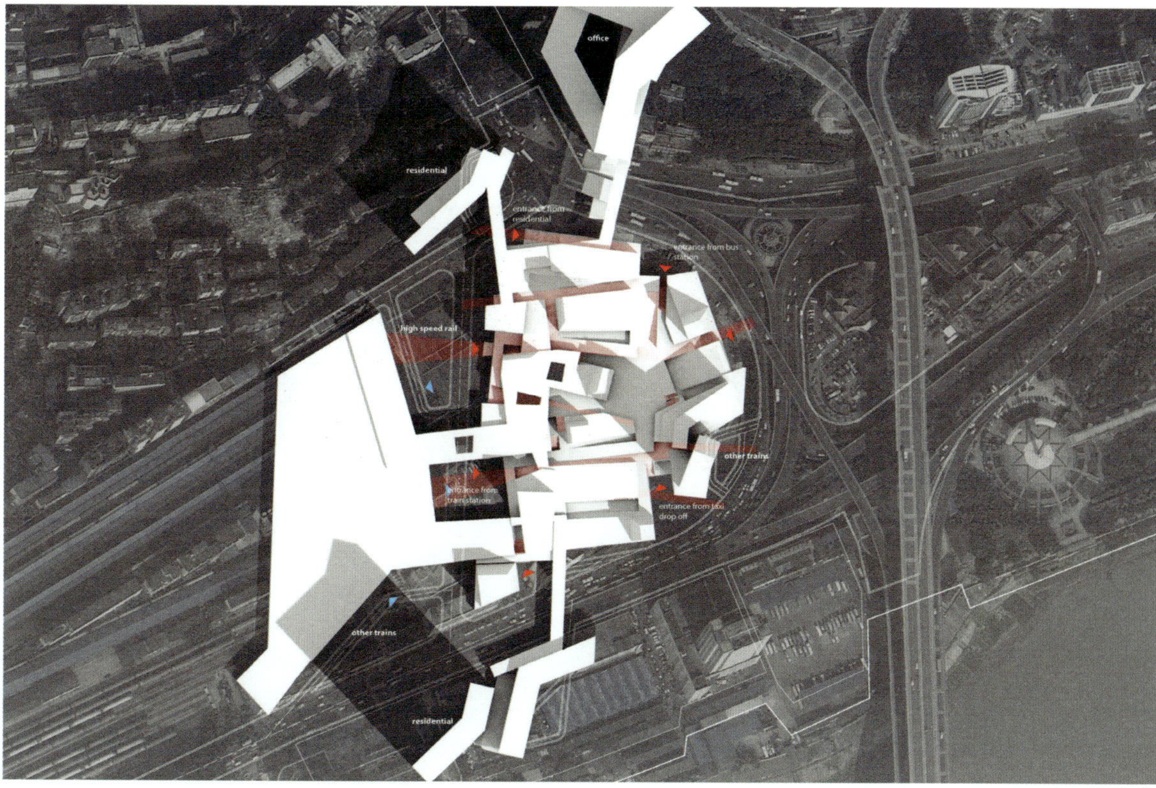
office
residential
entrance from residential
entrance from bus station
high speed rail
other trains
entrance from train station
entrance from taxi drop off
other trains
residential

02

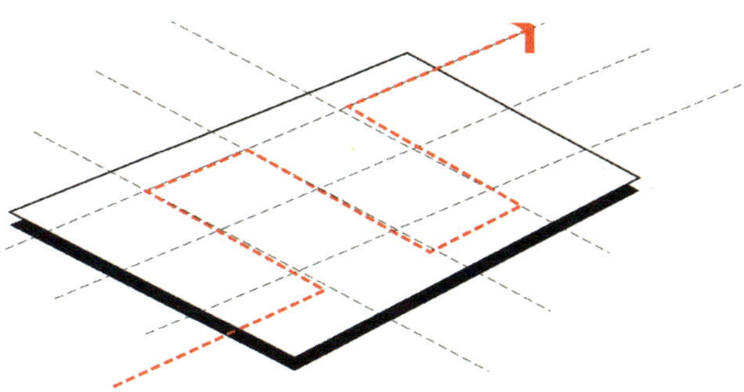

03

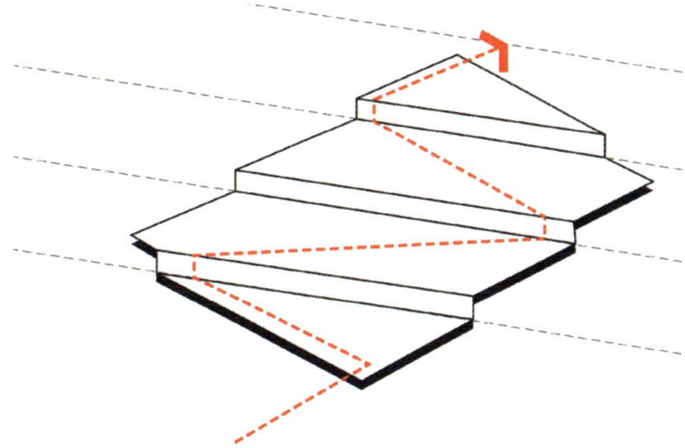

04

05

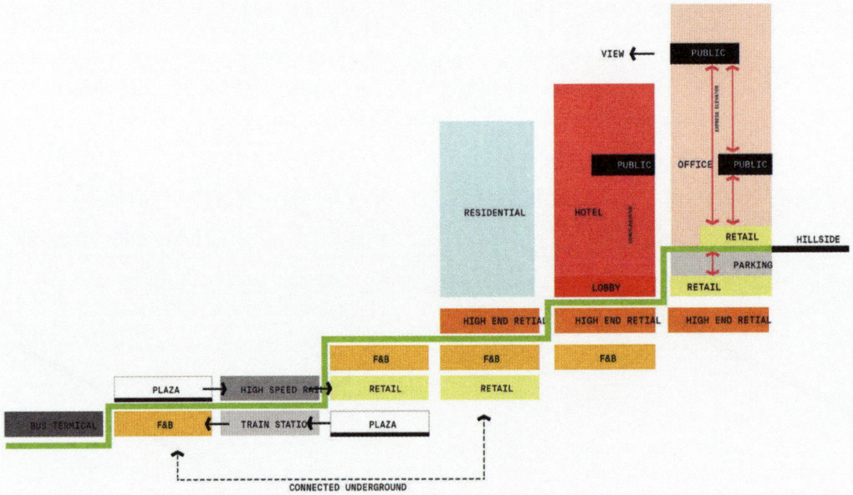
VIEW
PUBLIC
PUBLIC
OFFICE
PUBLIC
RESIDENTIAL
HOTEL
RETAIL
HILLSIDE
PARKING
LOBBY
RETAIL
HIGH END RETIAL
HIGH END RETIAL
HIGH END RETIAL
F&B
F&B
F&B
PLAZA
HIGH SPEED RAI
RETAIL
RETAIL
BUS TERMICAL
F&B
TRAIN STATIO
PLAZA
CONNECTED UNDERGROUND

06

05 North-south section.

06 Horizontal versus vertical connectivity. The program changes from retail to hotel and office based on elevation within the site, with public space woven through the massing.

07 Ground-floor plan.

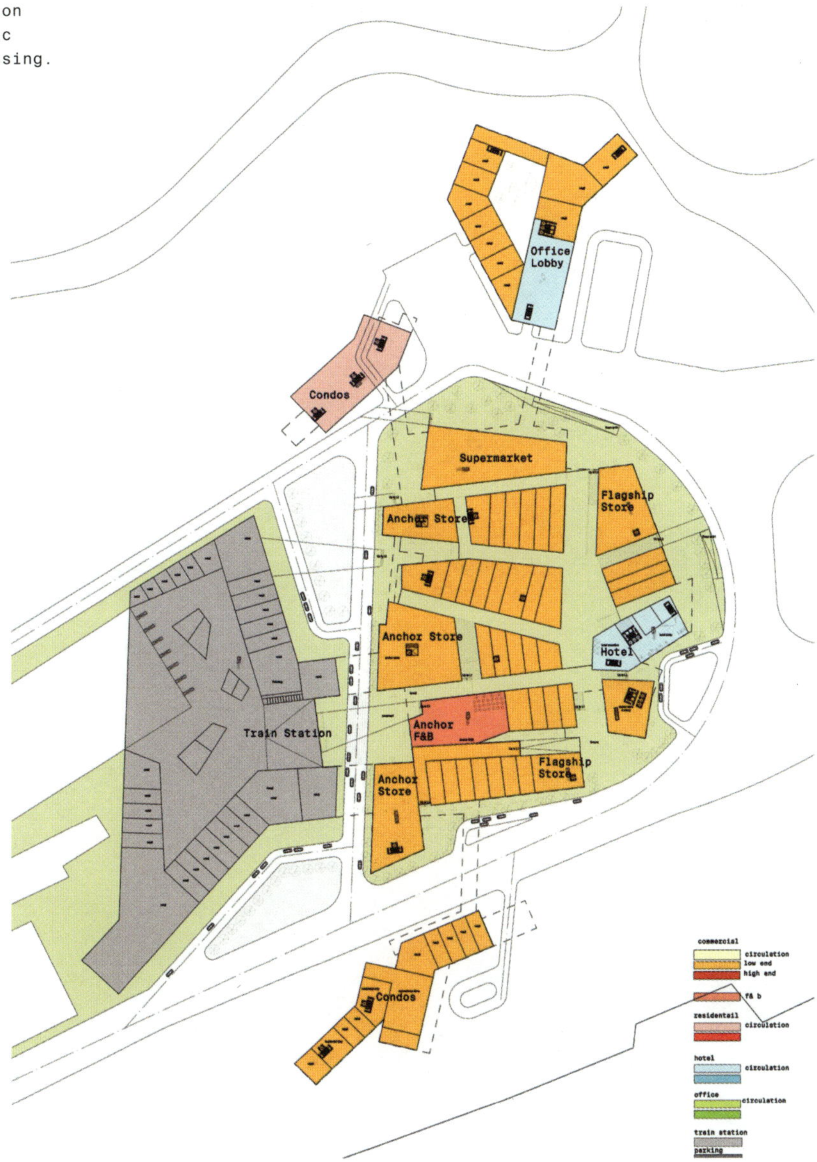

07

08

09

08 The central piazza is a focal point of the retail podium, with connections up and down.

09 View of the project looking north.

provide services to business and first-class travelers on the high-speed-rail system. Sandwiched between the low-end and high-end zones is the mid-level general retail zone, attracting local customers from the city. To facilitate the connection between the different levels, a landscape ramp is introduced, connecting from the drop-off area at the south to the plaza in the center and, finally, to the high-rise buildings at the north. A luxury, mid-rise hotel tower is situated at the southern entrance of the village, reinforcing the overall image of Chongqing Village while providing another consistent flow of customers for the high-end retail level.

The transition from the general retail in the lower levels to a life-style-based consumer experience on the upper levels signifies the current official narrative of transformation in Chongqing's and, as a whole, China's economy.

5.4.2.

Terminal Chongqing

—

Emmett Zeifman

This project is an attempt to articulate an alternative to the superblock planning and sprawling development of the contemporary Chinese city. It uses the massive scale of public infrastructure to produce another ground for the city's residents, juxtaposing two primary forms of collective space with two organizational logics: the civic square and the urban street. Formally, each portion of the project is held in tension between the clear definition of the square and the extensive element of the street, which bridges back toward the city and the river, offers connections to the existing populations and infrastructural networks, and suggests a possible logic for the proliferation of this mega-structural mixed-use building form. In both cases, the emphasis is on the definition of a public space in which urban communities and identities can form.

The project includes a hierarchy of public spaces, with a diverse range of scales and constituencies. The massive public square is defined by three pieces of urban infrastructure: the rail terminal, the bus terminal, and the retail center. In turn, each of these elements is organized around a large, central hall. Set above this center is a series of streets that reinforce the form of the square. These streets also establish a connection between the public-transit infrastructure and dense populations of the hills to the north and the riverfront park to their south. At each intersection of these elevated streets, a smaller square is formed. Major public vertical circulation between grounds is set at these junctures. A minor retail street in the form of a square spiral is inscribed around the central plaza and offers an alternative to the elevator.

01 Program distribution.

02/03 Site plans. Cloistered central form connects to the context at multiple levels.

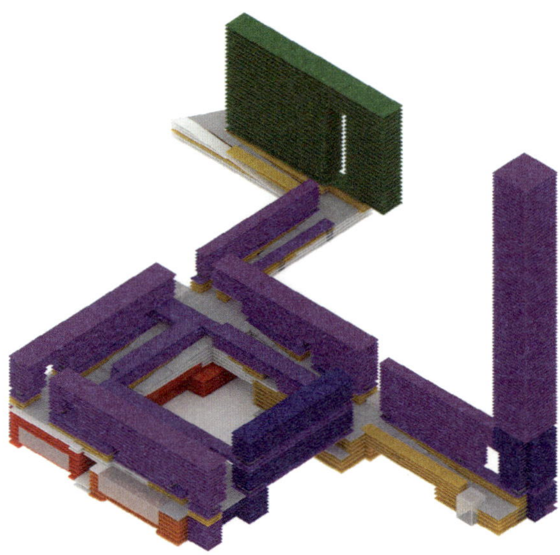

01

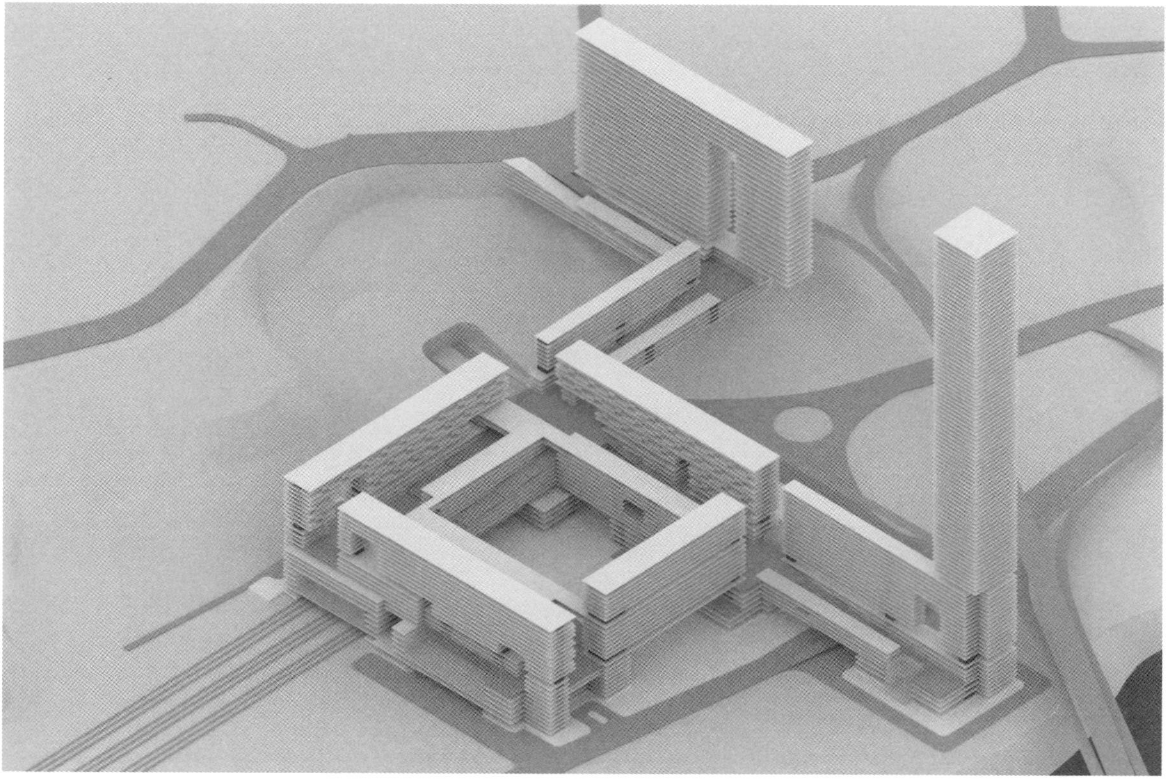

02

03

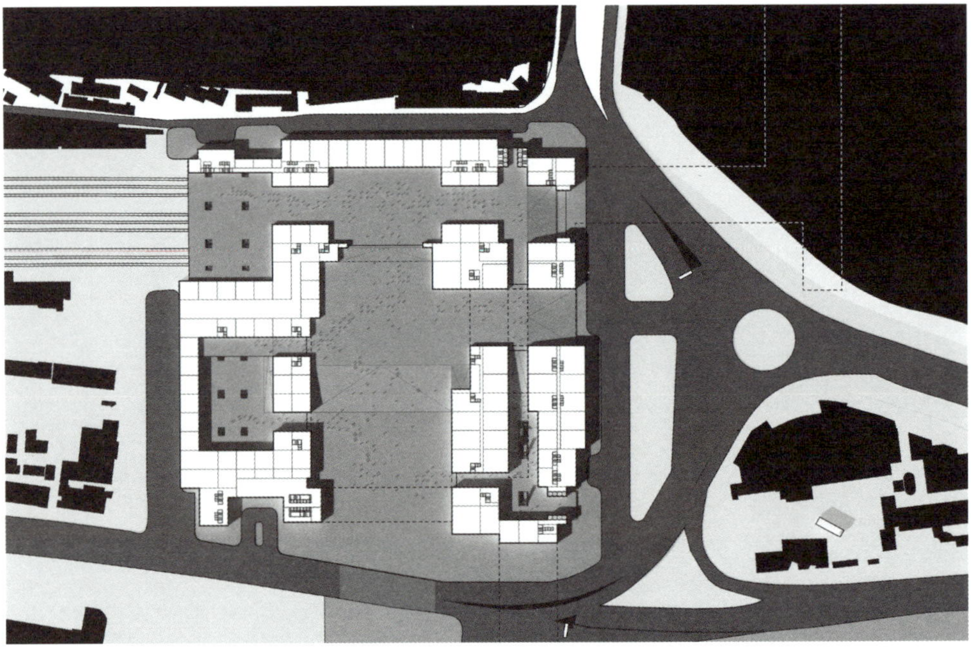

04

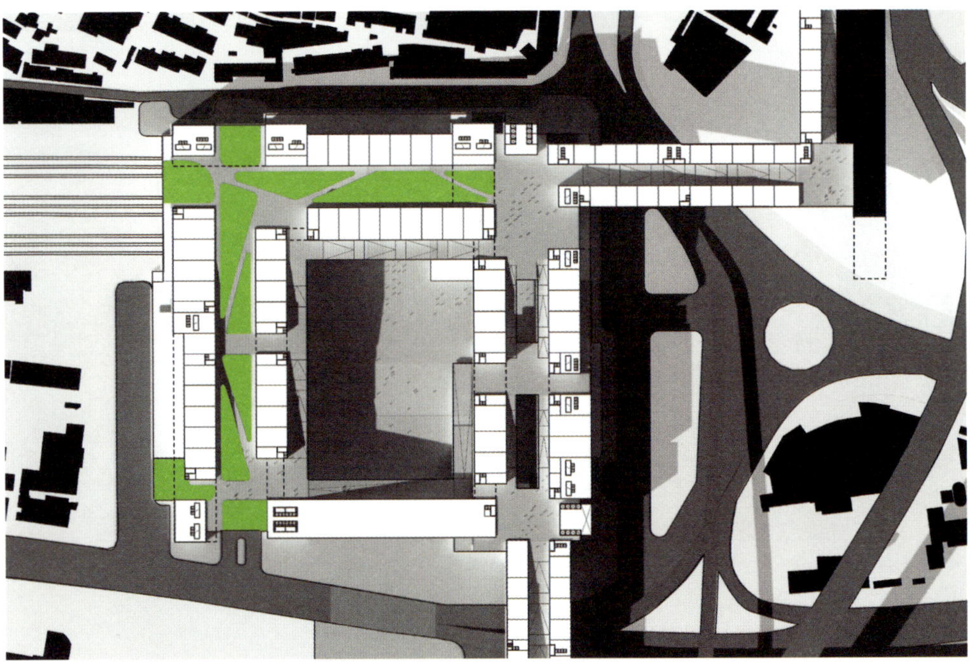

05

04 Ground-level plan. Major public spaces occupy the ground plan and provide access to the train station.

05 Upper-level plan. The upper-level pedestrian streets are lined with mid-rise residential slab buildings.

06 The upper-level street reaches out to connect with the waterfront and Central Business District.

06

07

08

07 Aerial view of central square and elevated streets.

08 View of Medium project from the river.

PP.190/191 Construction is rampant both in the older, well-developed areas of Chongqing, as well as newly developed suburbs and city-centers.

P.192 The skyline of central Chongqing seen from the plaza of the new Chongqing Opera House.

Resisting the impetus to disperse density into discrete point towers, the primary residential typology here is the slab. Duplex apartments with deep balconies overlook the streets and squares. Large openings carved through the slabs allow light and air to penetrate into the center of the development and serve as public gathering spaces for residents of the buildings. An open lobby floor separates the residential slabs from the below commercial and live-work spaces , which face directly onto the project's elevated streets. While, above the retail center, the slabs lining the east side of the square define a linear connection between hill and river, the north and west slabs, which are above the rail and bus terminals, frame urban rambles and complete the square. Green space is introduced into the project at multiple levels and scales, from the balconies and voids in the slabs to the linear parks they frame.

The ultimate ambition of the project is to suggest forms that can support the formation of neighborhoods and collectives and, at the same time, the enormous scales and population movements of China's urban development. The project is not a self-contained exception or contextual urban infill, for neither approach is possible given the site's complexity of populations, uses, geography, and infrastructure. By superimposing the typologies of the superblock, the mid-rise, and street-wall development onto the site, Terminal Chongqing probes the limits of livable density. It tests the urban possibilities of an unexpected scale and form in order to challenge the inextricably linked desires of capitalism and the collective in contemporary China.

5.5.0.

Comments from the Final Review at Yale

Marianne Kwok: It's difficult when you aren't given a program and when the site isn't very well defined to make up your mind as to what you want to do. But I think, that every student seemed to have a point of view that they pursued.

Paul Katz: What's interesting is that there was very little discussion today of the tower—in fact, there was really almost no discussion of the tower. All the discussion was about the ground, and the towers almost glided by as if they weren't there. In that sense, maybe we didn't quite achieve our objective, or maybe we did achieve our objective by showing how we could integrate the towers into these urban schemes.

John Alschuler: One thing that is impressive is that the students were all struggling with the right set of questions. There were different approaches, but how they handled the level of the city, the level of the highway, the level of the ground plane, the transitions between them, the grid relationship, the open space—they were all variations on the right set of questions. And if you solved them, you got things right. Also, I find it interesting that these projects made me more dubious of the megastructure as potential for a space that would work as a development. The projects had to be so radical in their separation of the context that they gave you something very simple, very clear, but very difficult to grapple with.

Demetri Porphyrios: I expected high-density, high-rises, with no ground at all—just the sky—but I was impressed by the fact that you all looked at the project from a starting part of a diagram, that was not just a functional diagram but a narrative. There were narratives that had to do with function, with program, and the relationship between those uses. There were narratives that had to do with the landscape—and by "landscape" I don't mean just green, but the entire siting of the project. There were other narratives that addressed the idea of connection—connection with the existing town, connection from the station. The architectural promenades were fantastic. And the other narrative, of course, was the narrative of the public realm. I was really delighted to see that the ground level—and by "ground level" I mean levels four, five, six, seven, eight, nine, ten, eleven, twelve—was a theme within each narrative. Also, I'd like to congratulate a few of you who specifically looked at the typological elements out of which the whole composition was made. I'm glad to see that the size of the commission is not the size of the building. I think you have to be congratulated because you've actually understood the sense of scale, the sense of landscape, and orientation.

Alex Twining: What also separated the students into different groups was the mess of infrastructure on this site. A lot of our discussion was about how you can deal with the infrastructure in two ways. Some of the earlier schemes created a "stepping down" and tried to erase the infrastructure. There were others that just said, "Look, you can't erase all that infrastructure. Let's just leave it there and do something bigger and grander that makes its own statement." In China, you don't have to deal with phasing, which is the big challenge in the U.S., where we can't build a few million square feet at a time, let alone ten million. That would add yet another challenge.

Demetri Porphyrios: On the issue of sustainability, usually the plan was not specific, and in that sense it was re-usable. That's the greatest part of sustainability, not the green stuff.

Patricia Patkau: Well, I think sustainability is systematic—it's all the stuff. But even the parking garage, if it's a ramped parking garage, it's much harder to use.

Alan Plattus: In our Yale-China joint studios, we struggle constantly, just as KPF does in its practice, with the problem of the podium at a superblock scale. It's very different in Shanghai, which is absolutely flat, but Chongqing has this amazing topography of the peninsula and the dramatic slope down to the water. The things that a podium is asked to do are complex and difficult, and it's not surprising that towers becomes somewhat—and I don't mean this in a bad way—somewhat ornamental vis-à-vis the more challenging problem of how that podium mediates the functions and the infrastructure and the connections. Also, there was a level of design resolution that made it very easy to get quickly to the critical points that the jury wanted to make about the schemes, and that's a great credit to the students.

Bill Pedersen: In concept, it's better to do the right thing badly than the wrong thing well. If I were to make any sort of criticism, I would have preferred to have seen more continuity in the process, from beginning to end—a series of progressive steps, in terms of your own thinking, in which you were constantly challenging your own point of view. I think it is necessary in our profession to be constantly challenging your own point of view. Everybody's in school right now, everybody is focusing on architecture, a certain level of aspiration, but that level is only achieved if you are able to constantly tell yourself over the next forty or fifty years that you are going to keep progressing, step by step by step. It is not going to happen in the next ten years, it's not going to happen in the next twenty years. It's going to take at least fifty years to get to the point where you can really achieve what you want to accomplish. You are off to one hell of a start. [*Laughter*] It's an incredibly exciting time in history, and with projects like this emerging, what you are going to be exposed to is amazing. You picked the right profession.

Albert Chan: This studio reinforced my idea that I wouldn't hire a single architect to do ten million square feet, unless Mr. Lo told me to. [*Laughter*]. Because when you do ten million square feet, no matter where it is, you are really building a part of the city. You are not building a project. As architects, we always want to put our mark on the environment, but I think, with ten million square feet, we have to ask ourselves how much we can do, no matter how talented we are. I think some of the better schemes left some crux of the projects undesigned or less designed and left some of the parts to be designed by somebody else. They left a framework for the project to mature. We do have to worry about phasing. We don't build everything at once, especially not ten million square feet. So, I think the more successful projects, in reality, would be those that leave some of this open. As architects, when any developer asks us to build more, to make it bigger, it's not necessarily the right answer. The scale of human beings remains the same. We have to remember that, or sometimes it just gets to be too big, too wild. We have to remember scale and humility. Maybe it is a good lesson that we are learning here. Some schemes recognize the limits, and those schemes are more realistic.

Jamie von Klemperer: Remember when we first visited the site, and we went underground to a series of spaces where someone was selling illegal gambling equipment and other things I shouldn't describe here, and three of you, I think, got lost? For me, it's a little bit of a metaphor, because, in the process of investigating this problem, you had the courage to lose yourselves a little bit before you found an answer. Where Mr. Kahn might have said it's better to do something well but not thoroughly, rather than thoroughly but not well, some other architect might have said that it's better to try the things that you're not sure will work before finding the thing that will work. And that does take courage, because you are exposing yourselves to a group of really tough critics.

Vincent Lo: For a project of this magnitude, you must take the whole city into perspective. It is not known in Chongqing whether this project is going to be developed, but if news got out that there were so many good schemes being prepared . . . [*Laughter*].

中太建设集团承建国泰广场深

6. TRANSLATION

中文翻译

—

Celeste Ma 翻译：马建杰

目录

1.1.1. 爱德华 P. 巴斯“建筑学杰出访问学者”奖学金项目

爱德华 P. 巴斯（Edward P. Bass）先生1967年毕业于耶鲁大学，并且是耶鲁大学建筑学院1972届的学生。2003年，他资助成立了这个奖学金项目：邀请地产开发商来到大学，与设计学院导师合作，带领高级设计工作室的创作。Bass 先生是一名环保主义者，1991年他资助了位于亚利桑那州 Oracle 地区的“生物圈二号”开发项目；作为一名开发商，他负责德克萨斯州沃斯堡城市中心的复兴工程，他的圣丹斯广场将旧建筑的翻新与新建筑结合，将原本沉寂的都市转变成活力四射的区域中心。在 Bass 先生所有的作品中，他始终坚信：建筑设计是一个将宏伟愿景和日常现实相融合的社会艺术。

巴斯奖学金项目确保学校课程充分认可地产开发商在设计过程中不可或缺的角色。它让开发商走进校园，与教育工作者和建筑系学生并肩工作，开展关于建筑在当代实践中的广泛论述。首个巴斯工作室于2005年由 Gerald Hines、 Louis I. Kahn 以及客座教授 Stefan Behnisch 带领，并结集成《诗篇、地产 和空间 Poetry, Property, and Place》一书(2006年出版)。2006年，第二个巴斯工作室由 Stuart Lipton, Saarine 客座教授 Richard Rogers(62届) 和工程师 Chris Wise 以及建筑师 Malcolm Smith(97届) 组建，并结集成书 《捍卫未来 Future-Proofing》 (2007年出版)。 《人类城市 The Human City》 (2008年出版) 中记载了 Roger Madelin 和 Bishop 客座教授 Demetri Porphyrios 共同合作的耶鲁工作室。2009年出版的《城市一体化: Bishopsgate Goods Yard》中记载了由 Nick Johnson 和 FAT 建筑事务所合作领导的工作室；2010年，由 Charles Atwood 和建筑师 David M. Schwarz's 领导的工作室作品出版为《向拉斯维加斯学习 Learning in Las Vegas》。2011年出版了《城市一体化: Sao Paulo》一书，是房地产开发商 Katherine Farley 和兼职教授 Deborah Berke 合作的工作室作品。现在，我们十分荣幸地展示由香港开发商罗康瑞协同纽约 KPF 建筑师事务所的 Paul Katz, Jamie von Klemperer 和 Forth Bagley 领导的工作室及其课题研究，后者都曾经担任过耶鲁大学的 Saarinen 荣誉教授。

1.1.2. 工作室简介

重庆的再思考：多功能和高密度 — 耶鲁大学建筑学院爱德华 P. 巴斯“建筑学杰出访问学者”奖学金项目书籍之七 — 集合了耶鲁工作室的设计研究和建议，该工作室由瑞安地产主席罗康瑞、KPF 建筑事务所的执行总监 Paul Katz、James (Jamie) von Klemperer，总监 Forth Bagley (99届本科，01届硕士) 教授，耶鲁教师 Andrei Harwell (06届) 协助教授。工作室以重庆市一个重要地块为例，对高密度开发项目的限制及其与城市设施、都市设计的错综关系进行了探讨。

重庆是中国四大直辖市之一，正经历着一场蓬勃的发展。其独特的地形、高密度的城市中心区域、复杂的交通设施给学生们带来了挑战传统都市开发模式的机会，他们需要设计一个100万平方米规模的项目，这是一项令人生畏的任务。

本书首先采访了爱德华 P. 巴斯（Edward P. Bass）项目的客座建筑学教授罗康瑞，其次是对 Eero Saarinen 客座教授 Paul Katz, Jamie von Klemperer 以及 Forth Bagley 的采访。继工作室介绍及学生面临的建筑和城市问题的总结后，还有一篇由同济大学副校长伍江纂写的文章和一篇由“去西部（Go West Project）”项目总监 Michel Hulshof 和 Daan Roggeveen 纂写的文章，“去西部（Go West Project）”是一个多学科研究工作室，将重庆的都市化放在当今中国的大背景下，为项目的理解提供了一个框架。

“先例”部分的图片和计算是工作室最初三周研究内容的分类，在这三周中，要求学生们制定详细全面的上海、香港和日本综合体及高密度类项目的研究，并准备瑞安地产在上海“新天地”这一开创式改建项目的详细分析。在第四周，学生参观了上海和重庆，会见并采访了重庆市各官员，例如：副市长凌月明，市对外贸易经济委员会副主任李世蓉，他们与工作室共同探讨了重庆政府对地块开发以及重庆未来发展的期望。返回耶鲁所在的New Haven后，围绕着新火车站和公共空间，学生们认真地开始了设计工作，经过与瑞安地产设计团队的咨询，学生在各自的设计中配置住宅、写字楼、酒店和会展空间等功能。本书对学生作品按照类型编排：相连的塔楼，巨型结构，宏大空间和城市肌理。最后的评论是建筑师和规划师的观点集锦，他们分别是 John Alschuler, Albert Chan, Paul Katz, Jamie von Klemperer Marianne Kwok, Vincent Lo, Patricia Patkau, Bill Pedersen, Alan Plattus, Demetri Porphyrios 和 Alex Twinin。

在此感谢所有参与工作室工作的学生，他们的贡献对本书意义重大， 他们是 Yijie Dang, William Gridley, Keith Johns, Alfie Koetter, Kee Lew, Qiwei Liang, Katsunori Shigemi, Brian Spring, Danh Thai 以及 Emmett Zeifman。同样还要感谢我们的编辑 David Delp；平面设计：来自 MGMT. design 的 Sarah Gephart；翻译：来自 KPF 的马建杰。——本书编辑 Andrei Harwell, Nina Rappaport, and Emmett Zeifman

2.1.1. 与罗康瑞先生访谈

以下与罗康瑞的访谈发生于2011年。

Nina Rappaport: 请问您第一次进行项目开发是什么时候？怎么开始的？

Vincent Lo: 我1976年开始开发第一个项目，作为私营公司参加香港政府的项目，为符合条件的香港居民提供买得起的住宅。但我从中收获最多的是上海的新天地项目，因为它在上海是将保留建筑与新的餐饮娱乐中心相结合的首例。首先，我要理解市场需要的和能接受的是什么，因为这对中国来说是一个新概念。由于这个项目的成功，我的公司收到很多城市的邀请，去建设类似的项目。

NR: 作为开发商，在1985年中国城市初发展时期，在上海是怎样的状况？你的开发方式有多么不同？

VL: 中国的改革在初步阶段，刚刚实施开放。房地产市场并没有形成，因为政府分配所有住宅，所以几乎没有购买力。
所以，我的第一个项目是作投资，与共青团合作，开发上海市中心的一个小型三星级酒店。市场没有准备好接受来自中国以外的开发商，在此数年以后，我们才进入房地产开发市场。
项目是与政府一起规划的，因为政府控制所有的土地资源。随着改革政策生根，中国经济持续快速发展，产生了对高端办公、商业和住宅的巨大需求。自从完成上海新天地项目以来，瑞安与多地政府紧密合作，为其所在城市发现合适的发展机会。我们对相关城市进行了大量的研究，调查它们的经济设施、历史、竞争力、资源以及机遇和挑战。然后，与政府一起，提议一项新的地标性城市中心开发项目。

NR: 如何与政府合作协调项目？购买地块的程序是怎样的？你在中国的合同与美国相比有哪些不同？当你有合作方的时候，你怎样协调整个过程，特别是在开发和拓展未来市场的过程中？

VL: 在发现一块适合开发的地块后，我们会准备一个总体规划提交给政府。在获得相关政府部门批准之后，地块会公开招标或挂牌。因为我们已经为项目做了一些工作，所以我们比其它开发商在购买土地上更具竞争力。
土地的购买与美国很不同，因为在中国没有私人自由持有的土地。土地只可从政府手中租用。当你与政府合作开发时，通常合同只列出一些基本条款。例如，我们在上海的项目，成本可能高达40亿，但30年前我们与政府签的合同只有6页，但是实施效果相当好。如果我们有合作方，我们走同样的程序，但是政府要求我的公司作为领导方，因为他们曾与我们合作并对我们很信任。

NR: 新天地是您最知名的项目。是什么导致您形成保留核心、开发新建筑、创建独特环境的概念？对尺度的保留是怎样的重要问题？你怎样与建筑师和政府一起把对历史地块的保留纳入您的规划之中？

VL: 新天地对上海和中国来说是一个创新的发票概念。我们承担了这个项目是因为它与中共一大会址相邻。
政府要求我们保留街道尺度和氛围，附近不允许建高楼。所以，我们必须考虑怎样最好地利用上海的历史性石库门建筑，怎样在现代保留并利用这些建筑。由于石库门建筑并不真正适合现代居住或作商业用途，我们只能把它改成餐饮和娱乐用途。
当时，中国没有人有类似的经验，所以我们邀请了 Benjamin Wood，一个美国建筑师与我们合作，他参与了波士顿 Faneuil Hall 项目的规划和设计。Wood 在上海花了几个月时间研究石库门建筑，在街道漫步，体会现场的氛围，以融合在其设计中。我们觉得并不建议只是把它建设成游客观光点，我们的首要客户是本地人群。所以，我们也邀请了同济大学的教授，一位研究石库门建筑的专家，为我们提供建筑和设计所需要的细节。有些建筑我们不得不拆除，从建筑上拆下来的旧材料我们也重新利用，这样使得新天地外观很独特。

NR: 为什么您没有聘请那些研究历史建筑的中国建筑师？

VL: 我们没有聘请中国建筑师设计新天地项目是因为这类保护和改建项目对中国来说是全新的，包括香港，所以我们邀请了 Ben Wood，他在这类项目的规划和设计上经验丰富。

NR: 您是如何把开发与建设相结合的？

VL: 例如，我们在上海的项目，可能成本高达40亿，但30年前我们和政府的合同只有6页，但它实施效果很好。如果我们有合作方，我们走同样的程序，但政府会要求我们作为领导方，因为政府与我们有过合作，对我们比较信任。

NR: 您是怎样影响政府在项目和经济增长方面的想法的？

VL: 2002年，上海政府希望通过科学技术来提升经济增长，但那只是个口号，而没有实质行动计划。那么，我们就主动提议在上海开发一个社区，模仿硅谷，促进创新、高科技和科研。我们相信，如果高新技术想获得成功，需要风险投资的支持。上海政府对此很兴奋，邀请我们确定一个地块，并准备一份可实施的详细计划。我就提议了一个地块，政府和我们组成了合作企业共同开发这个项目。6年了，项目已基本建成，它在杨浦区，叫创智天地。

NR: 您采用怎样的方式了解并实现项目的灵活性？您允许在一个项目中预留未来改变的空间吗？

VL: 我们项目中并不留太多灵活性，因为在我们开始总体规划之前，我们已经做了大量细致研究，了解城市未来的需要和变化。但如果市场条件剧烈变化，我们在说服政府修改规划方面没有太多困难。在我们接受重庆项目之前，我们对重庆作了大量研究，我们很清楚地了解城市将以什么样的方式发展，将来需要什么样的设施。我们把这些都体现在了我们的总体规划中，我们每年都会审核我们的总体规划。目前为止，在6年之后，没有任何需要修改我们总体规划的要求。我以施工承包商起家，后来才进入开发商领域，但现在这是我们的主要业务，我们也利用了我们在施工方面的专业能力协助开发业务。

NR: 您之前教授过建筑师吗？您最感兴趣、最想与他们分享的部分是什么？

VL: 我之前从来没教过建筑师，但我与他们亲密共事了30年。我希望我在耶鲁的教学有助于理解香港和中国的大型开发项目，理解市场是怎样运作的，我们怎样与政府合作。我也希望学生能从开发商的角度来看问题。

NR: 您觉得您的方式如何在全球新开发项目中进行推广？

VL: 我认为中国的方式不适合在其它地方推广，因为它太特别了，它的市场是巨大的，经济增长速度非常快，急需大量高品质开发项目。

NR: 随着您进入中国西部地区，那里的新挑战和新机遇是什么？对于中国的变化速度，最困难的问题是什么？

VL: 中国的改革开放从东部沿海城市开始，在三十年的发展之后，沿海和西部之间的分化严重，所以，中央政府坚定地制定了加快开发西部的策略。我们到中、西部开发已经有近十年的时间，城市在这期间经历了巨大的发展。我们开发的挑战在于，作为开发商和投资者，我们必须判断变化的速度，中国政府经常让全世界惊讶，包括我这样在中国有很多经验的人，他们经常很快就作出重大决定，然后在短时间内加以实施。目前，西部省份的机遇更多，因为这里的发展速度比沿海要快。最大的挑战是要紧跟政府变化莫测的政策。

2.1.2. 采访 KPF 建筑事务所

KPF 建筑事务所的 Jamie von Klemperer, Paul Katz 和 Forth Bagley 讨论他们在中国的工作。

Nina Rappaport: KPF 参与过无数由开发商主导的大型项目。你们认为，与非最终用户的客户合作，对你们的实际工作有什么样的影响？你们在指导建筑项目功能与用途方面扮演着怎样的角色？

Jamie von Klemperer: 相比在建筑上附加单个功能，开发商的工作范围更广。那些优秀开发商一直将自身融入到功能之中。如果建筑中包含商业，开发商就会涉足售卖、经营和品牌推广。而如果建筑属性是住宅区，他们就会变为公寓布局和家具陈设方面的专家。作为他们的建筑师，我们也已经成为了各方面功能的专家。与优秀的开发商共事，就像打一场网球比赛：我们把灵感发过去，他们把球打回来。

Paul Katz: 在与开发商的共事中，让我们深感欣慰的一点是，几乎所有的客户都是老客户。出于这些良好的关系，我们不用花大量时间找寻新的项目，而是从上个项目结束的位置开始。这可以节省从零开始准备的时间，并最终有助于我们完成更好、更复杂的建筑。

NR: 优秀的客户通常肩负着充满冒险的设计或是全新的功能类型，因为他们在财务方面更为充裕。你们是从什么时候开始影响开发商更改设计任务书，并帮助他们用新的视角看到重新组织功能和用途的？比如说，针对你们在中国的项目。你们是怎么在中国开始的？

JvK: 关于我们是如何影响开发模型的，典型的例子就是我们是如何从上世纪90年代开始在中国启动的。那个时候，中国的本土开发人员还刚刚起步。我们的介入主要是通过香港和东京的海外开发商；他们与中国的关系紧密，把我们带入到了这个新的环境中。我们首次合作的开发商是恒隆，项目是对一座在建项目的外表进行重新处理。这个项目很小，但是我们通过设计增加了价值。随后他们要求我们设计位于上海的恒隆广场。这座建筑定义了国际性商业办公楼所能达到的最高水平，同时是当时上海最高档的奢侈品商场。
实际上，开发商并没有预料到会有这样的成功。不过很快，中国其他区域的政府领导希望能有同样的建筑类型。这迅速成为了一个开发品牌。开发商在天津、沈阳、武汉及十多个其他城市中再现了这种建筑形态语言和流畅的动线平面。假如开发商在指定建筑师前就开始这样的工作，那么项目就会失去其所有的动感。

Forth Bagley: 我们与其他客户的合作中，也存在类似的案例。人们在讨论中国的时候，似乎总是认为这个国家的快速发展和城市化进程是不可避免的。然后，并没有什么限定中国的增长模式。这一切都是由于我们这样的建筑师和瑞安房地产这样的开发商合作，与政府一起解决问题，从前所未有的经济发展中获益。

NR: 伴随着北京奥运会之际、中国的第二波发展浪潮，在对你们工作的认知和你们肩负的项目类型方面，是否让你们感受到了巨大的不同？你们的声誉是如何传播的？

JvK: 我们已经开始了在中国的实践，但是同时，中国的国企也对聘用我们充满自信。突如其来的是，中国的公司开始聘用我们设计一次性的总部项目。他们审视了恒隆广场和我们的环球金融中心项目（后者目前是中国最高的建筑，这让我们达到了任何广告也无法企及的高度），看到了广受认可的记录成就。我们与中国设计标准之间的差异也许并未产生非常大的影响。比如说，过去数十年中中国最有影响力的建筑是 CCTV 大楼。这是一项杰作，但并未在样式上引领变革。因为它与传统的开发项目形态之间的区别太大了，不像是渐进式创新，因此对塑造中国的建筑环境并没有特别大的影响。

NR: 你们是如何看待高建筑密度对可持续发展的影响的，特别是在中国这样特殊的地方？像城市交通和保留公共空间这样的话题，我们已经讨论了很多年了。

PK: 对我们事务所而言，密度这一主题是一个深化的重点，因为事实上，我们从一开始就是专攻高层建筑。高层建筑曾经像是一块白面包，是带有投机性质的、用途单一的塔楼。然而，随着时间的推移，特别是在亚洲，塔楼慢慢的变成了多功能的垂直城市，在建筑形态上增添了新的维度。塔楼的这种植入横向基建网络的潜力，就像一颗拥有众多根须的大树，在塑造城市中心节点的方式方面，扮演了一个重要的角色。随着对可持续发展的探究越来越成为潮流，以及在密度的重要性方面，倾向于选择换乘枢纽和交通中心来提升项目（不只是二十层或者四十层，而是更高），超高密度建筑已经成为应对杂乱布局的最明显也是最有效的手段。

FB: 关于这一现象，有几个例子，就是目前我们正在珠三角建造的三座超高层塔楼：香港环球贸易广场（ICC）、深圳平安金融中心和广州周大福中心。每座塔楼的高度都超过400米，是多功能的超高层建筑，作为其所在城市中新 CBD 的地标，与整个城市范围内的地铁交通紧密联系。在竣工后，它们都会连接一条高速轨道交通路线，使之以新的方式相联系。位于香港 ICC 中的两万人与位于深圳平安金融中心的两万人之间，只有二十分钟的距离，通行者无需走到室外。

PK: 当你有八百万或者一千万人口的城市，以这样一种方式——即超高层建筑摆放在通道的战略性门户位置——相连接的时候，会改变人们对于这些建筑的期许。他们不再是单纯的办公楼了。

JvK: 在这个问题上，一个反面的例子是，我们的其中一个项目并没有在中国进行推广。我们设计项目，与学生交流，进行演讲。有人非法销售我们的书，并翻译成中文。我们看到自己的作品被盗版。从某种意义上说，我们认为应该颁布一条法令，让中国每个大城市里都有一座400米高的大楼；这是因为，在深圳、苏州、沈阳、广州和天津等城市，我们一直看到这样的设计要求。说到底，设计并呈现高质量的建筑本身就是最好的广告形式。

NR: 你们是如何在从设计到施工的过程中，保持对项目而不仅仅是图纸的控制的？你们对建筑施工文化的改变起到了哪些积极作用？

PK: 建筑师们相信，在1994年的中国，打造一座牢固、有趣并且耐久的建筑是非常困难的事情。平凡的大楼就是与众不同的。到现在，这种观点已经错了。从一开始，我们就定下了一条规矩，即所接手的项目，在外墙和公共区域方面不低于对施工图控制。这和其他建筑师事务所的方法不同。这使得我们在细节和执行方面保持独特的控制水准。
我们的纽约办公室与工程师和承包商团队（一间意大利外墙公司或是一名菲律宾幕墙工程师）一起，共同提升施工的水准。有大量的国际专业先驱在中国工作。

JvK: 当然，现如今，格局已经开始改变了。世界上最大的幕墙公司位于中国北方城市沈阳。KPF 也在适应这一变化。尽管设计主要还是以纽约为中心，但我们位于香港、上海和其他地区的办公室已经开始协助完成复杂的项目。

NR: 在新型的垂直城市设计项目中，你们有哪些创新？

JvK: 对我们来说，这些高层建筑创新在于，当一座大楼每天有三万人出入的时候，实现与基础设施和换乘系统的联系就关系重大。香港和日本的密度极高，因而在这方面的开发形式是最高水准的。我们事务所在这些地区进行了逐步的创新。

PK: 的确如此。这是一个渐进的过程。目前我们有一个大型项目正在建造中期，位于上海市中心。这个位于静安区的项目所围绕的故居，毛泽东年轻时曾住过六个月，那是在中国共产党诞生之前。项目包含塔楼和地下建筑，规模接近洛克菲勒中心，但是由形态更为自由的建筑群组成，目的是配合从地面一直延伸到300米高度的塔楼。我们的目的，是让它成为一座歌剧和文化的中心，同时又是一座企业办公楼和一个居住的场所。

NR: 这样一种切入历史性场所的安排是如何与周边相呼应的？

JvK: 这个问题很有意思。因为这是在上海这座曾经的租界城市，像是在做拼接。上海并不是一个真正的中国城市，它是由法国人、俄罗斯人和其他人共同建造的。大片建于二十世纪初、带有当地特色的住宅构成了巨大的城市街区。区域之间有宽阔的道路隔开；区域之间有机地排布开放空间和各种规格的道路，包括公路、半开放街道和私人花园。我们试图在设计大型项目时，以一种不同的规模，重新捕捉这种开放和私密空间的 DNA。这不是出于怀旧心理，而是让上海成为一个特别富有吸引力、适合闲逛和生活的地方。

PK: 不抹掉过去是有价值的。很早以前，罗康瑞先生（Vincent Lo）就看到了这一点。来到中国城市的人们一般都会碰到大量30层高的楼，这很让人丧气。我们在美国时的一个想法就是，文化遗产是有正面意义的。通过将其深层地运用到中国的城市中，产生了非常有价值的建筑结果。

NR: 在耶鲁工作坊的项目上，你们是怎么和罗康瑞先生合作的？

PK: 罗康瑞先生是当今最活跃的开发商之一。罗先生对新天地项目对二十世纪上海的意义，就像上世纪三十年代洛克菲勒中心对纽约的意义那样。总的来说，要超越他对上海和中国城市的影响是不可能的。因此，当我们决定为耶鲁课堂应对中国西部高密度城市化的问题的时候，我们就马上想到了他。

JvK: 此外，他从新天地项目中取得了很多收获，包括找到新的项目模型和对中国城市的未来发展作出积极贡献。他对建设这样的项目充满兴趣。他愿意接受建筑师会感兴趣的各种挑战。罗先生很受中国政府的尊重。

FB: 如果没有这样密切的关系，你就没有办法真正探讨中国的城市规划。他可以分享这种变化，而这种变化正是我们希望学生们完成的。

NR: 您认为在多功能火车站融入城市格局方面，课堂是否真的能在中国对新建筑类型产生影响？

JvK: 是的。项目所在的地点是重庆的中央火车站，地处市中心，体量非常巨大，但是与外界缺乏联系。在中国，交通系统是与商业项目割裂开来的。我们想看到的是，如果学生依据新天地的建筑模型进行设计，并增加密度，来反映火车站在城市中心的重要性，会产生什么样的结果？新天地项目是公共和私人空间、功能以及建筑类型的融合。我们能够达到多大的密度？这个项目会如何呼应快速的城市化进程和日益全球化的中产阶级？会如何提升现在的开发模型？实际上，这个课堂项目会改变中国建筑和城市的历史，因为我们的开发商认为这是一种非常有趣的想法。

PK: 我们真正感兴趣的，是和学生一起研究城市化的进程，为这个前所未有的增长与全球化相结合的时刻塑造形态。

2.2.1. 工作室介绍

工作室问题概述

在过去的15年里，由上海浦东 CBD 所延伸开来的城市化模型已经在中国的城市化进程中占据了主导地位，这就是彼此独立的大型多功能街区。现在，中国和西部的开发者普遍认为，这种模型鼓励的是城区扩张和开车，代替统一的、适合行人并以换乘为为导向的周边环境。同时这种模型更倾向于公共空间，而不是更为便利的公园和广场。随着城市化进程，和经济的发展深入到中国西部的城市中，当地的规划者正在寻求其他的开发模型，目的是打造具有可持续性的动态城市项目。

新天地是一个位于上海市中心的多功能街区项目。瑞安房地产在这个项目上的成功提供了一个更为丰富和更具持续性的模型，和公共换乘、适合行人的街道以及公共绿地相连接。学生从上半学期开始研究新天地和其他的综合项目，然后把学到的经验运用到重庆中央火车站地块超高密度综合项目的计划书中。

受到开发商和执行建筑师专业的指引，“Edward P. Bass 杰出建筑旅行奖学金”(Edward P. Bass Distinguished Visiting Architecture Fellowship) 试图将创新的学术理念渗透到现当代开发项目中。重庆工作室的目的是探索高速城市化中超高密度综合项目的极限，并进一步为中国西部的新开发充当实验案例。从一开始，这个瑞安和 KPF 合力打造的大规模项目就在地理环境、基础设施和经济上面临着挑战。学生们需要特别注意综合功能和地块，以便打造一个有可持续性的并且宜居的城市空间，同时具有远景和现实意义。这些项目在密度和用途多样性上都超过了以往，在应对重庆等西部城市的发展步伐和规模上，提出了新的开发方向。

背景

在过去20年里，中国的经济总量从世界最小一跃成为第二大，仅次于美国。这种快速的经济发展所伴随的，是几百万的人们前所未有地从中西部迁徙到东部沿海地区的大城市中。这个人类有史以来的最大迁徙过程使得中国的城市开始急速扩张，从根本上改变了他们的城市属性。

很少有城市经历了像上海那样剧烈的变革。上海所经历的城市化进程与世界历史中的任何一次都不相同。在浦东这个黄浦江畔和老城区之间曾经遍布稻田和小村庄的地方，新中央商务区（CBD）的天际线已经可以媲美世界上任何一个新建的城市。这个被规划为未来高密度城市的区域影响着中国一代城市的总体规划。由此导致的结果是，被超宽道路分割的、体量巨大的独立街区（浦东的基本城市形态）成为了中国几乎所有大城市新开发项目的标准。

巨型项目在西方被嘲讽成多余、奢侈和浪费，但在中国却占据主导地位，这是因为它在增加城市的密度方面，是一种有效、合法、经济和符合建筑学的解决方法。尽管这些大型项目在法理和所获得的经济利益方面毋庸置疑，但其带来的对建筑和城市的影响却不太明确。建筑师在与开发商的合作中所设计的大楼塑造了多功能大型街区的新形态，粉碎了对于单一项目营造内部城市领域的能力的假设，然而宽阔的街道、预定的用途和这些街区互相割裂的本质不断地削弱着独立地块中的城市环境。

随着城市人口不断增加，大型单体项目的限制越来越明显，中国的城市规划者已经开始寻找其它的项目开发途径。他们不再推崇美国式的、以汽车为导向的城市增长模式，而是转而寻求更为复杂和更有层次的方法，来打造具有持续性、富有效率并充满生命力的城市。

新天地

瑞安房地产旗下的上海新天地项目自2001年开放以来，从根本上重塑了人们对于中国城市未来的期待。这个项目将新的建筑项目、公园空间与对旧式低层建筑区的改造和修整相结合，由此创造了一个别具一格的融合体。这个融合体中有着传统的、利于行人的城市构造，有着现代化的高密度建筑群，更有着各色多样的功能来保持着新社区日夜不休的活力。在这之前，中国从未有开发者尝试过一边保护历史建筑，一边在现有的城市环境内结合新的建筑项目，并通过种类繁多的功能组合来提升城市体验。

瑞安的项目将现当代中国最重要历史遗迹之一的中共第一次全国代表大会会址，融入到现代化的酒店、零售、娱乐、居住、办公、大型公园和城市内部街道中。因此，这个上海的“洛克菲勒中心”立即成为了吸引居民、游客和商业的胜地，说明开发商可以在单个业主的总体规划项目中营造出传统城市二十四小时生活的感觉。随着中国东部地区城市化进程的减缓，政府官员逐渐将重心转移到发展西部城市的经济和环境上。成都、武汉、南宁和重庆等城市现在就在不断地效仿东部地区过去二十年的成长模式。

随着浦东发展模式的利弊被逐渐深入了解，寻求其他方式以维持经济增长、提供城市密度的规划师们将目光锁定在了新天地这个模型上。怎样才能让这个模型给密集的城市街区增添活力？当其他模型、综合项目的规模以及基础设施计划与这个新模型结合时，又会发生什么？

基地

重庆被群山环抱，与东部沿海地区隔绝，三千多万人口分布在南加州面积的土地上。重庆历史悠久的市中心坐落在长江和嘉陵江交汇处的丘陵半岛上，拥有大约一千万居民。重庆与上海、北京和天津并列为中国四大直辖市。与其他所有的城市相比，这四个城市在经济方面享有更高的地位，自治和规划的权力超过副省级城市——后者通常拥有省一级的规划权。重庆于1997年成为直辖市，但直到最近才开始快速发展。这主要归功于其日渐增长的制造业（主要在汽车和技术领域）以及对基础设施和交通的投资。这些投资使其在中国的房地产开发市场上占据了首要地位。这座城市大部分结构正经历着重新构思和重新定位。

课堂项目所在的地块是重庆火车站。这里是这座城市主要的轨道交通终点站，囊括了周边轨道交通上方和下方的区域，以及临近的基础设施组合和公共开放空间。这一片杂乱的设施如果想在城市发展的阵痛中生存下来，就需要合理布置、重新调整和改进。这个复杂的地块挤在山丘和嘉陵江之间，周围环绕着高架和铁路等基础设施，是重要的城市交通节点，大量连接着区域性和本地的换乘交通。

重庆市政府邀请瑞安房地产参与改造重庆火车站的投标。而瑞安房地产要求学生（以建筑师身份）完成对这个基地的分析，然后设计一系列的开发方案。基地的容积率为20，但对功能和高度没有限制，学生可以在各自项目中自行决定。政府部门指出，招标将在以下方面衡量设计能力：

- 建立一个高密度，并能够与中国西部其他城市相适应的模型。
- 打造这座城市持续发展能力、吸引力和繁荣程度的象征。
- 改善公共设施，推崇环保且可持续的生活方式。
- 将商业、零售和城市生活吸引到市中心。

方法

在上半个学期中，学生研究了新天地和其他的多功能超大型开发项目，针对这些项目的形态、功能及其与城市周边的关系作出了综合性的分析图表。在这个阶段，学生来到上海和重庆，参观过往案例并视察基地。身在中国期间，他们还与瑞安的资深团队、重庆副市长及其他当地官员见面，对当代开发模式、重庆的历史和经济条件及项目本身做了更深入的了解。学生们为重庆基地设计了初步项目方案，并向瑞安资深团队提交了初步计划书。

他们的案例研究涵盖了广泛的多功能和轨道项目。学生们从上海开始，两人一组，将瑞安的新天地开发方式与上海早期的综合项目进行对比，重点关注独立功能类型和周边环境，以及恒隆广场、静安综合项目、人民广场、上海国金中心和上海环球金融中心的效果。随后，学生们结对对新天地的多样功能和住宅楼、商业娱乐区域、酒店、办公、停车场和文化设施等业态模式进行了综合分析。

在对上海进行深入的调查之后，学生来到香港和日本，拓展对于综合项目重要性和创新性的理解。这两个地区对了解重庆基地的潜力提供了既有补充性又有对比性的土壤。香港的密度，对基础设施联系的重视，及其公共和私营公司的整合，衬托了上海开发的历史。此外，学生分析了太古广场、香港火车站/国金中心、九龙站/环球贸易广场、置地广场和信德中心的周边关系、交通联系和总体品牌推广与设计。在私人与公共项目关系（特别是与日本著名的铁路网络整合）方面，日本的六本木新城、东京中城、名古屋站、东京站和京都站等综合项目也提供了有趣的内容参考。

参观重庆以后，学生们开始设计各自的综合项目。他们从项目任务书着手，结合咨询课堂评论员后获得的一系列城市发展目标，开始为项目设计三套方案。在中期评审时，学生需要深化其中一套方案，清楚地陈述其设计任务和功能组合与周边环境的联系。中期评审之后，学生们致力于细化方案设计，即基于上半学期对上海、香港和其他国际性模型的形态研究，设计一系列项目，包含综合性超高层和超大型街区的方案。这些项目中很多试图结合重要的案例，以便最大化密度和连接能力。它们综合在一起，形成一套关于未来中国西部城市可能性的有趣问题。

2.3.1. 重庆新开发：挑战与机遇

伍江，同济大学副校长

在过去的30年里，中国经历了人类历史上前所未有的大规模快速城市化进程。在此期间，中国的城市人口以每年1%的速度增长，从低于总人口的20%提高到了人口总数的50%。现如今，城市人口每年的增长达到了一千三百万。如果未来二三十年中，中国的经济增长预期正确，那么中国城市化的规模和步伐会继续稳定向前。

在这过去30年的增长中，中国的城市化主要集中在东部沿海地区。珠江三角洲（以广东和深圳为中心）、长江三角洲（以上海为中心）和环渤海经济圈（以北京和天津为中心）都已经成长为坐拥众多大小型城市的都市地带。大多数重大的建筑项目和城市项目都诞生在这些广阔的城市居民区中。然而，随着快速而持续性的经济增长将城市化进程带到中国中西部地区，中央政府雄心勃勃地提出了西部开发政策来引导这股潮流。
这个由瑞安房地产和 KPF 共同教授的毕业生工作室位于重庆。这是中国西部最大的城市。在二战期间，重庆是国民政府的陪都，并因此奠定了其在政治、经济以及特别在工业方面的重要城市地位。从那时起，这座山城就是中国西部长江上游经济区重要的城市和经济中心。近年，重庆被定为中国第四个直辖市，位列北京、上海和天津之后。现如今，这个以重庆为中心、拥有三千两百万人口和8.2万平方公里面积的特大城市（在四个直辖市中排名第一）正进入一个新的发展阶段。

和很多中国西部城市一样，重庆正面临着追赶其他三个位于东部沿海的直辖市的压力，努力在国内范围达到它们的经济水平。重庆50%的人口还居住在郊区，因而其城市发展水平与北京、上海和天津相比，存在着巨大的发展差距。然而，重庆也有其自身的发展优势：在这四个城市中，重庆的人口最多，土地资源也更为丰富。此外，在上世纪六七十年代重工业向西部迁徙时期，重庆就是受益的城市之一，因此它拥有扎实的工业基础，能够吸引中国最好的工人和知识分子。现在，中央的西部大开发政策给重庆提供了一个非常好的改变经济和城市基础设施的机会。

重庆位于中国西部山区，因而得名“山城”。历史悠久而人口众多的重庆市中心位于长江和嘉陵江交汇处的丘陵半岛。快速发展的新城区环绕着这片因地理环境而形成的区域。由于地形的原因，重庆的空间分配与上海、天津和北京的城市格局迥然不同，因此给城市规划和设计提出了大量特殊的挑战。

重庆的现代化开发中包含了大量高楼。在老城区中，丰富的地貌为塔楼的开发提供了有趣的空间条件。这是因为山丘的坡度营造了不同的平面，使得单体建筑可以从周边进入，并与周边环境产生联系。与此形成对比的是，在快速发展的周边地区，这些塔楼大多以传统的方式坐落在大面积、用于开发的开放性地块上。复杂的高速公路网和快速发展的轨道交通系统在多个地点跨越长江和嘉陵江，连接着上述区域和重庆市中心。

重庆在发展过程中可以参考中国东部城市化的成功经验。但是在环境保护、生态平衡和文化延续性方面，重庆是否能表现得更好？拥挤而复杂的城市基础设施必须应对重大地形的挑战（如穿越河流）。轨道和公共换乘系统的缺乏，导致了对私家车的过于依赖。地形的限制和基础设施的安排使行人活动非常困难。市中心现有的建筑群逐渐老化，也不足以容纳日渐增加的人口和日益发展的服务型经济。一方面，这个直辖市想要增加工业产出，向更加平衡的服务业和工业经济混合体转型，并满足其大规模农村人口的快速城市化，而另一方面，规划者希望能够保留重要的历史格局、垂直建筑形态和其美不胜收（却面临农业挑战）的地貌。

耶鲁课堂为学生提供了一个面对如此规模、限制、和应对当代城市开发挑战的机会。学生们不仅要投入到重庆火车站这个项目地块的复杂地形和基础设施中去，还要制作一份针对一百万平方米综合项目（即一个超级街区）的任务书，用以指导他们的设计。来自瑞安和 KPF 的专家与来自耶鲁大学的教师对开发十个全面并经过深思熟虑项目起到了至关重要的作用。每个项目都以自己的方式解决课堂范围内提出的空间和功能挑战。

综合来说，这些设计概念打破了重庆旧有的牢固形象，体现了一种活泼的城市个性，来反映地块的地理特征。更为重要的是，学生们成功地将综合城市项目和动态城市空间结合到了一体化的建筑项目中。

2.3.2. CBD 模型：中国中部的金丝雀码头

一由 Michiel Hulshof 与 Daan Roggeveens 撰写，两人是《中国的大型新城》(How the City Moved to Mr Sun : China's New Megacities) 的作者

记者 Michiel Hulshof 是 Tertium 的合伙人；Daan Roggeveen 是上海 MORE Architecture 的创始人和香港大学/上海研究中心的馆长。

2009年，他们共同创办了“去西部”项目。这是一个重点关注日益增长的巨型城市的多学科研究室。他们在2011年共同出版了《中国的大型新城》(How the City Moved to Mr Sun : China's New Megacities)一书。

重庆和中国中西部的其他城市正在努力竞争获得外资。中国已经从一个农业国转型成为一个制造业大国。发展高端服务业的时刻已经到来了。正如上世纪八九十年代经济特区的概念对工业发展产生了刺激，中央商业区（CBD）的提出旨在促进金融和服务领域的发展。城市管理者将 CBD 视为城市转型成现代大都市的最高成就。

自从上世纪九十年代初上海将浦东转变成为国际金融中心，每个雄心勃勃的中国城市都希望拥有自己的 CBD。CBD 中的高层写字楼容纳跨国公司、银行、律师事务所、投资公司、保险公司和咨询公司的地区性总部，勾勒出一条壮观的天际线。于是，北京修建了朝阳 CBD，广州建成了天河 CBD，天津开发了滨海 CBD。这个概念是如此的流行，以至于 CBD 这个缩写本身成为了汉语中的一个词。

就像每一个拥有自尊心的中国城市一样，重庆在两江（嘉陵江和长江）交汇处的老城区中心打造了自己的城市规划馆。馆内陈列着一个未来城市的巨大模型。在这个未来城市中，投资者可以从今后十年内将被建造的 CBD 中进行挑选。

这些位于中国中部的新 CBD 不仅仅是中国经济快速发展的标志。遍布全国、不计其数的新商务区也可能是中国城市化开发模型中的隐患结果。在武汉这个位于中国中部的重庆竞争城市，我们就

看到了这样的问题。

我们第一次见到于一丁教授是在2009年的秋天。这位武汉规划局的副局长一支接一支的抽着当地的红金龙牌香烟。他是在一间典型的学术性办公室里接见我们的。他的书桌上满是论文和报告。柜子上堆放着书籍和一个木制地球仪，纸板箱里装着几瓶矿泉水。在这样的气氛里，他向我们解释了武汉着手成为经济中心的历程。

上世纪九十年代，于一丁还是武汉大学的教授。搬迁王家墩军用机场的讨论就是在那时开始的。随着城市的快速发展，机场的跑道和塔台被武汉城区占据了。军用基地完全被居民区包围。2002年，于一丁离开了武汉大学，进入规划局工作。他的时机非常好。不到一年，武汉人大就决定拆除王家墩机场。这是每个城市规划者的梦想：在武汉这个千万人口、快速发展的城市中心，突然拥有了一块七千平方米的空地，面积是纽约中央公园的两倍。

在接下来的五年中，于一丁一直在考虑如何利用这片巨大的空地。在与我们谈话时，他从桌上拿起了一张武汉地图，铺开到一张低矮的木桌上。他指着曾经的机场这块战略要地，谈起了在规划局中那次激烈的争辩："我们怎么利用这块区域？可以把它改造成住宅区、公园甚至是一片森林。但是这些主意似乎都不是太好。地方主管部门在改造基地上已经花了很多钱，希望能把成本收回来。很快，我们就清楚地发现应该做一些别的东西。"于一丁和他的同事们最终决定在这个城市的中心打造一个中央商务区，这也是每一个雄心勃勃的中国城市的梦想。

在中国超级大城市的一期规划中，越来越多的国际咨询公司扮演了建筑师和规划者的角色。在武汉，麦肯锡推动着于一丁和本地规划者在机场地块中打造一个中央商务区。这家咨询公司研究了世界范围内三十个不同的商务区，包括东京新宿、巴黎拉德芳斯、法兰克福银行区和芝加哥卢普区。他们的代表团访问了几个欧洲的商务区寻找灵感。最终，麦肯锡建议武汉的规划者参考伦敦金丝雀码头，并建议他们不仅仅模仿总体规划，还要采用类似的私营公司的手段，而不是由政府决定。通过引入公司和股东的理念，防止建造那些空洞的、会闲置数年的项目。

办公楼、餐厅、商场、美发店、酒店和公寓等设施堆叠在一起，形成了中式城区的混合功能，共同营造出无与伦比的生机。当代中国的规划仍然牢牢地遵守着现代主义的准则，即工作、居住、娱乐和交通分门别类。拟建的商业区遵循着这个理念，功能极为单一：它们的目标是吸引公司职员，而不是创造多功能的综合体。这种手段意味着，和金丝雀码头、拉德芳斯及曼哈顿中城一样，这些地方在晚上和周末是闲置的。中国的 CBD 旨在促进其周边的发展，在规划图中占据极为重要的地位。位于武汉的中央塔楼就表达了对未来的雄心：这座玻璃和钢铁结构的建筑高达428米，差不多是金丝雀码头中加拿大广场一号的两倍。

中国城市的另外一个重要特征是城市的随性：公共空间内充斥着商贩、夜市、街巷和各种人群。这种理念不符合现代商务中心的形象，无法在新的商务区中占有一席之地。房地产开发商只会允许顶级品牌店铺。

上海和北京在国际政治、经济和文化上占有重要的地位，因此公平的说，他们可以被称为国际化大都市。随着中国国际地位的提升和内部的发展，一部分中部的城市也会成为国际化都市的一员。尽管这一点尚未成真，但政府部门雄心百倍。通过吸引外资公司和跨国集团，他们希望创造就业岗位，获得资金，并改善自己城市的国际化履历。管理者对于成功也有个人的想法。从回应选民这个角度来说，中国也许不是一个竞选意义上的民主国家，但是执政党需要市长和其他高层政府官员对他们的表现负责。Richard McGregor 在《政党》(The Party) 一书中写道：省长或市长等在位高官的考评成绩都基于一长串量化指数，看起来像是管理咨询公司拟定的，经济增长、投资、当地空气和水的质量、公共秩序等在理论上都是考评标准。到目前为止，最重要的考量标准就是经济增长指数。如果官员能够展示最高水准的经济增长，他们就可以升迁到更大的城市或是中央政府部门。各个城市在吸引外资方面各尽所能，因为外资是经济发展最重要的推动力之一。

市长们正在不断地推动城市发展和建筑来吸引潜在的投资商。这一幕发生在所谓的城市规划中心——这些中心在规模和形式上描绘着未来的国际化都市。每一个充满抱负的中国大都市都设计了这样一个匠心独具的舞台来吸引外资代表团。来访者首先看到的是一组政府高层的照片，随后是一幅幅展示城市历史图片和该区域的地图。随后，他们来到一个神圣的大厅，大厅内是一个巨大的模型，描绘出这座城市2020年的面貌。在俯瞰模型的 VIP 包厢内落座后，灯光变暗，华美的声乐演出开始，向惊愕不已的来访者呈现纯粹的雄心壮志。观众可以亲眼看到，他们所访问的城市在得到投资后将很快具有世界性的地位。一个实体模型和一段 3D 动画胜过千万张 Excel 表格。而整个介绍中的点睛之笔，就是未来商业区的天际线。

很多中国城市都在计划开发 CBD，借此吸引外国公司。郑州、成都、重庆和石家庄都希望拥有自己城市中办公楼组成的天际线。正如武汉地质大学的研究人员Li和 Chibamba 所说，新 CBD 这样的超大型项目是中国城市为了吸引外资而进行僵化竞争的最好证据。

这具有十分重要的意义。在争夺美元或是日元的过程中，中国可能正在建造远远超过需要的 CBD。在一段冗长但却十分公开的访谈中，贵州省规划院副院长 Shan Xiaogang 告诉我们，他有意地避免参与到这种狂热气氛中。他说："真正的 CBD 是拥有公司总部，并获得金融机构和咨询公司支持的商业区。作为城市规划者，你可以复制那些建筑，但是无法复制他们的内涵。大多数的中国城市还没有达到那个发展水平。我们这么说吧：如果你想开一家管理咨询公司，我还是建议你去上海。"

这场争创中国内陆最佳银行区的战斗，很像当初迪拜、多哈和阿布扎比争建机场，希望成为阿拉伯半岛最主要的航空枢纽。很明显，会有一名赢家。这些新 CBD 中大多数的办公楼、酒店和文化中心在竣工后都将空置。中国队建造的重视优于使用，这是因为政府主导着大多数的开发项目。看到如此新的重大基础设施处于闲置状态，不禁让人联想到前苏联时期的巨大工程浪费。

为了建造一个具有国际化吸引力的 CBD，各个城市向大型的国际性设计公司征求意见。在城市规划方面，他们找到了像 SOM、Atkins、Obermeyer 这样的建筑师事务所，或是请某个中国大型设计院提交计划书。这种多方有偿提交设计的“方案比选”是非常典型的中国特色。客户选择几个其最喜欢的元素，把它们融合成一个。这种实用主义手段在西方的城市开发中是根本不存在的。在方案比选中，最终总体规划的质量取决于客户的质量。

在开发进程中，城市向开发商拍卖大宗土地，而开发商随后自行设计建筑。他们必须遵守总平面图中规定的一些限制条件，比如限高、最大密度和最低绿地面积。由此产生的结果在中国到处可见。就像上海浦东商业区那样，独立的街区被异常宽阔的道路分开，互无联系。行人们因此不愿走访此类社区中的大部分空间，从而使这些地方弥漫着荒凉。

在这样的 CBD 中闲逛时，你会看到宽阔的马路、高大的塔楼、矗立着市政中心的中央广场、文化中心、五星级酒店和会议大楼。塔楼的设计似曾相识，让人感觉可能在亚洲或者世界某个地方某个城市的某个商务区看到过。与位于中国和世界上其他地方的无数商务区类似，这个 CBD 中坐落着同样昂贵的办公楼、商店、酒店和服务式公寓。与别处相同的是，会议中心和大型电影院一定能吸引首批访客。“高起点、高标准、高效率、高水平”——从当地政府工作者编撰的毫无意义的计划任务书中，可以看到他们在有意地鼓励复制黏贴的操作。由同样的国际建筑师执笔，更进一步导致了一致性。SOM 依据伦敦金丝雀码头的总平面图规划了北京、芝加哥和天津的 CBD，也是武汉新 CBD 的规划者。

中国各地的政府部门都在邀请同样的建筑师提交设计，哪怕这样的设计是针对最高楼、博物馆或是大剧院等标志性建筑。法国人 Paul Andreu 为北京、上海、济南、苏州、成都和太原等地的商务区设计了文化建筑。由于他一直在设计中使用球形，中国的建筑师说，他在中国的每个城市都下了一个蛋。

中国的政府部门能够推动这样的开发，这是因为他们只需要几个月时间就能把小型的试验推广成大规模的城市开发项目。他们能够强迫村庄售卖土地，用来重新开发。这一事实引起了土地所有权的变更和地块面积的高速增长，因为对地方政府来说，拍卖大块土地更为容易。与这种面积增长保持一致的是，土地多样的用途变为了单一功能。现代化抹去了多功能的可能性，剩下的只是城市，由大路连接多个岛屿。

假如房地产开发商和地方政府尊重中国城市周边土地的所有权，那么这些地方会和亚洲其他城市一样充满生机，遍布多样化的建筑。尊重土地所有权之后，地块会保持较小的面积，进而形成渗透性更好、也更适合行走的城市格局。创业者可以建造自己的住房或是小型商业街区。生活、工作、教育和购物可以互相混合。公共空间将成为不同背景的人们会面和交往的场所。市场中有不同的建筑类型。由于不同的功能唾手可得，不再需要驾车出行，机动车也可以减少。中国城市的周边地区可以像东京、台北或是曼哈顿下城那样，拥有同等水平的城市、建筑和社交质量。

重庆以及中国其他超级大城市的政府主管部门还没有作出结论。他们还在继续投资型的增长模式，为此建造新的建筑地标和办公楼，等待白领前去填充。一个中央商务区还没有建完，城市规划者就把注意力投到了下一个。

两年后，我们再次见到了于一丁。武汉新商务区的建设早已开始。武汉塔的地基正在浇灌。在曾经的机场的海报栏上，市政府的梦想被压缩成了一幅巨大的海报，上面是纽约、巴黎、香港和上海的天际线，流畅地同化成未来的武汉。

武汉规划设计院搬迁到了一座新楼里。于一丁在他新的办公室里接见了我们。这间办公室位于拐角，俯瞰着武汉和长江。除了那个木质地球仪之外，已经没有什么可以让人想到我们第一次见面时候那个乱糟糟的地方。我们来到一间5X15米的会议室。乳白色的地毯上没有桌子，只有一张很大的红色沙发。地毯中央印着设计院的 logo。

“在曾经的机场上规划 CBD 仍然十分有意思”，于一丁说，“但是政府的速度太慢了。我们改变了目标。”助理给他一个小包，里面是给访客的礼物——一条印着城市规划图的丝质围巾。于一丁用这条围巾展示了自己的抱负。“我们非常需要在这里开发一个新区”，他指着城市另一边的武昌区说，“这是我们未来发展的新重心。”这次开发中的最关键项目是一座625米高的塔楼。

4.1.0. 会晤与访谈

凌月明，重庆市副市长

作为一位训练有素的经济学家和工程师，凌月明自2008年开始担任重庆市政府副市长和重庆市委员会委员。他会见了来访的学生们并讨论了城市近期的发展和规划目标策略。

重庆是中国四个直辖市之一，因此，近年来我们目睹了它的快速发展。

在此之前，我们的城市规划和建设局限于市中心，不到230平方公里的城市内环。去年，我们开始了一个庞大的计划就是将城市扩展到二环，面积从230平方公里到2200平方公里。内环高速长78公里，二环高速长186公里。

在新的环线内，有二十一处建设区域会成为我们未来的开发重点。每组区域计划容纳20-25万人口。如今，重庆市中心人口数已达650万。我们计划将这一区域建设成为可容纳1000万人口的核心区。如此迅速的城市发展和扩张完全是基于重庆市经济的快速发展。根据政府的最新数据，去年全球经济增长为4.3%；在亚洲，同一时期的经济增长为7.8%；然而，重庆的经济增长则高达17.1%。

在过去的一年里，重庆的房地产行业共售出3.5亿平方米，面积等同于整个欧洲国家的数量。

在过去，重庆主要产业是摩托车和汽车。从去年开始我们着手发展信息技术，除了其他六家工厂1亿台个人电脑的合同，我们还与美国惠普公司和台湾宏基签订了协议。我非常有信心在未来3-5年内，所有在座的各位朋友，两人中其中一人的电脑将是在重庆制造。

李世蓉，重庆市对外贸易经济委员会副主任

李世蓉是重庆对外贸易和经济委员会副主任，负责本市外商投资推广。她还是重庆大学施工管理系的教授。她曾任重庆市副市长负责城市建设和发展。她与来自耶鲁大学的学生们讨论了重庆市经济和发展的前景。

我想先描述一下重庆的特点以及它是如何吸引外资企业入驻的问题。我们称重庆是世界上最大的城市，但首先要对“城市”有一个定义。在中国，你会发现城市被分为五个不同的级别。重庆市属于城市的最高级别，被称之为直辖市。所以，举例来说，当人们让我拿重庆和成都做比较时，我会说这是毫无意义的因为它们是两个完全不同类型的城市。成都是四川省的省会，但作为一个直辖市重庆本身就像是一个省会。重庆包含了近40个区县，分布在82000平方公里的土地上，其中超过一半的区县至少有800, 000人生活在那里，重庆总人口数为3200万。许多游客到重庆看到的只是中央核心区，最发达的地区，那里的人口现在已超过500万。到2020年，人口将增加一倍至1000万。到那个时候，重庆一半的人将生活在市核心区，另外一半人则生活在这些区县内。通过这种比较方式，重庆又不同于上海和其他的直辖市，它们的人口大多集中在市中心。

根据重庆的发展策略，城市化是工业化和重点区域城市化。在1998年，城市人口占18%，而现今已达53%。到2020年，我们的城市人口比重将达70%或超过2000万人。每年将有40-50万人被城市化。事实上，每天重庆都在创建小城市，这意味着我们要为新的城市居民创建基础设施、建筑和市政功能。

让我们简要的看一下重庆的基础设施建设。我们计划扩展道路网络，并设定目标，其中包括八小时内可到达周边城市，四小时内到达重庆市内任何地方。过去十年里我们已建造了2000平方公里的高速公路，在未来五年，我们还将建造1000多公里高速。关于铁路规划，我们设下从重庆出发八小时内到达中国其它主要城市的目标，包括北京七小时，上海八小时，广州五小时。广州也属于规划中用于欧洲贸易的轨交路线沿站。当然重庆的港口发展也很迅速，很快将成为中国最大的内陆港口，我们的机场和内河港口相组合，比中国其它自由贸易区更有优势。我们的机场也在迅速成长，每年载客量达1600万人次。

当中国人说“西部开发”，他们往往指的是中国内地市场的潜力，但在重庆这只是我们成长的因素之一。如果你近期看到惠普公司入驻重庆，那么未来90%的产品将被出口，这也是重庆不同于其它内陆城市的原因。在我看来，比起沿海自由贸易区，重庆从外贸角度看更具吸引力。例如，在2010年，重庆拥有120亿美元的对外贸易。到2015年这一数字将达到1000亿美元。到达沿海地区的距离很短，无论从哪里出发，重庆和沿海城市相比，空中旅行几乎感觉不到距离差异。而在铁路方面，我们的地理位置优于沿海城市。如果你想去北京、上海、香港或广东旅行，重庆位于这些城市的中心，是最方便的。

我们的工业随着城市化进程共同发展，重点行业发展迅猛。依次为机械、化工和信息技术。如今，由于汽车摩托车的生产，机械仍然是最大的产业。我们的化工行业增长速度非常快，因为重庆有天然气，这将是我们一年内最大的产业。但是在2009年，我们决定将信息技术发展成未来最大的产业，而近期与惠普和其它公司的协议便是该决定的结果。此外，我们还有强大的农业发展，一些美国公司已搬迁到重庆开始种植橘子。

关于外国企业方面，在20世纪70年代初期，重庆没有一家外企。我们经历了很长一段时间才达到现在的状态，但是在2008年，2009年和2010年，却有着质的飞跃。外商投资的增长速度超过重庆的 GDP 和总投资。2007年，外商投资的比重还低于中国平均水平。而在2009年，已经超出中国平均水平。因此，随着重庆的发展，外商投资将在总投资中发挥更大的作用。如今，我们已进入第十二个五年计划，在这五年计划结束时，我们的国内生产总值将增加一倍。

5.1.0. 相连的塔楼

5.1.1. 不拥堵的高密度空间 - 设计者：William Gridley

重庆的高铁站位于本地、地区乃至全国的地理和基础设施的中心，势必成为21世纪全球商业和消费的中国枢纽。为了既满足开发商对密度和利润的要求，同时也实现市政府避免城市拥堵的目标，本项目为重庆带来了一种新的都市形态：不拥堵的高密度空间。面对这两个看似矛盾的要求，通过“不拥堵的高密度空间”将物理和视觉的网络与功能的分布和叠加相结合，实现了一种富有生机的建筑类型，解决社会、经济增长带来的挑战，实现都市和文化的可持续发展。

本项目首先建议在现有设施上环绕地块进行建设，从而为交通、停车建立不同的层次，同时在新的地面层之下提供设施，与毗邻的都市肌理相连。这些物理上的连接将地块扩展到现有的孤岛之外，融入邻近环境中，其中包含一个历史遗留下来的山边集贸市场，其将成为未来的中央商务区，以及地铁、轮渡、和滨江公园。其次，一百万平米的功能垂直分布于塔楼和连接各地块的连桥内，通过各层面的活动和动线，将不同的特色连接起来，形成一个不拥堵但超高密度的网络，并延伸至地块之外。

高铁站位于地块心脏部位，是首要的连接点，同时也是建筑的中心，吸引沿着精心布置的景观轴线上的人群，也将铁路乘客分散至周围的广场。三种不同的商场类型既吸收密度，也有助于为地块上的大型办公、住宅和酒店除去拥堵。首先，大型旗舰店坐落在塔楼底部，吸引广场上的访客，同时也作为塔楼和连桥的垂直动线的关键入口。其次，具有亲密空间的零售村沿江布置，激活了公园，与未来的轮渡站相连，在江面形成一条长长的景观长廊。再次，在连续、阶梯状的天桥内设有架空的购物中心，将地块北侧的商务中心区与南侧滨江相连。天桥为通勤人员和访客提供了有效的流通方式，刺激了商业和消费，提供了城市观光，横跨于多变的地形之上，与重庆历史上形成的山城特点相呼应，为项目设立标志性的建筑身份。矗立于带状地形之上的是塔楼本身，它们形成雕塑般的组合，无论是功能还是美观，都新颖而具有开创性。考虑到不同功能的规划要求，每栋高楼内的楼面都向大厦核心处靠近，为重要功能创建理想空间，如大堂、连桥中庭、交易楼层以及高性能活动空间。

通过与周边环境的结合，建筑、设施和都市元素提供了高密度而不拥堵的空间。其成果具有标志性，可成为重庆的新模式；它满足一个变化的全球性社会的要求，建立高效可持续的都市空间，为21世纪的社会、文化和商业带来动力、成长和互动。

5.1.2. 重庆快速道 – 设计者：Kee Lew

本项目重现了一座城市的经济地位与其对建筑的实践之间的关系，这种关系通过对建筑和都市设施的策略性垂直规划与多样化得以体现。高密度高层空间内各功能的规划布置与周边环境和设施的地理位置相呼应，着眼于新挑战和机遇进行建筑内部的功能规划和外部的形体设计。

重庆这座城市正在经历前所未有的发展，由此产生对城市中心区域的交通、商业和住房的需求增长。由于汽车市场仍然对整个制造工业和城市形象有着很大影响，本项目的目标在于为高端汽车零售和商业提供一座高密度的综合体建筑，以及为前述功能起辅助作用的高端住宅和酒店功能。

为在地块内布置大量的功能空间，须解决两个主要问题：地面无序的机动车停车以及服务于行人的零售相当有限。尽管现有广场拥有足够空间应对一年中可能出现的大客流，但并无任何其他公共活动。同时，该区域饱受拥堵之苦，原因在于多条交叉道路，停车不足，以及街区周边机动车动线效率低下。交通拥堵过于严重，以至于每天的公共活动无法支持可持续的零售商业。

本项目没有用交通动线将基地进一步划分，也没有将公共空间平均分布于各街区，而是将各种类型的零售商业 – 包括大型百货公司、超级市场和汽车零售店 – 围绕一个开放的公园空间组成一个大型综合体。零售的类型中，需要更繁忙、更快速交通的百货商场和超市布置在靠近火车站处，而汽车零售店则位于靠近高速公路的一端。

第二个策略则是将停车提升至零售空间之上，将周边各条高架路引入项目中。由于项目被山围绕，有多条倾斜高速路和隧道穿过基地。基地是重庆南部进入半岛的入口，因此可作为纽带，服务于出入于城市的人群。由于地面的大幅度倾斜，机动车交通和停车功能严重不足，并且由于紧挨着地面以上或以下的建筑会造成更多的拥堵，因此设置了一座5层的停车桥，与高速公路直接相连。

通过将停车场抬升到足够高度，项目脱离了地面拥堵，也与整个城市更好地连接。机动车无须通过隧道或下坡即可直接进入停车天桥。零售商场的顾客可从停车所在楼层乘坐扶梯下来，穿过高档零售区，同时可欣赏城市与中心公园的全景。

同时，汽车公司总部的顾客和用户可享受提升的大堂，如进入商务区的新入口，周围多座摩天大楼矗立，盘旋升向高空。在塔楼内部，那些需要较大楼面投影且需要与大堂邻近的功能，如汽车公司总部和会展酒店，布置于塔楼地区；而那些更私密的功能，如精品酒店和高端公寓，占据了塔楼高区。在两座塔楼之间的过渡层，多层花园和中庭将成为私密功能的大堂，可俯瞰城市以及公司总部的开放式休闲区。

5.1.3. 重庆都市桃花源 – 设计者：Brian Spring

重庆“都市桃花源”是城市多个区域辐射影响的中心所在。它是连接西侧的科技发展区，东侧的老商务区，北侧的中央商务区和南侧的传统文化中心的纽带。本项目提案书意在平衡这些连接功能，同时满足重庆从一个工业化经济向服务型经济过渡的要求。本设计提案目标为：使地块密度达到最大，同时提供大量的市政设施，为后工业时代的周边区域服务。

主要考虑到将来对办公空间的需求，本项目功能分布为：55%办公，24%商业；8% 酒店；5%住宅；5%各类车站站厅；3%会展。这些主要功能的分配布置使得项目具有可渗透性，同时又与邻近设施保持连接。三座塔楼在江对岸沿着菜园路战略性地布置于基地内，入口先后有序，为通过各类交通到达的人群形成了独特的视觉形象。塔楼的高度错落有致，从210米，到260米，而最南端则达到600米。在塔楼投影内使得容积率达到最大，尽可能实现建筑面积最大，从而给地面层留有余地，布置绿色设施，方便行人流线和出入的管理。这类绿色设施分布于整个项目的不同层面，作为公共设施在大范围内提供服务，但在公共活动领域之上，通过悬挑和桥梁结构进行操作。桥梁连接着三座塔楼，进一步增强其作为项目纽带的功能。这一纽带呈带状、阶梯状分布，提供各类截然不同的体验，穿插于各类特色铺地与大量绿色植物之间。各层之间的台阶和坡道与各办公楼层直接相通，悬挑于50米高处，为租户带来畅通的公园式体验。商场裙房布置为圈状（有利于商场的效率和商铺的曝光率），并避免布置在中心位置，从而满足站点的大客流。裙房的绿色屋顶向顾客开放，同时面向邻近的办公楼层，增强塔楼与裙房之间的连接。重庆“都市桃花源”开创了一种开发模式，通过提高塔楼的建筑面积，在各层面布置绿色植被，减轻高密度带来的拥堵，从而成为后工业时代的都市隐逸之所。

5.2.0. 巨型结构

5.2.1. 重庆大桥 – 设计者：Katsunori Shigemi

本设计建议通过“大桥“的形式将建筑与基础设施融合，将铁路车站与长江和中央商务区相连。本项目将成为高密度开发的有效例证，支持重庆市的发展，解决其由于人口涌入而面临的严重基础设施不足和土地短缺问题。“大桥”项目将建成3个各有特色但相互联系的建筑要素：一片新的地面层解决密度问题，大桥内部的功能空间，零售商场的屋顶。这一新设施将车站及周边地区转变为一处吸引商业、居住和旅行的新场所，同时解决了地块目前面临的都市症结。

一片新地面

“大桥”将成为地块的新地面，在车站、长江和中央商务区之间建立车辆和人行动线，其高出临近的山坡75米。同时，它提供了一座全新的平台，沿着这个平台，7座塔楼临江而建。这条在“大桥”上的新的悬空街道穿过山顶和山脚的街道，这样商业人士在商务区和车站之间的行程时间将缩短，缓解车站周边的大量交通。高端办公、住宅和高档酒店可有各自独立的落客区，与车站位于不同层面，避免与大量车站客流的冲突。

一组新空间

“大桥”下的空间规划为精品办公和研究机构，如重庆技术院，与生产企业建立双赢的关系，支持新兴的高科技产业。“大桥”内的办公和科研空间完全可从广场、地块周边和附近的高速路上看到。该计划呈现了一个新颖而特别的建筑形象，代表重庆作为高科技工业城市的新身份，同时也解决了现有城市高密度难题。

一座新屋顶

考虑到大桥横跨车站广场所需要的结构深度，大桥的室内规划为功能空间。广场为无柱空间，上覆玻璃屋顶，从巨型结构悬挂而下。大桥将车站围起，保护客流免受重庆恶劣天气之苦；此外，它网格状的几何形态可让阳光穿过到广场，增加舒适度。在广场层，天空一览无余，大桥内的办公和商业功能也毫无遮挡。这种独特的三维体验是通过将巨型结构穿插在塔楼和裙房各层之间实现的，活跃了公共和商业空间。

为基地设计“大桥”是有益举措，因为它将丰富的功能、舒适的都市空间与重庆的高密度相结合。通过三项功能的组合，“大桥”为多功能的基地形成组织结构，同时带来丰富的空间体验和特色供公众欣赏、共享。本项目利用大型设施将密度提高两倍，它将成为重庆当今和未来的重要门户。

5.2.2. 创想重庆 – 设计者：Keith Johns

通常，超高密度项目的物理外形是一座突兀的塔楼。尽管高层塔楼作为都市发展的一种形式而得到发展和成功，但它霸气、目空一切、特立独行的形象威胁着都市的可持续发展。如果建筑在于持续地服务于文明史上的最大规模人类迁徙 – 而目前正在中国发生，那我们必须另外探寻可通过多种方式运作的高密度建筑空间类型。本项目为此提供了一种建议。

本项目设计充分考虑了地块的垂直变化，由两个主要部分组成。第一部分是楼板，横跨于基地上方距东北中央商务区高度75米处。在创造新功能的同时，楼板为 CBD 商业肌理带来了延续性，提供了一个水平方向的发展策略。第二部分位于楼板腹地，是大型林荫道。在为机动车提供进入大楼通道的同时，林荫道上布置了办公大堂与入口，将上方楼板与下方商铺与零售商店连为一体。与纽约市的高架桥释放其下铁路路网运能的概念类似，林荫大道允许在中央商务区上方布置新的商业空间。办公部分楼板完全脱离地面杂乱的街道和高速道路设施。

从架空的楼板向下延伸，主要布置了商场功能，并形成了一个圈。在商业圈的西北角是火车站，旅客可无缝进入商场或穿过大型中央广场出去，中央广场可容纳数以万计的候车旅客。商场圈形成了非常内化的空间，刺激比较传统的零售消费，而上方的办公功能则是外向的空间，适合重庆崭露头角的创新经济。玻璃楼板由于其通透性，将成为城市的留言板、火车站的标志、生产发展的智囊媒介。

5.2.3. 全商业空间 – 设计者：Alfie Koetter

本设计提案充分考虑了重庆努力从生产型经济向消费型经济转变的目标。重庆在地理位置上处于内陆，远离出口交通网络，从而鼓励其发展面向本地和国内消费市场的产业，包括食品生产、汽车生产、纺织和电子。这些产业即使在没有类似于其它中国城市的出口区的情况下仍繁荣发展。今天，重庆是中国第三大汽车生产城市，中国最大型的钢铁、铝的生产城市之一。尽管在工业上获得了成功，重庆希望在未来十年内转型成为一个消费性社会。

鉴于此，“全商业”充分考虑了消费主义，通过经济和社会的多样化零售枢纽的形式得以呈现，同时它也是本地、地区、全国乃至全球的目的地。
建议的商业功能面积达40万平方米。以此为中心，辅以办公和酒店功能，各为25万平方米。办公功能与商场运营直接相关，为厂商、品牌提供商务空间。酒店功能为来访“全商业”的客人提供长期或短期住宿。

同样重要的是，本提案为重庆各类人群提供了一个全新的公共空间，吸引人们来此聚集。以京都火车站和上海恒隆广场为先例，本项目通过内化的开放式公共空间，缓解了中国大型体量带来的问题。

上海恒隆广场的面积为6万平方米，相比其它西方国家的城市体量，这个数字是相当大的。比如，通常的纽约市建筑体量为1.6万平方米，芝加哥通常为1.35万平方米。恒隆广场采用很多美国建筑采用的方式缓减大尺度问题：通过分解的方式。通过引入一系列人行通道，每个体量被有效地分解成一组易于掌控的小型体量。

京都车站提供了另一种模式：在单个建筑内，既实现功能的分配，又作为都市公共空间。 作为火车站，京都车站的功能类型极其多样，包括大量的零售商业，以及各类市民和文化功能。大厦核心筒处半开放的凹口提供了巨大的公共空间，不仅可被旅客使用，也可给整个城市利用。在形式上，“全商业”项目将京都火车站的尺寸变窄拉长，得到了一个更大型的四合院型体量。

“全商业”的四合院形式使得其可容纳不同的零售种类，将通常不可兼容的零售类型统一布置在一个商场圈内。高端和低端商业没有分布在一条线的两端，而由火车站将两者连接起来。通过这一技巧，可发现低端品牌和高端品牌之间的相似之处；进而，之前被不同品牌分隔的人群可相互融合。随着人群在“全商业”圈内的流动，店铺的尺度、组织和品牌不停变化。例如，当一位顾客在一处开放式商铺附近流连时，另一位顾客在另一处更典型的单层零售长廊穿越。尽管零售“四合院”可能被理解为四个院落分别面向不同的人群，但本提案并无意向将他们分开；而是通过连续的商场圈消除各人群之间的区别。

5.3.0. 宏大空间

5.3.1. 重庆广场 – 设计者：Qiwei Liang

本提案探讨了建筑密度与中国城市人口密度问题之间的关系，集中关注火车站，以重庆火车站作为研究案例。虽然节假日火车站过度拥挤是个严重的问题，但它具有刺激消费的潜力。本项目探讨创建一个都市活跃空间，吸引人群以及其购买力。

有两种中国建筑类型是相关的先例。一是裙房，大量零售商业占据低层楼层，支持相对小而高耸的塔楼。这类项目占据大量土地，但无法提供足够的密度应对重庆站的大规模客流。另一个中国传统建筑类型则具有相反的形式：大型公共广场，用来在特别场合容纳客流，但由于其没有合适密度的功能支持而受到冷落。

至于火车站，有三个挑战。一是旅客和访客，这类人群不仅应被容纳，而应刺激其购物。二是地块本身，应在此建立可持续的开放绿化空间，这也是重庆的建设目标。第三是功能，应提供一个舒适、流畅的换乘体验，方便衔接山区的地理环境。

对应这三个问题，本提案结合了裙房和广场的形式。项目的核心部位是大型裙房，大得超出人们通常的理解；但它提供公共空间的基础设施。裙房之上是各种建筑类型，由此产生的密度有别于裙房与广场。这样的密度是半集中式的：顾客被商场和娱乐功能吸引过来，但他们所处空间不一定有墙包围。这座宏大的裙房广场是均衡的：它形成一个自由的面，但当不同类型建筑插入时，则在这个自由面上创造出不同的密度区和功能区，且相互之间没有阻隔。在插入这些建筑类型后，我们在第二个景观面上将这个巨大的广场分解成7个小广场。景观面呈倾斜状，强调流动感和空间之间的渐变转换。中央广场是对称的标志空间，此外，还有供聚会活动的下沉式广场，车站广场，商业广场，住宅广场，更有绿化广场临江而建，略微倾斜的角度使之成为俯瞰城市的阳台。不同区域之间的界限被淡化，这样在诸如春节之类的特殊场合，可增强流动性，人群可被吸收。通过这些处理方式，项目既满足商业开发的价值和密度，又可像任何公共设施一样服务于大规模人群。

5.3.2. 重庆火车站和博览中心 – 设计者：Danh Thai

本提案充分考虑了中国的城际铁路网规划以及重庆不断增长的人口数量。它满足大型火车站的功能要求，从而服务于超高密度的人口，同时以汽车和摩托车工业为中心，为城市发展规划了一个特别的主题。这一主题通过特别而具有标志性的功能得以体现：一个以重庆的汽车和摩托车工业的成功为主题的博览中心。

地块上全新的都市景象通过五个元素来表达：一座重新布置的火车站，包括换乘功能；新的博览中心；多功能商业；高层带阳台的高端住宅；一条空中街道为地块带来更有效的动线。项目的设计不仅包含超高速道路和大型中央枢纽，它更像是一个自成一体的世界，车流承载着人们的生活在其上下自由流动。设计的目标在于创建一座综合的都市结构，在其中，各类设施和公共元素融合形成一个大集合。重庆站目前是终点站，但将来轨道可能延伸至城市中心；同时，博览中心作为枢纽，可以一种创新而高品质的方式促进汽车和摩托车工业的发展。

战略性的功能布置充分利用了地块上各关键节点。项目包含西端的一个体量和东端的两个体量。客流穿梭在其间。车站的位置在更往西处，比现有车站更大，在车站与地块北侧新的中央商务区之间，可容纳更现代化的功能。地块的东北区域布置了博览中心，从北侧来的大量交通将从博览中心一侧经过，驶向长江方向。博览中心对面是多功能办公楼，是现有商业和商务区的延伸。再往上，地块的北侧是高端住宅楼，在水平方向延伸布置，与山城的地理风貌保持一致，也可充分享用滨江景观。这一都市新节点建立在动感的模式基础之上。

重庆车站和博览中心是繁荣的商业和文化中心，有能力容纳重庆市举办的各类高端会展和活动。项目所处的中心地理位置非常便捷，不仅是举办大型活动的首选之地，也为新的活动创造了机会。

5.4.0. 都市肌理

5.4.1. 重庆村 – 设计者：Yijie Dang

本项目旨在拓展重庆的都市生活和城市形象。"重庆村"项目将滨江地带与山腰相连，同时在中央创建了一个商业文化村，它有别于其它中国城市的都市新开发项目，也为来到重庆车站的旅客展示了一种新的城市生活模式。

高层住宅和办公楼沿着山腰布置，充分利用了交通和江景优势，可直达现有的高架路和将来的地铁站。低层商业休闲村位于塔楼底部。整个村沿着山坡向下延伸直到滨江地带，项目的整个形态与当地的建筑类型相呼应。

新的火车站将两大类人群加以区分：一类是乘坐本地或普通轨道交通的通勤人员；另一类是乘坐城际或地区高速火车的旅客。尽管这两类人群利用同一栋楼，但各自有不同的大堂和候车区，落客区和室外广场也各自不同。

零售村位于车站的西端，吸收着大客流，但将他们根据消费类型加以区分。从低层往上，零售村按照购买力的增加而分成不同区间，并各自有其出入口。最下层主要是餐饮，与车站直接相连，服务于本地乘客，而高端零售商铺和会所为高铁商务旅客服务。在高端区与低端区之间是中间档普通零售区，吸引市内本地顾客。为方便各层之间的连通，布置了一个景观坡道，将南侧的落客区与广场中心相连，最后通往北侧高层建筑。村子南入口处布置了一栋高端酒店塔楼，中等高度，增强重庆村的整体形象，同时为高端零售区带来持续客流。

从低层普通零售向高层时尚消费体验过度的形式印证了目前重庆乃至全国的经济转型。

5.4.2. 重庆车站 – 设计者：Emmett Zeifman

本项目进行了一次尝试，为当代中国城市的超大体量规划和大范围开发提供一种不同的方式。它利用大规模的公共设施，为城市居民提供了一层新的地面，将两种主要空间形式通过两种组织分布逻辑并列布置：即市民广场和都市街道。在形式上，项目的两个组成部分为定义清晰的广场和内容丰富的街道，是连通城市和长江的桥梁，与现有城市人口和市政设施网络相连，为这座超大型结构的多功能大楼提供了逻辑依据。无论是那种空间形式，都着重于定义公共空间的都市社区身份。

项目包括不同层次的公共空间，规模尺度大小各异。大型公共广场由三组都市设施组成：火车站，公交车站和零售商业中心。而每个组成部分都围绕一个大型中央大厅布置。在这个中央大厅之上是一组街道，增强广场的形式。这些街道为公共设施、北侧山上的高密度人口和南侧滨江公园之间建立了连接关系。在挑高的街道的交叉口，又可分别形成一个小型广场。各层之间主要的垂直公共动线即布置在此。在中央广场周围又形成了一个正方形盘旋上升的次要商业街，提供了除电梯外的另一种流通方式。

设计中抵制了将密度分布于各塔楼的冲动，本项目主要的住宅类型是楼板。带有深阳台的复式公寓俯瞰街道和广场。楼板上留有大型开洞，阳光和空气可穿过进入项目中心，是建筑居民的公共聚会场所。同时，设有开放大堂的楼层将住宅部分与其下的商业和办公空间隔开，直接面对项目的挑高街道。在商业中心上，楼板与广场东侧边缘对齐，在山与江之间形成线型连接；北侧和西侧位于火车和公交车站之上的楼板形成了都市步道，组成了完整的广场。各种尺度的绿化空间布置于项目中的不同层面，从阳台和楼板的中空部位，到形成的长条形公园。

项目的最终目标是想建议一种建筑形式，既可支持社区与集体的生活形式，同时也适合中国都市的大规模发展和人口流动。项目不是一个独立的例外空间，也不是都市肌理上的外来建筑，因为这两者在本基地如此复杂的人口、功能、地理和设施情况下，都是不可能的。通过将超大体块、中等高度建筑和街道规模空间引入项目，"重庆车站"探寻可居住密度的极限。它测试了超常规模和形式在都市中的可能性，从而挑战资本主义与当今中国集体主义所固有的欲望。

5.5.0. 在耶鲁举行的最终评审

Marianne Kwok: 如果项目的功能规划没有确定，地块的定位也不清晰，在这种情况下要决定做什么是比较困难的。不过我觉得每个同学都对自己要做的有一个明确的观点。

Paul Katz: 有意思的是今天对塔楼的讨论很少 – 事实上对塔楼几乎没有讨论。所有的讨论都是关于土地，塔楼一闪而过，就像不存在一样。这样的话，我们或许没有达到我们的目标，或许我们达到了我们的目标，通过将塔楼融合在都市肌理中这一方式。

John Alschuler: 令人印象深刻的是所有学生要努力解决的问题都是正确的问题。 方式不同，但是他们解决城市高度问题，高速路高度问题，首层楼面高度问题，之间的过渡转换，轴线关系，开放空间，等等，所有这些都是同一个问题的不同形式。只要解决了这些问题，就是正确的。并且，我发现这些项目使我对巨型结构的开发效果持怀疑态度。项目需要与所在环境如此彻底地分开，从而使其简单清晰，但却很难把控。

Demetri Porphyrios: 我原来以为这些高密度、高层建筑会设计得像空中楼阁一样，但是每个人都以图纸的形式开始项目设计，不仅是功能图纸，还有设计描述，这给我留下很深印象。描述解释了功能、用途，及不同用途之间的关系。其中有对“景观”的描述，这里的“景观”不仅指绿地，而是整个项目坐落的基础。也有关于连接的描述－与现有城镇的连接，与车站的连接。步行道设计很棒。其它描述是关于公共领域的。我很高兴看到“地面层”，并且这里的“地面层”是指第四层、第五层、第六、第七、第八、第九、第十、第十一、第十二层，并且是每个设计描述涉及的主题。并且我要祝贺有些同学，你们特别关注了组成整个项目的各元素的类型。我也很高兴看到各建筑的规模并不是整个项目的规模。你们值得祝贺，因为你们事实上了解了规模、景观和朝向等概念。

Alex Twining: 对基地上基础设施的处理将学生分成不同的组别。我们很多讨论都是关于如何用两种方式来处理基础设施。之前很多方案都采用“阶梯式下行“，试图抹掉基础设施。还有些人说：”看，你没法抹掉这些基础设施，那就让它留在那儿吧，我们另外做一个更大的，自成一体。”在中国，你无需考虑分期开发的问题，在美国这是个很大的挑战，我们没法一次建设几百万平方英尺的建筑，更别提几千万级的建筑。这会构成另一个挑战。

Demetri Porphyrios: 关于可持续发展，通常计划都不明确，在这种情况下通常指可反复利用。这是可持续最关键的部分，而不是绿色的东西。

Patricia Patkau: 我认为可持续是系统性的，就是那些东西。就算是停车场，如果那是个斜坡，将很难利用。

Alan Plattus: 在我们耶鲁-中国合作工作室，我们一直在努力解决大型体量的裙房问题，就像 KPF 努力实践的一样。在上海，情况完全不同，因为那里是平原，但重庆的地貌相当特殊，它是半岛，以很大的坡度通向长江。裙房的任务复杂而困难，这样塔楼变得像是装饰，我这样说没有贬义，同样，更具挑战性的问题是裙房怎样调节功能、设施和连接关系。另外，设计已达到了相当的水平，评审团很容易就可找到方案的评论点，这对学生是很大的表扬。

Bill Pedersen: 从概念上来说，一件好事没做好比做好了一件坏事要好。如果让我来评价的话，我更愿意看到整个过程的进步，从开始到结束，是你思想的不断进步，在过程中不断挑战自己的观点。在你们的职业生涯中，我认为必须不断挑战你自己的观点。现在大家都还在学校，大家都专注于建筑，有一定的热情，但只有你在未来四十年或五十年的时间中，不断地告诫自己，要不停地更上一层楼，才能达到应有的水平。至少要50年的时间，你才能达到从心所欲的境界。你们站在一个美妙的起点。（笑声）这是历史上一个非常激动人心的时刻，随着像这类项目的涌现，你们将面临非常棒的机遇。你们选择了正确的职业。

Albert Chan: 这个工作室让我更加相信，我不会只请一个建筑师来完成一个千万平方英尺的项目，除非罗先生让我这么干。（笑）。因为当你做一个千万平方英尺的项目时，无论它在哪里，那将是城市的一部分。你不仅仅在做一个项目。作为建筑师，我们总是会说我们考虑了环境，但我想，面对几千万平方英尺，我们要问问自己能做多少，无论我们多么有才华。一些比较好的方案中，项目的一部分没有设计或只略微设计了一点，让它们由其他建筑师来设计。为项目的成熟留下框架。我们确实要担心分期开发问题。我们不会一下造好所有内容，特别有几千平方英尺。因此，我认为，在现实中，成功的项目预留了待开发的余地。作为建筑师，如果有开发商让我们做得更多，做得更大，这不一定是正确的答案。人的尺寸就这么大。我们要记住这一点。有些时候项目就是太大、太过了。我们要记住规模和谦逊。这次对我们可能是一个很好的教训。有些方案意识到了限度，这些方案更现实。

Jamie von Klemperer: 记得我们第一次参观现场的时候，我们在多个地下空间走了一下，有人在那里卖非法赌博用品，还有一些东西我不便在这里说，你们中有三个人走丢了吧？对我来说，这是一个小小的比喻，因为在探讨问题的过程中，你们有勇气迷失，然后找到问题的答案。Kahn 可能说过，一件事做好了但是不彻底，比做得彻底但不好要好；还有建筑师说过，在发现真正有效的方法之前，应尝试你不确认是否有效的方法。这确实需要勇气，因为你们确实面对着一堆艰难的问题。

Vincent Lo: 对于这样量级的项目，你应该着眼于整个城市。重庆还不知道是否会开发这个项目，但是如果传出消息说有这么多好的方案已经准备好了。。。。。。(笑)